FIVE GREAT
MODERN
IRISH PLAYS

The Playboy of the Western World
BY JOHN M. SYNGE

Juno and the Paycock BY SEAN O'CASEY

Riders to the Sea BY JOHN M. SYNGE

Spreading the News BY LADY GREGORY

Shadow and Substance BY PAUL VINCENT CARROLL

WITH A FOREWORD BY
GEORGE JEAN NATHAN

THE
MODERN LIBRARY
NEW YORK

Random House IS THE PUBLISHER OF

THE MODERN LIBRARY

BENNETT A. CERF · DONALD S. KLOPFER · ROBERT K. HAAS

Manufactured in the United States of America

Printed by Parkway Printing Company   Bound by H. Wolff

Acknowledgments

For permission to include the following plays, acknowledgment is here made to the authors of the plays and the publishers under whose imprint they were issued:

Juno and the Paycock reprinted by permission of The Macmillan Company.

Riders to the Sea and *The Playboy of the Western World* reprinted by permission of the Executors of J. M. Synge and the Modern Library, Inc.

Shadow and Substance reprinted by permission of Paul Vincent Carroll and Random House, Inc.

Spreading the News reprinted by permission of G. P. Putnam's Sons.

Contents

Foreword

BY

GEORGE JEAN NATHAN

I TAKE it there is small critical question, save alone in the lands
of dictated appraisal, that the modern Irish drama leads what is
left of the European theatre. Even here in America, where the
theatre enjoys a vitality unimpaired and ever increasing, there
are with one or two exceptions—O'Neill the foremost—never-
theless no playwrights who have in them the rich singing humor
and beauty of an O'Casey, the mordant lyric passion of a Synge
or the spiritual current of even a Carroll. Our theatre is quick
and alive and in many ways admirable, but its plays come mainly
out of galvanic impulse rather than deep meditation. And only
out of such meditation is true drama born.

Surely, in searching the stage of the world theatre of the later
years it is difficult to find a body of drama possessed of the Celtic's poetic pulse. Surely, except in sporadic instances, that quality
which insinuates into the mind and emotion its peculiarly linger-
ing after-image is rare in the plays of men nurtured by other
soils. It isn't, certainly, that all the plays that are coming out of
the Eire soil are masterpieces. Very, very far from that. But, as
I have written in the past, in even the poorest of them one finds
a probity, a passionate undertone, a brave resolve, and a hint of
spiritual music that one all too infrequently encounters in the
present dramaturgy of other peoples. And in the finer plays
there is a poetic sweep, a surgery of human emotions and a warm
golden glow that even the best drama of other countries most
often lacks.

Perhaps the outstanding mark of the Irish dramatists by and large is their shameless emotional candor. They write what they honestly feel, however possibly embarrassing. Other playwrights will sometimes not hesitate to write what they honestly think, however in turn possibly embarrassing, but when it comes to exposing their fundamental, naked emotions they often, fearful of being taken for too sentimental souls, equivocate and indulge themselves in a superficial protective coloration of wit, humor, oblique apology and extenuation, and even extra-character ridicule. But seldom the Irish. The Irishman wears not only his heart on his coat-sleeve but this very emotional gizzard as well. And that, unless I am mistaken, is where any genuine dramatist must wear his heart and even his gizzard. For it is hardly news that the drama is primarily an instrument of emotion and that thought is merely the occasional lubricating grease.

While on the subject of the heart, previous words may be paraphrased. The latter-day English playwrights have seldom plumbed it much beneath the modish Bond Street waistcoat that covers it. The latter-day French, with but few exceptions, traditionally and habitually appear to confuse it with an organ biologically somewhat less ecclesiastical. The Nazi aesthetes identify its beat with that of a military drum and its contour with that of the swastika. The aesthetes of the Soviet generally either view it as a political organ or loftily dismiss it as an uneconomical wart; the Hungarians, before racial edict robbed them of their pens, seemed to think that its beat was most often in three-quarter time and that every pale boulevard Emperor Jones was helplessly tomtomed by it into a lady's arms; and our American playwrights usually interpret it either in terms of Cab Calloway's baton or a lace valentine, or make wisecracks about it. The Irish alone as a playwrighting nation appear to appreciate it for what in all its strange and various moods it is, and the Irish alone with a profligate beauty and a lyric artlessness permit it to tell its true and often aching story.

To the great witty line of Congreve and Farquhar, of Sheridan and Wilde and Shaw, the Irish drama has added in our modern times the profound emotional dynamics of such further notables as Synge and Yeats and the earlier St. John Ervine and Sean O'Casey. Of all the still living, this O'Casey, Shaw aside, is in every respect the foremost. Not only is he at his best the best of all the Celts but even at his worst so much better than three-fourths of them at their best—and some of them are surely not to be sniffed at—that to fail to perceive it must remain the privilege of amateur criticism. If *The Plough And the Stars* is not one of the finest dramas in the modern theatre, if *Juno and the Paycock* is not one of the richest human comedies, if *The Silver Tassie* with all its admitted deficiencies is not one of the most honorable experiments, if *Within the Gates,* for all its lapses, is not beautiful, brave and thrilling song, if *Purple Dust* is not a ringing, moving melody orchestrated with a resounding slapstick, and if even the incontrovertibly poor *The Star Turns Red,* the feeblest play O'Casey has written, is not oddly invested with what may conceivably turn out to be a poet's prophetic vision—if these plays are not these things, then I am not the man to have been engaged to write this foreword.

The derogation of O'Casey by certain critics, first among them his fellow countryman and fellow playwright, Ervine, as —in the instance of *Juno and the Paycock*—mere superb music-hall seems to me not only obvious critical snobbery, for superb music-hall remains nonetheless still superb, but equally obvious critical superficiality, inasmuch as it overlooks the play's rare comedy scenes' deep roots in dramatic character, their deep penetration into human eccentricity, and withal their beautiful, drunken dramatic literature. They are Molière full of Irish whiskey, now and again Shaw off dietetic spinach and full of red meat, Flanagan and Allen (if such critics insist) in the classical garb of Falstaff and Dogberry. Furthermore, to derogate O'Casey as a mere hint of a poet, which these same critics do, is an even larger betrayal of critical sense. Where in the drama of living Irishmen is there greater and more genuine dramatic poetry than you will find in the mighty sweep of *The Plough and the Stars,* or in the boozy low measures of parts of *Juno,* or in the riff-raff of *Within the Gates* and their periodic utterance, or in the speech of the workmen in *Purple Dust,* or even in passages of the otherwise largely dubious *The Star Turns Red?*

The answer is: nowhere. Dunsany has his valued poetic moments, and so has Carroll, and so, at least in *The Moon in the Yellow River,* has Denis Johnston, but even at their most deserving and eloquent there is missing in them something of the profundity of feeling, something of the real pity and sorrow and pain and joy, something of the true, shooting beauty of life tragically experienced and life triumphantly lived that lies innermost in and is awakened by the O'Casey pen.

Of those who have gone to their Maker, Synge stands preeminent in after-glory. The two plays included in this volume represent him at his best, and at the opposite poles of his fulgent dramatic writing. *The Playboy of the Western World* has not its match in Celtic satirical drama, and one would have to search far and deep for an equivalent of the melodious pain in *Riders to the Sea.* Both are classics of the modern Irish—of the modern world—theatre. And both testify to the genius that combined in itself an ironic humor of rare and juicy puissance and a compassion for humanity drenched in the tears of a great pity's understanding.

Lady Gregory's moralized fables, folk comedies and little symbolical and allegorical plays constitute simpler theatre. They are agreeable and sometimes piquant pastimes with the occasional glint of a drollish mind. Intellectual vaudeville is a phrase that may perhaps best be used to describe a number of them. They are, often, trifles—but trifles of a peculiar sheen and glimmer.

Returning to the still living, there remains Carroll. His best plays, *Shadow and Substance* and *The White Steed,* indicate him to be the possessor of a sharp wit and a lyric spirituality, both of which he is expert in dovetailing into valid drama. In each of these plays he vouchsafes sufficient illustration of his skill, and in each of them, again, much of that precious quality which allows to the Irish drama its distinctive place on the stage of the theatre of us hitherward peoples.

New York City
Fall, 1940

The Playboy of the Western World

A PLAY IN THREE ACTS

BY JOHN M. SYNGE

PREFACE

IN WRITING *The Playboy of the Western World,* as in my other plays, I have used one or two words only that I have not heard among the country people of Ireland, or spoken in my own nursery before I could read the newspapers. A certain number of the phrases I employ I have heard also from herds and fishermen along the coast from Kerry to Mayo, or from beggar-women and ballad-singers nearer Dublin; and I am glad to acknowledge how much I owe to the folk-imagination of these fine people. Anyone who has lived in real intimacy with the Irish peasantry will know that the wildest sayings and ideas in this play are tame indeed, compared with the fancies one may hear in any little hillside cabin in Geesala, or Carraroe, or Dingle Bay. All art is a collaboration; and there is little doubt that in the happy ages of literature, striking and beautiful phrases were as ready to the story-teller's or the playwright's hand, as the rich cloaks and dresses of his time. It is probable that when the Elizabethan dramatist took his ink-horn and sat down to his work he used many phrases that he had just heard, as he sat at dinner, from his mother or his children. In Ireland, those of us who know the people have the same privilege. When I was writing *The Shadow of the Glen,* some years ago, I got more aid than any learning could have given me from a chink in the floor of the old Wicklow house where I was staying, that let me hear what was being said by the servant girls in the kitchen. This matter, I think, is of importance, for in countries where the imagination of the people, and the language they use, is rich and living, it is possible for a writer to be rich and copious in his words, and at the same time to give the reality, which is the root of all poetry, in a comprehensive and

3

natural form. In the modern literature of towns, however, richness is found only in sonnets, or prose poems, or in one or two elaborate books that are far away from the profound and common interests of life. One has, on one side, Mallarmé and Huysmans producing this literature; and on the other, Ibsen and Zola dealing with the reality of life in joyless and pallid words. On the stage one must have reality, and one must have joy; and that is why the intellectual modern drama has failed, and people have grown sick of the false joy of the musical comedy, that has been given them in place of the rich joy found only in what is superb and wild in reality. In a good play every speech should be as fully flavoured as a nut or apple, and such speeches cannot be written by anyone who works among people who have shut their lips on poetry. In Ireland, for a few years more, we have a popular imagination that is fiery and magnificent, and tender; so that those of us who wish to write start with a chance that is not given to writers in places where the springtime of the local life has been forgotten, and the harvest is a memory only, and the straw has been turned into bricks.

J. M. S.

January 21, 1907

CHARACTERS

CHRISTOPHER MAHON

OLD MAHON (*his father, a squatter*)

MICHAEL JAMES FLAHERTY, called MICHAEL JAMES (*a publican*)

MARGARET FLAHERTY, called PEGEEN MIKE (*his daughter*)

WIDOW QUIN (*a woman of about thirty*)

SHAWN KEOGH (*her cousin, a young farmer*)

PHILLY CULLEN and JIMMY FARRELL (*small farmers*)

SARA TANSEY, SUSAN BRADY, and HONOR BLAKE (*village girls*)

A BELLMAN

SOME PEASANTS

The action takes place near a village, on a wild coast of Mayo. The first Act passes on an evening of autumn, the other two Acts on the following day.

The Playboy of the Western World

ACT ONE

SCENE. *Country public-house or shebeen, very rough and untidy. There is a sort of counter on the right with shelves, holding many bottles and jugs, just seen above it. Empty barrels stand near the counter. At back, a little to left of counter, there is a door into the open air, then, more to the left, there is a settle with shelves above it, with more jugs, and a table beneath a window. At the left there is a large open fire-place, with turf fire, and a small door into inner room. Pegeen, a wild-looking but fine girl of about twenty, is writing at table. She is dressed in the usual peasant dress.*

PEGEEN (*slowly as she writes*). Six yards of stuff for to make a yellow gown. A pair of lace boots with lengthy heels on them and brassy eyes. A hat is suited for a wedding-day. A fine tooth comb. To be sent with three barrels of porter in Jimmy Farrell's creel cart on the evening of the coming Fair to Mister Michael James Flaherty. With the best compliments of this season. Margaret Flaherty.

SHAWN KEOGH (*a fat and fair young man comes in as she signs, looks round awkwardly, when he sees she is alone*). Where's himself?

PEGEEN (*without looking at him*). He's coming. (*She directs the letter.*) To Master Sheamus Mulroy, Wine and Spirit Dealer, Castlebar.

SHAWN (*uneasily*). I didn't see him on the road.

PEGEEN. How would you see him (*licks stamp and puts it on letter*) and it dark night this half hour gone by?

SHAWN (*turning towards the door again*). I stood a while outside wondering would I have a right to pass on or to walk in and see you, Pegeen Mike (*comes to fire*), and I could hear the cows breathing, and sighing in the stillness of the air, and not a step moving any place from this gate to the bridge.

PEGEEN (*putting letter in envelope*). It's above at the cross-roads he is, meeting Philly Cullen; and a couple more are going along with him to Kate Cassidy's wake.

SHAWN (*looking at her blankly*). And he's going that length in the dark night?

PEGEEN (*impatiently*). He is surely, and leaving me lonesome on the scruff of the hill. (*She gets up and puts envelope on dresser, then winds clock.*) Isn't it long the nights are now, Shawn Keogh, to be leaving a poor girl with her own self counting the hours to the dawn of day?

SHAWN (*with awkward humour*). If it is, when we're wedded in a short while you'll have no call to complain, for I've little will to be walking off to wakes or weddings in the darkness of the night.

PEGEEN (*with rather scornful good humour*). You're making mighty certain, Shaneen, that I'll wed you now.

SHAWN. Aren't we after making a good bargain, the way we're only waiting these days on Father Reilly's dispensation from the bishops, or the Court of Rome?

PEGEEN (*looking at him teasingly, washing up at dresser*). It's a wonder, Shaneen, the Holy Father'd be taking notice of the likes of you; for if I was him I wouldn't bother with this place where you'll meet none but Red Linahan, has a squint in his eye, and Patcheen is lame in his heel, or the mad Mulrannies were driven from California and they lost in their wits. We're a queer lot these times to go troubling the Holy Father on his sacred seat.

SHAWN (*scandalized*). If we are, we're as good this place as another, maybe, and as good these times as we were for ever.

PEGEEN (*with scorn*). As good, is it? Where now will you meet the like of Daneen Sullivan knocked the eye from a peeler, or Marcus Quin, God rest him, got six months for maiming ewes, and he a great warrant to tell stories of holy Ireland till he'd have the old women shedding down tears about their feet. Where will you find the like of them, I'm saying?

SHAWN (*timidly*). If you don't, it's a good job, maybe; for (*with peculiar emphasis on the words*) Father Reilly has small conceit to have that kind walking around and talking to the girls.

PEGEEN (*impatiently, throwing water from basin out of the door*). Stop tormenting me with Father Reilly (*imitating his voice*) when I'm asking only what way I'll pass these twelve hours of dark, and not take my death with the fear. (*Looking out of door.*)

SHAWN (*timidly*). Would I fetch you the Widow Quin, maybe?

PEGEEN. Is it the like of that murderer? You'll not, surely.

SHAWN (*going to her, soothingly*). Then I'm thinking himself will stop along with you when he sees you taking on, for it'll be a long night-time with great darkness, and I'm after feeling a kind of fellow above in the furzy ditch, groaning wicked like a maddening dog, the way it's good cause you have, maybe, to be fearing now.

PEGEEN (*turning on him sharply*). What's that? Is it a man you seen?

SHAWN (*retreating*). I couldn't see him at all; but I heard him groaning out, and breaking his heart. It should have been a young man from his words speaking.

PEGEEN (*going after him*). And you never went near to see was he hurted or what ailed him at all?

SHAWN. I did not, Pegeen Mike. It was a dark, lonesome place to be hearing the like of him.

PEGEEN. Well, you're a daring fellow, and if they find his corpse stretched above in the dews of dawn, what'll you say then to the peelers, or the Justice of the Peace?

SHAWN (*thunderstruck*). I wasn't thinking of that. For the love of God, Pegeen Mike, don't let on I was speaking of him. Don't tell your father and the men is coming above; for if they heard that story, they'd have great blabbing this night at the wake.

PEGEEN. I'll maybe tell them, and I'll maybe not.

SHAWN. They are coming at the door. Will you whisht, I'm saying?

PEGEEN. Whisht yourself. (*She goes behind counter.* MICHAEL JAMES, *fat jovial publican, comes in followed by* PHILLY CULLEN, *who is thin and mistrusting, and* JIMMY FARRELL, *who is fat and amorous, about forty-five.*)

MEN (*together*). God bless you. The blessing of God on this place.

PEGEEN. God bless you kindly.

MICHAEL (*to men who go to the counter*). Sit down now, and take your rest. (*Crosses to* SHAWN *at the fire*) And how is it you are, Shawn Keogh? Are you coming over the sands to Kate Cassidy's wake?

SHAWN. I am not, Michael James. I'm going home the short cut to my bed.

PEGEEN (*speaking across the counter*). He's right too, and have you no shame, Michael James, to be quitting off for the whole night, and leaving myself lonesome in the shop?

MICHAEL (*good-humouredly*). Isn't it the same whether I go for the whole night or a part only? and I'm thinking it's a queer daughter you are if you'd have me crossing backward through the Stooks of the Dead Women, with a drop taken.

PEGEEN. If I am a queer daughter, it's a queer father'd be leav·ing me lonesome these twelve hours of dark, and I piling the turf with the dogs barking, and the calves mooing, and my own teeth rattling with the fear.

JIMMY (*flatteringly*). What is there to hurt you, and you a fine, hardy girl would knock the head of any two men in the place?

PEGEEN (*working herself up*). Isn't there the harvest boys with their tongues red for drink, and the ten tinkers is camped in the east glen, and the thousand militia—bad cess to them!— walking idle through the land. There's lots surely to hurt me, and I won't stop alone in it, let himself do what he will.

MICHAEL. If you're that afeard, let Shawn Keogh stop along with you. It's the will of God, I'm thinking, himself should be seeing to you now.

(*They all turn on* SHAWN.)

SHAWN (*in horrified confusion*). I would and welcome, Michael James, but I'm afeard of Father Reilly; and what at all would the Holy Father and the Cardinals of Rome be saying if they heard I did the like of that?

MICHAEL (*with contempt*). God help you! Can't you sit in by the hearth with the light lit and herself beyond in the room? You'll do that surely, for I've heard tell there's a queer fellow above, going mad or getting his death, maybe, in the gripe of the ditch, so she'd be safer this night with a person here.

SHAWN (*with plaintive despair*). I'm afeard of Father Reilly, I'm saying. Let you not be tempting me, and we near married itself.

PHILLY (*with cold contempt*). Lock him in the west room. He'll stay then and have no sin to be telling to the priest.

MICHAEL (*to* SHAWN, *getting between him and the door*). Go up now.

SHAWN (*at the top of his voice*). Don't stop me, Michael James. Let me out of the door, I'm saying, for the love of the Almighty God. Let me out (*trying to dodge past him*). Let me out of it, and may God grant you His indulgence in the hour of need.

MICHAEL (*loudly*). Stop your noising, and sit down by the hearth. (*Gives him a push and goes to counter laughing.*)

SHAWN (*turning back, wringing his hands*). Oh, Father Reilly and the saints of God, where will I hide myself to-day? Oh, St. Joseph and St. Patrick and St. Brigid, and St. James, have mercy on me now! (SHAWN *turns round, sees door clear, and makes a rush for it.*)

MICHAEL (*catching him by the coat-tail*). You'd be going, is it?

SHAWN (*screaming*). Leave me go, Michael James, leave me go, you old Pagan, leave me go, or I'll get the curse of the priests on you, and of the scarlet-coated bishops of the courts of Rome. (*With a sudden movement he pulls himself out of his coat, and disappears out of the door, leaving his coat in* MICHAEL'S *hands.*)

MICHAEL (*turning round, and holding up coat*). Well, there's the coat of a Christian man. Oh, there's sainted glory this day in the lonesome west; and by the will of God I've got you a decent man, Pegeen, you'll have no call to be spying after if you've a score of young girls, maybe, weeding in your fields.

PEGEEN (*taking up the defence of her property*). What right have you to be making game of a poor fellow for minding the priest, when it's your own the fault is, not paying a penny pot-boy to stand along with me and give me courage in the doing of my work? (*She snaps the coat away from him, and goes behind counter with it.*)

MICHAEL (*taken aback*). Where would I get a pot-boy? Would you have me send the bellman screaming in the streets of Castlebar?

SHAWN (*opening the door a chink and putting in his head, in a small voice*). Michael James!

MICHAEL (*imitating him*). What ails you?

SHAWN. The queer dying fellow's beyond looking over the ditch. He's come up, I'm thinking, stealing your hens. (*Looks over his shoulder*) God help me, he's following me now (*he runs into room*), and if he's heard what I said, he'll be having my life, and I going home lonesome in the darkness of the night.

(*For a perceptible moment they watch the door with curiosity. Some one coughs outside. Then* CHRISTY MAHON, *a slight young man, comes in very tired and frightened and dirty.*)

CHRISTY (*in a small voice*). God save all here!

MEN. God save you kindly.

CHRISTY (*going to the counter*). I'd trouble you for a glass of porter, woman of the house. (*He puts down coin.*)

PEGEEN (*serving him*). You're one of the tinkers, young fellow, is beyond camped in the glen?

CHRISTY. I am not; but I'm destroyed walking.

MICHAEL (*patronizingly*). Let you come up then to the fire. You're looking famished with the cold.

CHRISTY. God reward you. (*He takes up his glass and goes a little way across to the left, then stops and looks about him*) Is it often the police do be coming into this place, master of the house?

MICHAEL. If you'd come in better hours, you'd have seen "Licensed for the sale of Beer and Spirits, to be consumed on the premises," written in white letters above the door, and what would the polis want spying on me, and not a decent house within four miles, the way every living Christian is a bona fide, saving one widow alone?

CHRISTY (*with relief*). It's a safe house, so. (*He goes over to the fire, sighing and moaning. Then he sits down, putting his glass beside him and begins gnawing a turnip, too miserable to feel the others staring at him with curiosity.*)

MICHAEL (*going after him*). Is it yourself is fearing the polis? You're wanting, maybe?

CHRISTY. There's many wanting.

MICHAEL. Many surely, with the broken harvest and the ended wars. (*He picks up some stockings, etc., that are near the fire, and carries them away furtively*) It should be larceny, I'm thinking.

CHRISTY (*dolefully*). I had it in my mind it was a different word and a bigger.

PEGEEN. There's a queer lad. Were you never slapped in school, young fellow, that you don't know the name of your deed?

CHRISTY (*bashfully*). I'm slow at learning, a middling scholar only.

MICHAEL. If you're a dunce itself, you'd have a right to know that larceny's robbing and stealing. Is it for the like of that you're wanting?

CHRISTY (*with a flash of family pride*). And I the son of a strong farmer (*with a sudden qualm*), God rest his soul, could have bought up the whole of your old house awhile since, from the butt of his tailpocket, and not have missed the weight of it gone.

MICHAEL (*impressed*). If it's not stealing, it's maybe something big.

CHRISTY. (*flattered*). Aye; it's maybe something big.

JIMMY. He's a wicked-looking young fellow. Maybe he followed after a young woman on a lonesome night.

CHRISTY (*shocked*). Oh, the saints forbid, mister; I was all times a decent lad.

PHILLY (*turning on* JIMMY). You're a silly man, Jimmy Farrell. He said his father was a farmer a while since, and there's himself now in a poor state. Maybe the land was grabbed from him, and he did what any decent man would do.

MICHAEL (*to* CHRISTY, *mysteriously*). Was it bailiffs?

CHRISTY. The divil a one.

MICHAEL. Agents?

CHRISTY. The divil a one.

MICHAEL. Landlords?

CHRISTY (*peevishly*). Ah, not at all, I'm saying. You'd see the like of them stories on any little paper of a Munster town. But I'm not calling to mind any person, gentle, simple, judge or jury, did the like of me.

(*They all draw nearer with delighted curiosity.*)

PHILLY. Well, that lad's a puzzle-the-world.

JIMMY. He'd beat Dan Davies' circus, or the holy missioners making sermons on the villainy of man. Try him again, Philly.

PHILLY. Did you strike golden guineas out of solder, young fellow, or shilling coins itself?

CHRISTY. I did not, mister, not sixpence nor a farthing coin.

JIMMY. Did you marry three wives maybe? I'm told there's a sprinkling have done that among the holy Luthers of the preaching north.

CHRISTY (*shyly*). I never married with one, let alone with a couple or three.

PHILLY. Maybe he went fighting for the Boers, the like of the man beyond, was judged to be hanged, quartered and drawn. Were you off east, young fellow, fighting bloody wars for Kruger and the freedom of the Boers?

CHRISTY. I never left my own parish till Tuesday was a week.

PEGEEN (coming from counter). He's done nothing, so. (*To* CHRISTY) If you didn't commit murder or a bad, nasty thing, or false coining, or robbery, or butchery, or the like of them, there isn't anything that would be worth your troubling for to run from now. You did nothing at all.

CHRISTY (*his feelings hurt*). That's an unkindly thing to be saying to a poor orphaned traveller, has a prison behind him, and hanging before, and hell's gap gaping below.

PEGEEN (*with a sign to the men to be quiet*). You're only saying it. You did nothing at all. A soft lad the like of you wouldn't slit the windpipe of a screeching sow.

CHRISTY (*offended*). You're not speaking the truth.

PEGEEN (*in mock rage*). Not speaking the truth, is it? Would you have me knock the head off you with the butt of the broom?

CHRISTY (*twisting round on her with a sharp cry of horror*). Don't strike me. I killed my poor father, Tuesday was a week, for doing the like of that.

PEGEEN (*with blank amazement*). Is it killed your father?

CHRISTY (*subsiding*). With the help of God I did surely, and that the Holy Immaculate Mother may intercede for his soul.

PHILLY (*retreating with* JIMMY). There's a daring fellow.

JIMMY. Oh, glory be to God!

MICHAEL (*with great respect*). That was a hanging crime, mister honey. You should have had good reason for doing the like of that.

CHRISTY (*in a very reasonable tone*). He was a dirty man, God forgive him, and he getting old and crusty, the way I couldn't put up with him at all.

PEGEEN. And you shot him dead?

CHRISTY (*shaking his head*). I never used weapons. I've no license, and I'm a law-fearing man.

MICHAEL. It was with a hilted knife maybe? I'm told, in the big world it's bloody knives they use.

CHRISTY (*loudly, scandalized*). Do you take me for a slaughter-boy?

PEGEEN. You never hanged him, the way Jimmy Farrell hanged his dog from the license, and had it screeching and wriggling three hours at the butt of a string, and himself swearing it was a dead dog, and the peelers swearing it had life?

CHRISTY. I did not then. I just riz the loy and let fall the edge of it on the ridge of his skull, and he went down at my feet like an empty sack, and never let a grunt or groan from him at all.

MICHAEL (*making a sign to* PEGEEN *to fill* CHRISTY'S *glass*). And what way weren't you hanged, mister? Did you bury him then?

CHRISTY (*considering*). Aye. I buried him then. Wasn't I digging spuds in the field?

MICHAEL. And the peelers never followed after you the eleven days that you're out?

CHRISTY (*shaking his head*). Never a one of them, and I walking forward facing hog, dog, or divil on the highway of the road.

PHILLY (*nodding wisely*). It's only with a common week-day kind of a murderer them lads would be trusting their carcase, and that man should be a great terror when his temper's roused.

MICHAEL. He should then. (*To* CHRISTY) And where was it, mister honey, that you did the deed?

CHRISTY (*looking at him with suspicion*). Oh, a distant place, master of the house, a windy corner of high, distant hills.

PHILLY (*nodding with approval*). He's a close man, and he's right, surely.

PEGEEN. That'd be a lad with the sense of Solomon to have for a pot-boy, Michael James, if it's the truth you're seeking one at all.

PHILLY. The peelers is fearing him, and if you'd that lad in the house there isn't one of them would come smelling around if the dogs itself were lapping poteen from the dung-pit of the yard.

JIMMY. Bravery's a treasure in a lonesome place, and a lad would kill his father, I'm thinking, would face a foxy divil with a pitchpike on the flags of hell.

PEGEEN. It's the truth they're saying, and if I'd that lad in the house, I wouldn't be fearing the loosèd kharki cut-throats, or the walking dead.

CHRISTY (*swelling with surprise and triumph*). Well, glory be to God!

MICHAEL (*with deference*). Would you think well to stop here and be pot-boy, mister honey, if we gave you good wages, and didn't destroy you with the weight of work?

SHAWN (*coming forward uneasily*). That'd be a queer kind to bring into a decent quiet household with the like of Pegeen Mike.

PEGEEN (*very sharply*). Will you whisht? Who's speaking to you?

SHAWN (*retreating*). A bloody-handed murderer the like of . . .

PEGEEN (*snapping at him*). Whisht I am saying; we'll take no fooling from your like at all. (*To* CHRISTY *with a honeyed voice*) And you, young fellow, you'd have a right to stop, I'm thinking, for we'd do our all and utmost to content your needs.

CHRISTY (*overcome with wonder*). And I'd be safe in this place from the searching law?

MICHAEL. You would, surely. If they're not fearing you, itself, the peelers in this place is decent droughty poor fellows, wouldn't touch a cur dog and not give warning in the dead of night.

PEGEEN (*very kindly and persuasively*). Let you stop a short while anyhow. Aren't you destroyed walking with your feet in bleeding blisters, and your whole skin needing washing like a Wicklow sheep?

CHRISTY (*looking round with satisfaction*). It's a nice room, and if it's not humbugging me you are, I'm thinking that I'll surely stay.

JIMMY (*jumps up*). Now, by the grace of God, herself will be safe this night, with a man killed his father holding danger from the door, and let you come on, Michael James, or they'll have the best stuff drunk at the wake.

MICHAEL (*going to the door with men*). And begging your pardon, mister, what name will we call you, for we'd like to know?

CHRISTY. Christopher Mahon.

MICHAEL. Well, God bless you, Christy, and a good rest till we meet again when the sun'll be rising to the noon of day.

CHRISTY. God bless you all.

MEN. God bless you.

   (*They go out except* SHAWN, *who lingers at door.*)

SHAWN (*to* PEGEEN). Are you wanting me to stop along with you and keep you from harm?

PEGEEN. (*gruffly*). Didn't you say you were fearing Father Reilly?

SHAWN. There'd be no harm staying now, I'm thinking, and himself in it too.

PEGEEN. You wouldn't stay when there was need for you, and let you step off nimble this time when there's none.

SHAWN. Didn't I say it was Father Reilly . . .

PEGEEN. Go on, then, to Father Reilly (*in a jeering tone*), and let him put you in the holy brotherhoods, and leave that lad to me.

SHAWN. If I meet the Widow Quin . . .

PEGEEN. Go on, I'm saying, and don't be waking this place with your noise. (*She hustles him out and bolts the door*) That lad would wear the spirits from the saints of peace. (*Bustles about, then takes off her apron and pins it up in the window as a blind.* CHRISTY *watching her timidly. Then she comes to him and speaks with bland good-humour*) Let you stretch out now by the fire, young fellow. You should be destroyed travelling.

CHRISTY (*shyly again, drawing off his boots*). I'm tired, surely, walking wild eleven days, and waking fearful in the night. (*He holds up one of his feet, feeling his blisters, and looking at them with compassion.*)

PEGEEN (*standing beside him, watching him with delight*). You should have had great people in your family, I'm thinking, with the little, small feet you have, and you with a kind of a quality name, the like of what you'd find on the great powers and potentates of France and Spain.

CHRISTY (*with pride*). We were great surely, with wide and windy acres of rich Munster land.

PEGEEN. Wasn't I telling you, and you a fine, handsome young fellow with a noble brow?

CHRISTY (*with a flash of delighted surprise*). Is it me?

PEGEEN. Aye. Did you never hear that from the young girls where you come from in the west or south?

CHRISTY (*with venom*). I did not then. Oh, they're bloody liars in the naked parish where I grew a man.

PEGEEN. If they are itself, you've heard it these days, I'm thinking, and you walking the world telling out your story to young girls or old.

CHRISTY. I've told my story no place till this night, Pegeen Mike, and it's foolish I was here, maybe, to be talking free, but you're decent people, I'm thinking, and yourself a kindly woman, the way I wasn't fearing you at all.

PEGEEN (*filling a sack with straw*). You've said the like of that, maybe, in every cot and cabin where you've met a young girl on your way.

CHRISTY (*going over to her, gradually raising his voice*). I've said it nowhere till this night, I'm telling you, for I've seen none the like of you the eleven long days I am walking the world, looking over a low ditch or a high ditch on my north or my south, into stony scattered fields, or scribes of bog, where you'd see young, limber girls, and fine prancing women making laughter with the men.

PEGEEN. If you weren't destroyed travelling, you'd have as much talk and streeleen, I'm thinking, as Owen Roe O'Sullivan or the poets of the Dingle Bay, and I've heard all times it's the poets are your like, fine fiery fellows with great rages when their temper's roused.

CHRISTY (*drawing a little nearer to her*). You've a power of rings, God bless you, and would there be any offence if I was asking are you single now?

PEGEEN. What would I want wedding so young?

CHRISTY (*with relief*). We're alike, so.

PEGEEN (*she puts sack on settle and beats it up*). I never killed my father. I'd be afeard to do that, except I was the like of yourself with blind rages tearing me within, for I'm thinking you should have had great tussling when the end was come.

CHRISTY (*expanding with delight at the first confidential talk he has ever had with a woman*). We had not then. It was a hard woman was come over the hill, and if he was always a crusty kind when he'd a hard woman setting him on, not the divil himself or his four fathers could put up with him at all.

PEGEEN (*with curiosity*). And isn't it a great wonder that one wasn't fearing you?

CHRISTY (*very confidentially*). Up to the day I killed my father, there wasn't a person in Ireland knew the kind I was, and I there drinking, waking, eating, sleeping, a quiet, simple poor fellow with no man giving me heed.

PEGEEN (*getting a quilt out of the cupboard and putting it on the sack*). It was the girls were giving you heed maybe, and I'm thinking it's most conceit you'd have to be gaming with their like.

CHRISTY (*shaking his head, with simplicity*). Not the girls itself, and I won't tell you a lie. There wasn't anyone heeding me in that place saving only the dumb beasts of the field. (*He sits down at fire.*)

PEGEEN (*with disappointment*). And I thinking you should have been living the like of a king of Norway or the Eastern world. (*She comes and sits beside him after placing bread and mug of milk on the table.*)

CHRISTY (*laughing piteously*). The like of a king, is it? And I after toiling, moiling, digging, dodging from the dawn till dusk with never a sight of joy or sport saving only when I'd be abroad in the dark night poaching rabbits on hills, for I was a divil to poach, God forgive me, (*very naïvely*) and I near got six months for going with a dung fork and stabbing a fish.

PEGEEN. And it's that you'd call sport, is it, to be abroad in the darkness with yourself alone?

CHRISTY. I did, God help me, and there I'd be as happy as the sunshine of St. Martin's Day, watching the light passing the north or the patches of fog, till I'd hear a rabbit starting to screech and I'd go running in the furze. Then when I'd my full share I'd come walking down where you'd see the ducks and geese stretched sleeping on the highway of the road, and before I'd pass the dunghill, I'd hear himself snoring out, a loud lonesome snore he'd be making all times, the while he was sleeping, and he a man 'd be raging all times, the while he was waking, like a gaudy officer you'd hear cursing and damning and swearing oaths.

PEGEEN. Providence and Mercy, spare us all!

CHRISTY. It's that you'd say surely if you seen him and he after drinking for weeks, rising up in the red dawn, or before it maybe, and going out into the yard as naked as an ash tree in the moon of May, and shying clods against the visage of the stars till he'd put the fear of death into the banbhs and the screeching sows.

PEGEEN. I'd be well-nigh afeard of that lad myself, I'm thinking. And there was no one in it but the two of you alone?

CHRISTY. The divil a one, though he'd sons and daughters walking all great states and territories of the world, and not a one of them, to this day, but would say their seven curses on him, and they rousing up to let a cough or sneeze, maybe, in the deadness of the night.

PEGEEN (*nodding her head*). Well, you should have been a queer lot. I never cursed my father the like of that, though I'm twenty and more years of age.

CHRISTY. Then you'd have cursed mine, I'm telling you, and he a man never gave peace to any, saving when he'd get two months or three, or be locked in the asylums for battering peelers or assaulting men (*with depression*) the way it was a bitter life he led me till I did up a Tuesday and halve his skull.

PEGEEN (*putting her hand on his shoulder*). Well, you'll have peace in this place, Christy Mahon, and none to trouble you, and it's near time a fine lad like you should have your good share of the earth.

CHRISTY. It's time surely, and I a seemly fellow with great strength in me and bravery of . . .

(*Someone knocks.*)

CHRISTY (*clinging to* PEGEEN). Oh, glory! it's late for knocking, and this last while I'm in terror of the peelers, and the walking dead.

(*Knocking again.*)

PEGEEN. Who's there?

VOICE (*outside*). Me.

PEGEEN. Who's me?

VOICE. The Widow Quin.

PEGEEN (*jumping up and giving him the bread and milk*). Go on now with your supper, and let on to be sleepy, for if she found you were such a warrant to talk, she'd be stringing gabble till the dawn of day. (*He takes bread and sits shyly with his back to the door.*)

PEGEEN (*opening door, with temper*). What ails you, or what is it you're wanting at this hour of the night?

WIDOW QUIN (*coming in a step and peering at* CHRISTY.) I'm after meeting Shawn Keogh and Father Reilly below, who told me of your curiosity man, and they fearing by this time he was maybe roaring, romping on your hands with drink.

PEGEEN (*pointing to* CHRISTY). Look now is he roaring, and he stretched away drowsy with his supper and his mug of milk. Walk down and tell that to Father Reilly and to Shaneen Keogh.

WIDOW QUIN (*coming forward*). I'll not see them again, for I've their word to lead that lad forward for to lodge with me.

PEGEEN (*in blank amazement*). This night, is it?

WIDOW QUIN (*going over*). This night. "It isn't fitting," says the priesteen, "to have his likeness lodging with an orphaned girl." (*To* CHRISTY) God save you, mister!

CHRISTY (*shyly*). God save you kindly.

WIDOW QUIN (*looking at him with half-amazed curiosity*). Well, aren't you a little smiling fellow? It should have been great and bitter torments did rouse your spirits to a deed of blood.

CHRISTY (*doubtfully*). It should, maybe.

WIDOW QUIN. It's more than "maybe" I'm saying, and it'd soften my heart to see you sitting so simple with your cup and cake, and you fitter to be saying your catechism than slaying your da.

PEGEEN (*at counter, washing glasses*). There's talking when any'd see he's fit to be holding his head high with the wonders of the world. Walk on from this, for I'll not have him tormented and he destroyed travelling since Tuesday was a week.

WIDOW QUIN (*peaceably*). We'll be walking surely when his supper's done, and you'll find we're great company, young fellow, when it's of the like of you and me you'd hear the penny poets singing in an August Fair.

CHRISTY (*innocently*). Did you kill your father?

PEGEEN (*contemptuously*). She did not. She hit himself with a worn pick, and the rusted poison did corrode his blood the way he never overed it, and died after. That was a sneaky kind of murder did win small glory with the boys itself. (*She crosses to* CHRISTY's *left.*)

WIDOW QUIN (*with good-humour*). If it didn't, maybe all knows a widow woman has buried her children and destroyed her man is a wiser comrade for a young lad than a girl, the like of you, who'd go helter-skeltering after any man would let you a wink upon the road.

PEGEEN (*breaking out into wild rage*). And you'll say that, Widow Quin, and you gasping with the rage you had racing the hill beyond to look on his face.

WIDOW QUIN (*laughing derisively*). Me, is it? Well, Father Reilly has cuteness to divide you now. (*She pulls* CHRISTY *up*) There's great temptation in a man did slay his da, and we'd best be going, young fellow; so rise up and come with me.

PEGEEN (*seizing his arm*). He'll not stir. He's pot-boy in this place, and I'll not have him stolen off and kidnabbed while himself's abroad.

WIDOW QUIN. It'd be a crazy pot-boy'd lodge him in the shebeen where he works by day, so you'd have a right to come on, young fellow, till you see my little houseen, a perch off on the rising hill.

PEGEEN. Wait till morning, Christy Mahon. Wait till you lay eyes on her leaky thatch is growing more pasture for her buck goat than her square of fields, and she without a tramp itself to keep in order her place at all.

WIDOW QUIN. When you see me contriving in my little gardens, Christy Mahon, you'll swear the Lord God formed me to be living lone, and that there isn't my match in Mayo for thatching, or mowing, or shearing a sheep.

PEGEEN (*with noisy scorn*). It's true the Lord God formed you to contrive indeed. Doesn't the world know you reared a black lamb at your own breast, so that the Lord Bishop of Connaught felt the elements of a Christian, and he eating it after in a kidney stew? Doesn't the world know you've been seen shaving the foxy skipper from France for a threepenny bit and a sop of grass tobacco would wring the liver from a mountain goat you'd meet leaping the hills?

WIDOW QUIN (*with amusement*). Do you hear her now, young fellow? Do you hear the way she'll be rating at your own self when a week is by?

PEGEEN (*to* CHRISTY). Don't heed her. Tell her to go into her pigsty and not plague us here.

WIDOW QUIN. I'm going; but he'll come with me.

PEGEEN (*shaking him*). Are you dumb, young fellow?

CHRISTY (*timidly, to* WIDOW QUIN). God increase you; but I'm pot-boy in this place, and it's here I'd liefer stay.

PEGEEN (*triumphantly*). Now you have heard him, and go on from this.

WIDOW QUIN (*looking round the room*). It's lonesome this hour crossing the hill, and if he won't come along with me, I'd have a right maybe to stop this night with yourselves. Let me stretch out on the settle, Pegeen Mike; and himself can lie by the hearth.

PEGEEN (*short and fiercely*). Faith, I won't. Quit off or I will send you now.

WIDOW QUIN (*gathering her shawl up.*) Well, it's a terror to be aged a score. (*To* CHRISTY) God bless you now, young fellow, and let you be wary, or there's right torment will await you here if you go romancing with her like, and she waiting only, as they bade me say, on a sheepskin parchment to be wed with Shawn Keogh of Killakeen.

CHRISTY (*going to Pegeen as she bolts the door*). What's that she's after saying?

PEGEEN. Lies and blather, you've no call to mind. Well, isn't Shawn Keogh an impudent fellow to send up spying on me? Wait till I lay hands on him. Let him wait, I'm saying.

CHRISTY. And you're not wedding him at all?

PEGEEN. I wouldn't wed him if a bishop came walking for to join us here.

CHRISTY. That God in glory may be thanked for that.

PEGLEN. There's your bed now. I've put a quilt upon you I'm after quilting a while since with my own two hands, and you'd best stretch out now for your sleep, and may God give you a good rest till I call you in the morning when the cocks will crow.

CHRISTY (*as she goes to inner room*). May God and Mary and St. Patrick bless you and reward you, for your kindly talk. (*She shuts the door behind her. He settles his bed slowly, feeling the quilt with immense satisfaction*) Well, it's a clean bed and soft with it, and it's great luck and company I've won me in the end of time—two fine women fighting for the likes of me—till I'm thinking this night wasn't I a foolish fellow not to kill my father in the years gone by.

CURTAIN

ACT TWO

SCENE, *as before. Brilliant morning light.* CHRISTY, *looking bright and cheerful, is cleaning a girl's boots.*

CHRISTY (*to himself, counting jugs on dresser*). Half a hundred beyond. Ten there. A score that's above. Eighty jugs. Six cups and a broken one. Two plates. A power of glasses. Bottles, a school-master'd be hard set to count, and enough in them, I'm thinking, to drunken all the wealth and wisdom of the County Clare. (*He puts down the boot carefully*) There's her boots now, nice and decent for her evening use, and isn't it grand brushes she has? (*He puts them down and goes by degrees to the looking-glass*) Well, this'd be a fine place to be my whole life talking out with swearing Christians, in place of my old dogs and cat, and I stalking around, smoking my pipe and drinking my fill, and never a day's work but drawing a cork an odd time, or wiping a glass, or rinsing out a shiny tumbler for a decent man. (*He takes the looking-glass from the wall and puts it on the back of a chair; then sits down in front of it and begins washing his face*) Didn't I know rightly I was hand-some, though it was the divil's own mirror we had beyond, would twist a squint across an angel's brow; and I'll be grow-ing fine from this day, the way I'll have a soft lovely skin on me and won't be the like of the clumsy young fellows do be plough-ing all times in the earth and dung. (*He starts*) Is she coming again? (*He looks out*) Stranger girls. God help me, where'll I hide myself away and my long neck naked to the world?

(*He looks out*) I'd best go to the room maybe till I'm dressed again. (*He gathers up his coat and the looking-glass, and runs into the inner room. The door is pushed open, and* SUSAN BRADY *looks in, and knocks on door.*)

SUSAN. There's nobody in it. (*Knocks again.*)

NELLY (*pushing her in and following her, with* HONOR BLAKE *and* SARA TANSEY). It'd be early for them both to be out walking the hill.

SUSAN. I'm thinking Shawn Keogh was making game of us and there's no such man in it at all.

HONOR (*pointing to straw and quilt*). Look at that. He's been sleeping there in the night. Well, it'll be a hard case if he's gone off now, the way we'll never set our eyes on a man killed his father, and we after rising early and destroying ourselves running fast on the hill.

NELLY. Are you thinking them's his boots?

SARA (*taking them up*). If they are, there should be his father's track on them. Did you never read in the papers the way murdered men do bleed and drip?

SUSAN. Is that blood there, Sara Tansey?

SARA (*smelling it*). That's bog water, I'm thinking, but it's his own they are surely, for I never seen the like of them for whity mud, and red mud, and turf on them, and the fine sands of the sea. That man's been walking, I'm telling you. (*She goes down right, putting on one of his boots.*)

SUSAN (*going to window*). Maybe he's stolen off to Belmullet with the boots of Michael James, and you'd have a right so to follow after him, Sara Tansey, and you the one yoked the ass cart and drove ten miles to set your eyes on the man bit the yellow lady's nostril on the northern shore. (*She looks out.*)

SARA (*running to window with one boot on.*) Don't be talking, and we fooled to-day. (*Putting on other boot*) There's a pair do fit me well, and I'll be keeping them for walking to the priest, when you'd be ashamed this place, going up winter and summer with nothing worth while to confess at all.

HONOR (*who has been listening at the door*). Whisht! there's someone inside the room. (*She pushes door a chink open*) It's a man.

(*Sara kicks off boots and puts them where they were. They all stand in a line looking through chink.*)

SARA. I'll call him. Mister! Mister! (*He puts in his head*) Is Pegeen within?

CHRISTY (*coming in as meek as a mouse, with the looking-glass held behind his back*). She's above on the cnuceen, seeking the nanny goats, the way she'd have a sup of goat's milk for to colour my tea.

SARA. And asking your pardon, is it you's the man killed his father?

CHRISTY (*sidling toward the nail where the glass was hanging*). I am, God help me!

SARA (*taking eggs she has brought*). Then my thousand welcomes to you, and I've run up with a brace of duck's eggs for your food to-day. Pegeen's ducks is no use, but these are the real rich sort. Hold out your hand and you'll see it's no lie I'm telling you.

CHRISTY (*coming forward shyly, and holding out his left hand*). They're a great and weighty size.

SUSAN. And I run up with a pat of butter, for it'd be a poor thing to have you eating your spuds dry, and you after running a great way since you did destroy your da.

CHRISTY. Thank you kindly.

HONOR. And I brought you a little cut of cake, for you should have a thin stomach on you, and you that length walking the world.

NELLY. And I brought you a little laying pullet—boiled and all she is—was crushed at the fall of night by the curate's car. Feel the fat of that breast, mister.

CHRISTY. It's bursting, surely. (*He feels it with the back of his hand, in which he holds the presents.*)

SARA. Will you pinch it? Is your right hand too sacred for to use at all? (*She slips round behind him*) It's a glass he has. Well, I never seen to this day a man with a looking-glass held to his back. Them that kills their fathers is a vain lot surely.

  (*Girls giggle.*)

CHRISTY (*smiling innocently and piling presents on glass.*) I'm very thankful to you all to-day . . .

WIDOW QUIN (*coming in quickly, at door*). Sara Tansey, Susan Brady, Honor Blake! What in glory has you here at this hour of day?

GIRLS (*giggling*). That's the man killed his father.

WIDOW QUIN (*coming to them*). I know well it's the man; and

I'm after putting him down in the sports below for racing, leaping, pitching, and the Lord knows what.

SARA (*exuberantly*). That's right. Widow Quin. I'll bet my dowry that he'll lick the world.

WIDOW QUIN. If you will, you'd have a right to have him fresh and nourished in place of nursing a feast. (*Taking presents*) Are you fasting or fed, young fellow?

CHRISTY. Fasting, if you please.

WIDOW QUIN (*loudly*). Well, you're the lot. Stir up now and give him his breakfast. (*To* CHRISTY) Come here to me (*she puts him on bench beside her while the girls make tea and get his breakfast*) and let you tell us your story before Pegeen will come, in place of grinning your ears off like the moon of May.

CHRISTY (*beginning to be pleased*). It's a long story; you'd be destroyed listening.

WIDOW QUIN. Don't be letting on to be shy, a fine, gamey, treacherous lad the like of you. Was it in your house beyond you cracked his skull?

CHRISTY (*shy but flattered*). It was not. We were digging spuds in his cold, sloping, stony, divil's patch of a field.

WIDOW QUIN. And you went asking money of him, or making talk of getting a wife would drive him from his farm?

CHRISTY. I did not, then; but there I was, digging and digging, and "You squinting idiot," says he, "let you walk down now and tell the priest you'll wed the Widow Casey in a score of days."

WIDOW QUIN. And what kind was she?

CHRISTY (*with horror*). A walking terror from beyond the hills, and she two score and five years, and two hundredweights and five pounds in the weighing scales, with a limping leg on her, and a blinded eye, and she a woman of noted misbehavior with the old and young.

GIRLS (*clustering round him, serving him*). Glory be.

WIDOW QUIN. And what did he want driving you to wed with her? (*She takes a bit of the chicken.*)

CHRISTY (*eating with growing satisfaction*). He was letting on I was wanting a protector from the harshness of the world, and he without a thought the whole while but how he'd have her hut to live in and her gold to drink.

WIDOW QUIN. There's maybe worse than a dry hearth and a widow woman and your glass at night. So you hit him then?

CHRISTY (*getting almost excited*). I did not. "I won't wed her," says I, "when all know she did suckle me for six weeks when I came into the world, and she a hag this day with a tongue on her has the crows and seabirds scattered, the way they would cast a shadow on her garden with the dread of her curse."

WIDOW QUIN (*teasingly*). That one should be right company.

SARA (*eagerly*). Don't mind her. Did you kill him then?

CHRISTY. "She's too good for the like of you," says he, "and go on now or I'll flatten you out like a crawling beast has passed under a dray." "You will not if I can help it," says I. "Go on," says he, "or I'll have the divil making garters of your limbs to-night." "You will not if I can help it," says I. (*He sits up, brandishing his mug.*)

SARA. You were right surely.

CHRISTY (*impressively*). With that the sun came out between the cloud and the hill, and it shining green in my face. "God have mercy on your soul," says he, lifting a scythe; "or on your own," says I, raising the loy.

SUSAN. That's a grand story.

HONOR. He tells it lovely.

CHRISTY (*flattered and confident, waving bone*). He gave a drive with the scythe, and I gave a lep to the east. Then I turned around with my back to the north, and I hit a blow on the ridge of his skull, laid him stretched out, and he split to the knob of his gullet. (*He raises the chicken bone to his Adam's apple.*)

GIRLS (*together*). Well, you're a marvel! Oh, God bless you! You're the lad surely!

SUSAN. I'm thinking the Lord God sent him this road to make a second husband to the Widow Quin, and she with a great yearning to be wedded, though all dread her here. Lift him on her knee, Sara Tansey.

WIDOW QUIN. Don't tease him.

SARA (*going over to dresser and counter very quickly, and getting two glasses and porter*). You're heroes surely, and let you drink a supeen with your arms linked like the outlandish lovers in the sailor's song. (*She links their arms and gives them the glasses*) There now. Drink a health to the wonders of the western world, the pirates, preachers, poteen-makers, with the jobbing jockies; parching peelers, and the juries fill their stomachs selling judgments of the English law. (*Brandishing the bottle.*)

WIDOW QUIN. That's a right toast, Sara Tansey. Now, Christy.

(*They drink with their arms linked, he drinking with his left hand, she with her right. As they are drinking,* PEGEEN MIKE *comes in with a milk can and stands aghast. They all spring away from* CHRISTY. *He goes down left.* WIDOW QUIN *remains seated.*)

PEGEEN (*angrily, to Sara*). What is it you're wanting?

SARA (*twisting her apron*). An ounce of tobacco.

PEGEEN. Have you tuppence?

SARA. I've forgotten my purse.

PEGEEN. Then you'd best be getting it and not fooling us here. (*To the* WIDOW QUIN, *with more elaborate scorn*) And what is it you're wanting, Widow Quin?

WIDOW QUIN (*insolently*). A penn'orth of starch.

PEGEEN (*breaking out*). And you without a white shift or a shirt in your whole family since the drying of the flood. I've no starch for the like of you, and let you walk on now to Killamuck.

WIDOW QUIN (*turning to* CHRISTY, *as she goes out with the girls*). Well, you're mighty huffy this day, Pegeen Mike, and, you young fellow, let you not forget the sports and racing when the noon is by.

(*They go out.*)

PEGEEN (*imperiously*). Fling out that rubbish and put them cups away. (CHRISTY *tidies away in great haste*) Shove in the bench by the wall. (*He does so*) And hang that glass on the nail. What disturbed it at all?

CHRISTY (*very meekly*). I was making myself decent only, and this a fine country for young lovely girls.

PEGEEN (*sharply*). Whisht your talking of girls. (*Goes to counter—right.*)

CHRISTY. Wouldn't any wish to be decent in a place . . .

PEGEEN. Whisht I'm saying.

CHRISTY (*looks at her face for a moment with great misgivings, then as a last effort, takes up a loy, and goes towards her, with feigned assurance*). It was with a loy the like of that I killed my father.

PEGEEN (*still sharply*). You've told me that story six times since the dawn of day.

CHRISTY (*reproachfully*). It's a queer thing you wouldn't care to be hearing it and them girls after walking four miles to be listening to me now.

PEGEEN (*turning around astonished*). Four miles.

CHRISTY (*apologetically*). Didn't himself say there were only four bona fides living in the place?

PEGEEN. It's bona fides by the road they are, but that lot came over the river lepping the stones. It's not three perches when you go like that, and I was down this morning looking on the papers the post-boy does have in his bag. (*With meaning and emphasis*) For there was great news this day, Christopher Mahon. (*She goes into room left.*)

CHRISTY (*suspiciously*). Is it news of my murder?

PEGEEN (*inside*). Murder, indeed.

CHRISTY (*loudly*). A murdered da?

PEGEEN (*coming in again and crossing right*). There was not, but a story filled half a page of the hanging of a man. Ah, that should be a fearful end, young fellow, and it worst of all for a man who destroyed his da, for the like of him would get small mercies, and when it's dead he is, they'd put him in a narrow grave, with cheap sacking wrapping him round, and pour down quicklime on his head, the way you'd see a woman pouring any frish-frash from a cup.

CHRISTY (*very miserably*). Oh, God help me. Are you thinking I'm safe? You were saying at the fall of night, I was shut of jeopardy and I here with yourselves.

PEGEEN (*severely*). You'll be shut of jeopardy in no place if you go talking with a pack of wild girls the like of them do be walking abroad with the peelers, talking whispers at the fall of night.

CHRISTY (*with terror*). And you're thinking they'd tell?

PEGEEN (*with mock sympathy*). Who knows, God help you.

CHRISTY (*loudly*). What joy would they have to bring hanging to the likes of me?

PEGEEN. It's queer joys they have, and who knows the thing they'd do, if it'd make the green stones cry itself to think of you swaying and swiggling at the butt of a rope, and you with a fine, stout neck, God bless you! the way you'd be a half an hour, in great anguish, getting your death.

CHRISTY (*getting his boots and putting them on*). If there's that terror of them, it'd be best, maybe, I went on wandering like Esau or Cain and Abel on the sides of Neifin or the Erris plain.

PEGEEN (*beginning to play with him*). It would, maybe, for I've heard the Circuit Judges this place is a heartless crew.

CHRISTY (*bitterly*). It's more than Judges this place is a heartless crew. (*Looking up at her*) And isn't it a poor thing to be starting again and I a lonesome fellow will be looking out on women and girls the way the needy fallen spirits do be looking on the Lord?

PEGEEN. What call have you to be that lonesome when there's poor girls walking Mayo in their thousands now?

CHRISTY (*grimly*). It's well you know what call I have. It's well you know it's a lonesome thing to be passing small towns with the lights shining sideways when the night is down, or going in strange places with a dog noising before you and a dog noising behind, or drawn to the cities where you'd hear a voice kissing and talking deep love in every shadow of the ditch, and you passing on with an empty, hungry stomach failing from your heart.

PEGEEN. I'm thinking you're an odd man, Christy Mahon. The oddest walking fellow I ever set my eyes on to this hour to-day.

CHRISTY. What would any be but odd men and they living lonesome in the world?

PEGEEN. I'm not odd, and I'm my whole life with my father only.

CHRISTY (*with infinite admiration*). How would a lovely handsome woman the like of you be lonesome when all men should be thronging around to hear the sweetness of your voice, and the little infant children should be pestering your steps I'm thinking, and you walking the roads.

PEGEEN. I'm hard set to know what way a coaxing fellow the like of yourself should be lonesome either.

CHRISTY. Coaxing?

PEGEEN. Would you have me think a man never talked with the girls would have the words you've spoken to-day? It's only letting on you are to be lonesome, the way you'd get around me now.

CHRISTY. I wish to God I was letting on; but I was lonesome all times, and born lonesome, I'm thinking, as the moon of dawn. (*Going to door.*)

PEGEEN (*puzzled by his talk*). Well, it's a story I'm not understanding at all why you'd be worse than another, Christy Mahon, and you a fine lad with the great savagery to destroy your da.

CHRISTY. It's little I'm understanding myself, saving only that my heart's scalded this day, and I am going off stretching out the earth between us, the way I'll not be waking near you another dawn of the year till the two of us do arise to hope or judgment with the saints of God, and now I'd best be going with my wattle in my hand, for hanging is a poor thing (*turning to go*), and it's little welcome only is left me in this house to-day.

PEGEEN (*sharply*). Christy! (*He turns round*) Come here to me. (*He goes towards her*) Lay down that switch and throw some sods on the fire. You're pot-boy in this place, and I'll not have you mitch off from us now.

CHRISTY. You were saying I'd be hanged if I stay.

PEGEEN (*quite kindly at last*). I'm after going down and reading the fearful crimes of Ireland for two weeks or three, and there wasn't a word of your murder. (*Getting up and going over to the counter*) They've likely not found the body. You're safe so with ourselves.

CHRISTY (*astonished, slowly*). It's making game of me you were (*following her with fearful joy*), and I can stay so, working at your side, and I not lonesome from this mortal day.

PEGEEN. What's to hinder you from staying, except the widow woman or the young girls would inveigle you off?

CHRISTY (*with rapture*). And I'll have your words from this day filling my ears, and that look is come upon you meeting my two eyes, and I watching you loafing around in the warm sun, or rinsing your ankles when the night is come.

PEGEEN (*kindly, but a little embarrassed*). I'm thinking you'll be a loyal young lad to have working around, and if you vexed me a while since with your leaguing with the girls, I wouldn't give a thraneen for a lad hadn't a mighty spirit in him and a gamey heart.

(SHAWN KEOGH *runs in carrying a cleeve on his back, followed by the* WIDOW QUIN.)

SHAWN (*to* PEGEEN). I was passing below, and I seen your mountainy sheep eating cabbages in Jimmy's field. Run up or they'll be bursting surely.

PEGEEN. Oh, God mend them! (*She puts a shawl over her head and runs out.*)

CHRISTY (*looking from one to the other. Still in high spirits*). I'd best go to her aid maybe. I'm handy with ewes.

WIDOW QUIN (*closing the door*). She can do that much, and there is Shaneen has long speeches for to tell you now. (*She sits down with an amused smile.*)

SHAWN (*taking something from his pocket and offering it to* CHRISTY). Do you see that, mister?

CHRISTY (*looking at it*). The half of a ticket to the Western States!

SHAWN (*trembling with anxiety*) I'll give it to you and my new hat (*pulling it out of hamper*); and my breeches with the double seat (*pulling it off*); and my new coat is woven from the blackest shearings for three miles around (*giving him the coat*); I'll give you the whole of them, and my blessing, and the blessing of Father Reilly itself, maybe, if you'll quit from this and leave us in the peace we had till last night at the fall of dark.

CHRISTY (*with a new arrogance*). And for what is it you're wanting to get shut of me?

SHAWN (*looking to the* WIDOW *for help*). I'm a poor scholar with middling faculties to coin a lie, so I'll tell you the truth, Christy Mahon. I'm wedding with Pegeen beyond, and I don't think well of having a clever fearless man the like of you dwelling in her house.

CHRISTY (*almost pugnaciously*). And you'd be using bribery for to banish me?

SHAWN (*in an imploring voice*). Let you not take it badly, mister honey, isn't beyond the best place for you where you'll have golden chains and shiny coats and you riding upon hunters with the ladies of the land. (*He makes an eager sign to the* WIDOW QUIN *to come to help him.*)

WIDOW QUIN (*coming over*). It's true for him, and you'd best

quit off and not have that poor girl setting her mind on you, for
there's Shaneen thinks she wouldn't suit you though all is saying that she'll wed you now.

(CHRISTY *beams with delight.*)

SHAWN (*in terrified earnest*). She wouldn't suit you, and she
with the divil's own temper the way you'd be strangling one another in a score of days. (*He makes the movement of strangling
with his hands*) It's the like of me only that she's fit for, a quiet
simple fellow wouldn't raise a hand upon her if she scratched
itself.

WIDOW QUIN (*putting* SHAWN's *hat on* CHRISTY). Fit them clothes
on you anyhow, young fellow, and he'd maybe loan them to you
for the sports. (*Pushing him towards inner door*) Fit them on
and you can give your answer when you have them tried.

CHRISTY (*beaming, delighted with the clothes*). I will then. I'd
like herself to see me in them tweeds and hat. (*He goes into
room and shuts the door.*)

SHAWN (*in great anxiety*). He'd like herself to see them. He'll
not leave us, Widow Quin. He's a score of divils in him the
way it's well nigh certain he will wed Pegeen.

WIDOW QUIN (*jeeringly*). It's true all girls are fond of courage
and do hate the like of you.

SHAWN (*walking about in desperation*). Oh, Widow Quin,
what'll I be doing now? I'd inform again him, but he'd burst
from Kilmainham and he'd be sure and certain to destroy me.
If I wasn't so God-fearing, I'd near have courage to come behind
him and run a pike into his side. Oh, it's a hard case to be an
orphan and not to have your father that you're used to, and

you'd easy kill and make yourself a hero in the sight of all. (*Coming up to her*) Oh, Widow Quin, will you find me some contrivance when I've promised you a ewe?

WIDOW QUIN. A ewe's a small thing, but what would you give me if I did wed him and did save you so?

SHAWN (*with astonishment*). You?

WIDOW QUIN. Aye. Would you give me the red cow you have and the mountainy ram, and the right of way across your rye path, and a load of dung at Michaelmas, and turbary upon the western hill?

SHAWN (*radiant with hope*). I would surely, and I'd give you the wedding-ring I have, and the loan of a new suit, the way you'd have him decent on the wedding-day. I'd give you two kids for your dinner, and a gallon of poteen, and I'd call the piper on the long car to your wedding from Crossmolina or from Ballina. I'd give you . . .

WIDOW QUIN. That'll do so, and let you whisht, for he's coming now again.

(CHRISTY *comes in very natty in the new clothes.* WIDOW QUIN *goes to him admiringly.*)

WIDOW QUIN. If you seen yourself now, I'm thinking you'd be too proud to speak to us at all, and it'd be a pity surely to have your like sailing from Mayo to the Western World.

CHRISTY (*as proud as a peacock*). I'm not going. If this is a poor place itself, I'll make myself contented to be lodging here.

(WIDOW QUIN *makes a sign to* SHAWN *to leave them.*)

SHAWN. Well, I'm going measuring the race-course while the

tide is low, so I'll leave you the garments and my blessing for the sports to-day. God bless you! (*He wriggles out.*)

WIDOW QUIN (*admiring* CHRISTY). Well, you're mighty spruce, young fellow. Sit down now while you're quiet till you talk with me.

CHRISTY (*swaggering*). I'm going abroad on the hillside for to seek Pegeen.

WIDOW QUIN. You'll have time and plenty for to seek Pegeen, and you heard me saying at the fall of night the two of us should be great company.

CHRISTY. From this out I'll have no want of company when all sorts is bringing me their food and clothing (*he swaggers to the door, tightening his belt*), the way they'd set their eyes upon a gallant orphan cleft his father with one blow to the breeches belt. (*He opens door, then staggers back*) Saints of glory! Holy angels from the throne of light!

WIDOW QUIN (*going over*). What ails you?

CHRISTY. It's the walking spirit of my murdered da?

WIDOW QUIN (*looking out*). Is it that tramper?

CHRISTY (*wildly*). Where'll I hide my poor body from that ghost of hell?

(*The door is pushed open, and old* MAHON *appears on threshold.* CHRISTY *darts in behind door.*)

WIDOW QUIN (*in great amusement*). God save you, my poor man.

MAHON (*gruffly*). Did you see a young lad passing this way in the early morning or the fall of night?

WIDOW QUIN. You're a queer kind to walk in not saluting at all.

MAHON. Did you see the young lad?

WIDOW QUIN (*stiffly*). What kind was he?

MAHON. An ugly young streeler with a murderous gob on him, and a little switch in his hand. I met a tramper seen him coming this way at the fall of night.

WIDOW QUIN. There's harvest hundreds do be passing these days for the Sligo boat. For what is it you're wanting him, my poor man?

MAHON. I want to destroy him for breaking the head on me with the clout of a loy. (*He takes off a big hat, and shows his head in a mass of bandages and plaster, with some pride*) It was he did that, and amn't I a great wonder to think I've traced him ten days with that rent in my crown?

WIDOW QUIN (*taking his head in both hands and examining it with extreme delight*). That was a great blow. And who hit you? A robber maybe?

MAHON. It was my own son hit me, and he the divil a robber, or anything else, but a dirty, stuttering lout.

WIDOW QUIN (*letting go his skull and wiping her hands in her apron*). You'd best be wary of a mortified scalp, I think they call it, lepping around with that wound in the splendour of the sun. It was a bad blow surely, and you should have vexed him fearful to make him strike that gash in his da.

MAHON. Is it me?

WIDOW QUIN (*amusing herself*). Aye. And isn't it a great shame when the old and hardened do torment the young?

MAHON (*raging*). Torment him is it? And I after holding out with the patience of a martyred saint till there's nothing but destruction on, and I'm driven out in my old age with none to aid me.

WIDOW QUIN (*greatly amused*). It's a sacred wonder the way that wickedness will spoil a man.

MAHON. My wickedness, is it? Amn't I after saying it is himself has me destroyed, and he a liar on walls, a talker of folly, a man you'd see stretched the half of the day in the brown ferns with his belly to the sun.

WIDOW QUIN. Not working at all?

MAHON. The divil a work, or if he did itself, you'd see him raising up a haystack like the stalk of a rush, or driving our last cow till he broke her leg at the hip, and when he wasn't at that he'd be fooling over little birds he had—finches and felts—or making mugs at his own self in the bit of a glass we had hung on the wall.

WIDOW QUIN (*looking at* CHRISTY). What way was he so foolish? It was running wild after the girls maybe?

MAHON (*with a shout of derision*). Running wild, is it? If he seen a red petticoat coming swinging over the hill, he'd be off to hide in the sticks, and you'd see him shooting out his sheep's eyes between the little twigs and the leaves, and his two ears rising like a hare looking out through a gap. Girls, indeed!

WIDOW QUIN. It was drink maybe?

MAHON. And he a poor fellow would get drunk on the smell of a pint. He'd a queer rotten stomach, I'm telling you, and when I gave him three pulls from my pipe a while since, he was taken with contortions till I had to send him in the ass cart to the females' nurse.

WIDOW QUIN (*clasping her hands*). Well, I never till this day heard tell of a man the like of that!

MAHON. I'd take a mighty oath you didn't surely, and wasn't he the laughing joke of every female woman where four baronies meet, the way the girls would stop their weeding if they seen him coming the road to let a roar at him, and call him the looney of Mahon's.

WIDOW QUIN. I'd give the world and all to see the like of him. What kind was he?

MAHON. A small low fellow.

WIDOW QUIN. And dark?

MAHON. Dark and dirty.

WIDOW QUIN (*considering*). I'm thinking I seen him.

MAHON (*eagerly*). An ugly young blackguard.

WIDOW QUIN. A hideous, fearful villain, and the spit of you.

MAHON. What way is he fled?

WIDOW QUIN. Gone over the hills to catch a coasting steamer to the north or south.

MAHON. Could I pull up on him now?

WIDOW QUIN. If you'll cross the sands below where the tide is out, you'll be in it as soon as himself, for he had to go round ten miles by the top of the bay. (*She points to the door*) Strike down by the head beyond and then follow on the roadway to the north and east.

(MAHON *goes abruptly.*)

WIDOW QUIN (*shouting after him*). Let you give him a good vengeance when you come up with him, but don't put yourself in the power of the law, for it'd be a poor thing to see a judge in his black cap reading out his sentence on a civil warrior the like of you. (*She swings the door to and looks at* CHRISTY, *who is cowering in terror, for a moment, then she bursts into a laugh.*)

WIDOW QUIN. Well, you're the walking Playboy of the Western World, and that's the poor man you had divided to his breeches belt.

CHRISTY (*looking out: then, to her*). What'll Pegeen say when she hears that story? What'll she be saying to me now?

WIDOW QUIN. She'll knock the head of you, I'm thinking, and drive you from the door. God help her to be taking you for a wonder, and you a little schemer making up the story you destroyed your da.

CHRISTY (*turning to the door, nearly speechless with rage, half to himself*). To be letting on he was dead, and coming back to his life, and following after me like an old weasel tracing a rat, and coming in here laying desolation between my own self and the fine women of Ireland, and he a kind of carcase that you'd fling upon the sea . . .

WIDOW QUIN (*more soberly*). There's talking for a man's one only son.

CHRISTY (*breaking out*). His one son, is it? May I meet him with one tooth and it aching, and one eye to be seeing seven and seventy divils in the twists of the road, and one old timber leg on him to limp into the scalding grave. (*Looking out*) There he is now crossing the strands, and that the Lord God would send a high wave to wash him from the world.

WIDOW QUIN (*scandalized*). Have you no shame? (*Putting her hand on his shoulder and turning him round*) What ails you? Near crying, is it?

CHRISTY (*in despair and grief*). Amn't I after seeing the love-light of the star of knowledge shining from her brow, and hearing words would put you thinking on the holy Brigid speaking to the infant saints, and now she'll be turning again, and speaking hard words to me, like an old woman with a spavindy ass she'd have, urging on a hill.

WIDOW QUIN. There's poetry talk for a girl you'd see itching and scratching, and she with a stale stink of poteen on her from selling in the shop.

CHRISTY (*impatiently*). It's her like is fitted to be handling merchandise in the heavens above, and what'll I be doing now, I ask you, and I a kind of wonder was jilted by the heavens when a day was by.

(*There is a distant noise of girls' voices.* WIDOW QUIN *looks from window and comes to him, hurriedly.*)

WIDOW QUIN. You'll be doing like myself, I'm thinking, when I did destroy my man, for I'm above many's the day, odd times in great spirits, abroad in the sunshine, darning a stocking or stitching a shift; and odd times again looking out on the schooners, hookers, trawlers is sailing the sea, and I thinking on the gallant hairy fellows are drifting beyond, and myself long years living alone.

CHRISTY (*interested*). You're like me, so.

WIDOW QUIN. I am your like, and it's for that I'm taking a fancy to you, and I with my little houseen above where there'd be myself to tend you, and none to ask were you a murderer or what at all.

CHRISTY. And what would I be doing if I left Pegeen?

WIDOW QUIN. I've nice jobs you could be doing, gathering shells to make a whitewash for our hut within, building up a little goose-house, or stretching a new skin on an old curragh I have, and if my hut is far from all sides, it's there you'll meet the wisest old men, I tell you, at the corner of my wheel, and it's there yourself and me will have great times whispering and hugging. . . .

VOICES (*outside, calling far away*). Christy! Christy Mahon! Christy!

CHRISTY. Is it Pegeen Mike?

WIDOW QUIN. It's the young girls, I'm thinking, coming to bring you to the sports below, and what is it you'll have me to tell them now?

CHRISTY. Aid me for to win Pegeen. It's herself only that I'm seeking now. (WIDOW QUIN *gets up and goes to window*) Aid me for to win her, and I'll be asking God to stretch a hand to you in the hour of death, and lead you short cuts through the Meadows of Ease, and up the floor of Heaven to the Footstool of the Virgin's Son.

WIDOW QUIN. There's praying.

VOICES (*nearer*). Christy! Christy Mahon!

CHRISTY (*with agitation*). They're coming. Will you swear to aid and save me for the love of Christ?

WIDOW QUIN (*looks at him for a moment*). If I aid you, will you swear to give me a right of way I want, and a mountainy ram, and a load of dung at Michaelmas, the time that you'll be master here?

CHRISTY. I will, by the elements and stars of night.

WIDOW QUIN. Then we'll not say a word of the old fellow, the way Pegeen won't know your story till the end of time.

CHRISTY. And if he chances to return again?

WIDOW QUIN. We'll swear he's a maniac and not your da. I could take an oath I seen him raving on the sands to-day.

(*Girls run in.*)

SUSAN. Come on to the sports below. Pegeen says you're to come.

SARA TANSEY. The lepping's beginning, and we've a jockey's suit to fit upon you for the mule race on the sands below.

HONOR. Come on, will you?

CHRISTY. I will then if Pegeen's beyond.

SARA TANSEY. She's in the boreen making game of Shaneen Keogh.

CHRISTY. Then I'll be going to her now. (*He runs out followed by the girls.*)

WIDOW QUIN. Well, if the worst comes in the end of all, it'll be great game to see there's none to pity him but a widow woman, the like of me, has buried her children and destroyed her man. (*She goes out.*)

CURTAIN

ACT THREE

Scene, *as before. Later in the day.* JIMMY *comes in, slightly drunk.*

JIMMY (*calls*). Pegeen! (*Crosses to inner door*) Pegeen Mike! (*Comes back again into the room*) Pegeen! (PHILLY *comes in in the same state*) (*To* PHILLY) Did you see herself?

PHILLY. I did not; but I sent Shawn Keogh with the ass cart for to bear him home. (*Trying cupboards which are locked*) Well, isn't he a nasty man to get into such staggers at a morning wake? and isn't herself the divil's daughter for locking, and she so fussy after that young gaffer, you might take your death with drought and none to heed you?

JIMMY. It's little wonder she'd be fussy, and he after bringing bankrupt ruin on the roulette man, and the trick-o'-the-loop man, and breaking the nose of the cockshot-man, and winning al! in the sports below, racing, lepping, dancing, and the Lord knows what! He's right luck, I'm telling you.

PHILLY. If he has, he'll be rightly hobbled yet, and he not able to say ten words without making a brag of the way he killed his father, and the great blow he hit with the loy.

JIMMY. A man can't hang by his own informing, and his father should be rotten by now.

(OLD MAHON *passes window slowly.*)

PHILLY. Supposing a man's digging spuds in that field with a long spade, and supposing he flings up the two halves of that skull, what'll be said then in the papers and the courts of law?

JIMMY. They'd say it was an old Dane, maybe, was drowned in the flood. (OLD MAHON *comes in and sits down near door listening*) Did you never hear tell of the skulls they have in the city of Dublin, ranged out like blue jugs in a cabin of Connaught?

PHILLY. And you believe that?

JIMMY (*pugnaciously*). Didn't a lad see them and he after coming from harvesting in the Liverpool boat? "They have them there," says he, "making a show of the great people there was one time walking the world. White skulls and black skulls and yellow skulls, and some with full teeth, and some haven't only but one."

PHILLY. It was no lie, maybe, for when I was a young lad there was a graveyard beyond the house with the remnants of a man who had thighs as long as your arm. He was a horrid man, I'm telling you, and there was many a fine Sunday I'd put him together for fun, and he with shiny bones, you wouldn't meet the like of these days in the cities of the world.

MAHON (*getting up*). You wouldn't, is it? Lay your eyes on that skull, and tell me where and when there was another the like of it, is splintered only from the blow of a loy.

PHILLY. Glory be to God! And who hit you at all?

MAHON (*triumphantly*). It was my own son hit me. Would you believe that?

JIMMY. Well, there's wonders hidden in the heart of man!

PHILLY (*suspiciously*). And what way was it done?

MAHON (*wandering about the room*). I'm after walking hundreds and long scores of miles, winning clean beds and the fill of my belly four times in the day, and I doing nothing but telling stories of that naked truth. (*He comes to them a little aggressively*) Give me a supeen and I'll tell you now.

(WIDOW QUIN *comes in and stands aghast behind him. He is facing* JIMMY *and* PHILLY, *who are on the left.*)

JIMMY. Ask herself beyond. She's the stuff hidden in her shawl.

WIDOW QUIN (*coming to* MAHON *quickly*). You here, is it? You didn't go far at all?

MAHON. I seen the coasting steamer passing, and I got a drought upon me and a cramping leg, so I said, "The divil go along with him," and turned again. (*Looking under her shawl*) And let you give me a supeen, for I'm destroyed travelling since Tuesday was a week.

WIDOW QUIN (*getting a glass, in a cajoling tone*). Sit down then by the fire and take your ease for a space. You've a right to be destroyed indeed, with your walking, and fighting, and facing the sun (*giving him poteen from a stone jar she has brought in*). There now is a drink for you, and may it be to your happiness and length of life.

MAHON (*taking glass greedily and sitting down by fire*). God increase you!

WIDOW QUIN (*taking men to the right stealthily*). Do you know what? That man's raving from his wound to-day, for I met him a while since telling a rambling tale of a tinker had him destroyed. Then he heard of Christy's deed, and he up and says it was his son had cracked his skull. O isn't madness a fright, for he'll go killing someone yet, and he thinking it's the man has struck him so?

JIMMY (*entirely convinced*). It's a fright, surely. I knew a party was kicked in the head by a red mare, and he went killing horses a great while, till he eat the insides of a clock and died after.

PHILLY (*with suspicion*). Did he see Christy?

WIDOW QUIN. He didn't. (*With a warning gesture*) Let you not be putting him in mind of him, or you'll be likely summoned if there's murder done. (*Looking round at* MAHON) Whisht! He's listening. Wait now till you hear me taking him easy and unravelling all. (*She goes to* MAHON) And what way are you feeling, mister? Are you in contentment now?

MAHON (*slightly emotional from his drink*). I'm poorly only, for it's a hard story the way I'm left to-day, when it was I did tend him from his hour of birth, and he a dunce never reached his second book, the way he'd come from school, many's the day, with his legs lamed under him, and he blackened with his beatings like a tinker's ass. It's a hard story, I'm saying, the way some do have their next and nighest raising up a hand of murder on them, and some is lonesome getting their death with lamentation in the dead of night.

WIDOW QUIN (*not knowing what to say*). To hear you talking so quiet, who'd know you were the same fellow we seen pass to-day?

MAHON. I'm the same surely. The wrack and ruin of three score years; and it's a terror to live that length, I tell you, and to have your sons going to the dogs against you, and you wore out scolding them, and skelping them, and God knows what.

PHILLY (*to* JIMMY). He's not raving. (*To* WIDOW QUIN) Will you ask him what kind was his son?

WIDOW QUIN (*to* MAHON, *with a peculiar look*). Was your son that hit you a lad of one year and a score maybe, a great hand at racing and lepping and licking the world?

MAHON (*turning on her with a roar of rage*). Didn't you hear me say he was the fool of men, the way from this out he'll know the orphan's lot with old and young making game of him and they swearing, raging, kicking at him like a mangy cur.

(*A great burst of cheering outside, some way off.*)

MAHON (*putting his hands to his ears*). What in the name of God do they want roaring below?

WIDOW QUIN (*with the shade of a smile*). They're cheering a young lad, the champion Playboy of the Western World.

(*More cheering.*)

MAHON (*going to window*). It'd split my heart to hear them, and I with pulses in my brain-pan for a week gone by. Is it racing they are?

JIMMY (*looking from door*). It is then. They are mounting him for the mule race will be run upon the sands. That's the playboy on the winkered mule.

MAHON (*puzzled*). That lad, is it? If you said it was a fool he was, I'd have laid a mighty oath he was the likeness of my wandering son (*uneasily, putting his hand to his head*). Faith, I'm thinking I'll go walking for to view the race.

WIDOW QUIN (*stopping him, sharply*). You will not. You'd best take the road to Belmullet, and not be dilly-dallying in this place where there isn't a spot you could sleep.

PHILLY (*coming forward*). Don't mind her. Mount there on the bench and you'll have a view of the whole. They're hurrying before the tide will rise, and it'd be near over if you went down the pathway through the crags below.

MAHON (*mounts on bench,* WIDOW QUIN *beside him*). That's a right view again the edge of the sea. They're coming now from the point. He's leading. Who is he at all?

WIDOW QUIN. He's the champion of the world, I tell you, and there isn't a hop'orth isn't falling lucky to his hands to-day.

PHILLY (*looking out, interested in the race*). Look at that. They're pressing him now.

JIMMY. He'll win it yet.

PHILLY. Take your time, Jimmy Farrell. It's too soon to say.

WIDOW QUIN (*shouting*). Watch him taking the gate. There's riding.

JIMMY (*cheering*). More power to the young lad!

MAHON. He's passing the third.

JIMMY. He'll lick them yet!

WIDOW QUIN. He'd lick them if he was running races with a score itself.

MAHON. Look at the mule he has, kicking the stars.

WIDOW QUIN. There was a lep! (*Catching hold of* MAHON *in her excitement*) He's fallen! He's mounted again! Faith, he's passing them all!

JIMMY. Look at him skelping her!

PHILLY. And the mountain girls hooshing him on!

JIMMY. It's the last turn! The post's cleared for them now!

MAHON. Look at the narrow place. He'll be into the bogs!
(*With a yell*) Good rider! He's through it again!

JIMMY. He's neck and neck!

MAHON. Good boy to him! Flames, but he's in!

(*Great cheering, in which all join.*)

MAHON (*with hesitation*). What's that? They're raising him
up. They're coming this way. (*With a roar of rage and astonishment*) It's Christy! by the stars of God! I'd know his way of
spitting and he astride the moon.

(*He jumps down and makes for the door, but* WIDOW QUIN
catches him and pulls him back.)

WIDOW QUIN. Stay quiet, will you. That's not your son. (*To*
JIMMY) Stop him, or you'll get a month for the abetting of
manslaughter and be fined as well.

JIMMY. I'll hold him.

MAHON (*struggling*). Let me out! Let me out, the lot of you!
till I have my vengeance on his head to-day.

WIDOW QUIN (*shaking him, vehemently*). That's not your son.
That's a man is going to make a marriage with the daughter of
this house, a place with fine trade, with a license, and with poteen too.

MAHON (*amazed*). That man marrying a decent and a moneyed

girl! Is it mad yous are? Is it in a crazy-house for females that I'm landed now?

WIDOW QUIN. It's mad yourself is with the blow upon your head. That lad is the wonder of the Western World.

MAHON. I seen it's my son.

WIDOW QUIN. You seen that you're mad. (*Cheering outside*) Do you hear them cheering him in the zig-zags of the road? Aren't you after saying that your son's a fool, and how would they be cheering a true idiot born?

MAHON (*getting distressed*). It's maybe out of reason that that man's himself. (*Cheering again*) There's none surely will go cheering him. Oh, I'm raving with a madness that would fright the world! (*He sits down with his hand to his head*) There was one time I seen ten scarlet divils letting on they'd cork my spirit in a gallon can; and one time I seen rats as big as badgers sucking the life blood from the butt of my lug; but I never till this day confused that dribbling idiot with a likely man. I'm destroyed surely.

WIDOW QUIN. And who'd wonder when it's your brain-pan that is gaping now?

MAHON. Then the blight of the sacred drought upon myself and him, for I never went mad to this day, and I not three weeks with the Limerick girls drinking myself silly, and parlatic from the dusk to dawn. (*To* WIDOW QUIN, *suddenly*) Is my visage astray?

WIDOW QUIN. It is then. You're a sniggering maniac, a child could see.

MAHON (*getting up more cheerfully*). Then I'd best be going to the union beyond, and there'll be a welcome before me, I tell you (*with great pride*), and I a terrible and fearful case, the way that there I was one time, screeching in a straitened waistcoat, with seven doctors writing out my sayings in a printed book. Would you believe that?

WIDOW QUIN. If you're a wonder itself, you'd best be hasty, for them lads caught a maniac one time and pelted the poor creature till he ran out, raving and foaming, and was drowned in the sea.

MAHON (*with philosophy*). It's true mankind is the divil when your head's astray. Let me out now and I'll slip down the boreen, and not see them so.

WIDOW QUIN (*showing him out*). That's it. Run to the right, and not a one will see.

(*He runs off.*)

PHILLY (*wisely*). You're at some gaming, Widow Quin; but I'll walk after him and give him his dinner and a time to rest, and I'll see then if he's raving or as sane as you.

WIDOW QUIN (*annoyed*). If you go near that lad, let you be wary of your head, I'm saying. Didn't you hear him telling he was crazed at times?

PHILLY. I heard him telling a power; and I'm thinking we'll have right sport, before night will fall. (*He goes out.*)

JIMMY. Well, Philly's a conceited and foolish man. How could that madman have his senses and his brain-pan slit? I'll go after them and see him turn on Philly now.

(*He goes;* WIDOW QUIN *hides poteen behind counter. Then hubbub outside.*)

VOICES. There you are! Good jumper! Grand lepper! Darlint boy! He's the racer! Bear him on, will you!

(CHRISTY *comes in, in* JOCKEY'S *dress, with* PEGEEN MIKE, SARA, *and other girls, and men.*)

PEGEEN (*to crowd*). Go on now and don't destroy him and he drenching with sweat. Go along, I'm saying, and have your tug-of-warring till he's dried his skin.

CROWD. Here's his prizes! A bagpipes! A fiddle was played by a poet in the years gone by! A flat and three-thorned blackthorn would lick the scholars out of Dublin town!

CHRISTY (*taking prizes from the men*). Thank you kindly, the lot of you. But you'd say it was little only I did this day if you'd seen me a while since striking my one single blow.

TOWN CRIER (*outside, ringing a bell*). Take notice, last event of this day! Tug-of-warring on the green below! Come on, the lot of you! Great achievements for all Mayo men!

PEGEEN. Go on, and leave him for to rest and dry. Go on, I tell you, for he'll do no more. (*She hustles crowd out;* WIDOW QUIN *following them.*)

MEN (*going*). Come on, then. Good luck for the while!

PEGEEN (*radiantly, wiping his face with her shawl*). Well, you're the lad, and you'll have great times from this out when you could win that wealth of prizes, and you sweating in the heat of noon!

CHRISTY (*looking at her with delight*). I'll have great times if I win the crowning prize I'm seeking now, and that's your promise that you'll wed me in a fortnight, when our banns is called.

PEGEEN (*backing away from him*). You've right daring to go ask me that, when all knows you'll be starting to some girl in your own townland, when your father's rotten in four months, or five.

CHRISTY (*indignantly*). Starting from you, is it? (*He follows her*) I will not, then, and when the airs is warming in four months, or five, it's then yourself and me should be pacing Neifin in the dews of night, the times sweet smells do be rising, and you'd see a little shiny new moon, maybe, sinking on the hills.

PEGEEN (*looking at him playfully*). And it's that kind of a poacher's love you'd make, Christy Mahon, on the sides of Neifin, when the night is down?

CHRISTY. It's little you'll think if my love's a poacher's, or an earl's itself, when you'll feel my two hands stretched around you, and I squeezing kisses on your puckered lips, till I'd feel a kind of pity for the Lord God in all ages sitting lonesome in his golden chair.

PEGEEN. That'll be right fun, Christy Mahon, and any girl would walk her heart out before she'd meet a young man was your like for eloquence, or talk, at all.

CHRISTY (*encouraged*). Let you wait, to hear me talking, till we're astray in Erris, when Good Friday's by, drinking a sup from a well, and making mighty kisses with our wetted mouths, or gaming in a gap or sunshine, with yourself stretched back unto your necklace, in the flowers of the earth.

PEGEEN (*in a lower voice, moved by his tone*). I'd be nice so, is it?

CHRISTY (*with rapture*). If the mitred bishops seen you that time, they'd be the like of the holy prophets, I'm thinking, do be straining the bars of Paradise to lay eyes on the Lady Helen of Troy, and she abroad, pacing back and forward, with a nose-gay in her golden shawl.

PEGEEN (*with real tenderness*). And what is it I have, Christy Mahon, to make me fitting entertainment for the like of you, that has such poet's talking, and such bravery of heart?

CHRISTY (*in a low voice*). Isn't there the light of seven heavens in your heart alone, the way you'll be an angel's lamp to me from this out, and I abroad in the darkness, spearing salmons in the Owen, or the Carrowmore?

PEGEEN. If I was your wife, I'd be along with you those nights, Christy Mahon, the way you'd see I was a great hand at coaxing bailiffs, or coining funny nick-names for the stars of night.

CHRISTY. You, is it? Taking your death in the hailstones, or in the fogs of dawn.

PEGEEN. Yourself and me would shelter easy in a narrow bush, (*with a qualm of dread*) but we're only talking, maybe, for this would be a poor, thatched place to hold a fine lad is the like of you.

CHRISTY (*putting his arm around her*). If I wasn't a good Christian, it's on my naked knees I'd be saying my prayers and paters to every jackstraw you have roofing your head, and every stony pebble is paving the laneway to your door.

PEGEEN (*radiantly*). If that's the truth, I'll be burning candles from this out to the miracles of God that have brought you from the south to-day, and I, with my gowns bought ready, the way that I can wed you, and not wait at all.

CHRISTY. It's miracles, and that's the truth. Me there toiling a long while, and walking a long while, not knowing at all I was drawing all times nearer to this holy day.

PEGEEN. And myself, a girl, was tempted often to go sailing the seas till I'd marry a Jew-man, with ten kegs of gold, and I not knowing at all there was the like of you drawing nearer, like the stars of God.

CHRISTY. And to think I'm long years hearing women talking that talk, to all bloody fools, and this the first time I've heard the like of your voice talking sweetly for my own delight.

PEGEEN. And to think it's me is talking sweetly, Christy Mahon, and I the fright of seven townlands for my biting tongue. Well, the heart's a wonder; and, I'm thinking, there won't be our like in Mayo, for gallant lovers, from this hour, to-day. (*Drunken singing is heard outside*) There's my father coming from the wake, and when he's had his sleep we'll tell him, for he's peaceful then.

(*They separate.*)

MICHAEL (*singing outside*).
>   The jailor and the turnkey
>   They quickly ran us down,
>   And brought us back as prisoners
>   Once more to Cavan town.

(*He comes in supported by* SHAWN.)
>   There we lay bewailing
>   All in a prison bound. . . .

(*He sees* CHRISTY. *Goes and shakes him drunkenly by the hand, while* PEGEEN *and* SHAWN *talk on the left.*)

MICHAEL (*to* CHRISTY). The blessing of God and the holy angels on your head, young fellow. I hear tell you're after winning all in the sports below; and wasn't it a shame I didn't bear you along with me to Kate Cassidy's wake, a fine, stout lad, the like of you, for you'd never see the match of it for flows of drink, the way when we sunk her bones at noonday in her narrow grave, there were five men, aye, and six men, stretched out retching speechless on the holy stones.

CHRISTY (*uneasily, watching* PEGEEN). Is that the truth?

MICHAEL. It is then, and aren't you a louty schemer to go burying your poor father unbeknownst when you'd a right to throw him on the crupper of a Kerry mule and drive him westwards, like holy Joseph in the days gone by, the way we could have given him a decent burial, and not have him rotting beyond, and not a Christian drinking a smart drop to the glory of his soul?

CHRISTY (*gruffly*). It's well enough he's lying, for the likes of him.

MICHAEL (*slapping him on the back*). Well, aren't you a hardened slayer? It'll be a poor thing for the household man where you go sniffing for a female wife; and (*pointing to* SHAWN) look beyond at that shy and decent Christian I have chosen for my daughter's hand, and I after getting the gilded dispensation this day for to wed them now.

CHRISTY. And you'll be wedding them this day, is it?

MICHAEL (*drawing himself up*). Aye. Are you thinking, if I'm drunk itself, I'd leave my daughter living single with a little frisky rascal is the like of you?

PEGEEN (*breaking away from* SHAWN). Is it the truth the dispensation's come?

MICHAEL (*triumphantly*). Father Reilly's after reading it in gallous Latin, and "It's come in the nick of time," says he; "so I'll wed them in a hurry, dreading that young gaffer who'd capsize the stars."

PEGEEN (*fiercely*). He's missed his nick of time, for it's that lad, Christy Mahon, that I'm wedding now.

MICHAEL (*loudly with horror*). You'd be making him a son to me, and he wet and crusted with his father's blood?

PEGEEN. Aye. Wouldn't it be a bitter thing for a girl to go marrying the like of Shaneen, and he a middling kind of a scarecrow, with no savagery or fine words in him at all?

MICHAEL (*gasping and sinking on a chair*). Oh, aren't you a heathen daughter to go shaking the fat of my heart, and I swamped and drownded with the weight of drink? Would you have them turning on me the way that I'd be roaring to the dawn of day with the wind upon my heart? Have you not a word to aid me, Shaneen? Are you not jealous at all?

SHAWN (*in great misery*). I'd be afeard to be jealous of a man did slay his da.

PEGEEN. Well, it'd be a poor thing to go marrying your like. I'm seeing there's a world of peril for an orphan girl, and isn't it a great blessing I didn't wed you, before himself came walking from the west or south?

SHAWN. It's a queer story you'd go picking a dirty tramp up from the highways of the world.

PEGEEN (*playfully*). And you think you're a likely beau to go straying along with, the shiny Sundays of the opening year, when it's sooner on a bullock's liver you'd put a poor girl thinking than on the lily or the rose?

SHAWN. And have you no mind of my weight of passion, and the holy dispensation, and the drift of heifers I am giving, and the golden ring?

PEGEEN. I'm thinking you're too fine for the like of me, Shawn Keogh of Killakeen, and let you go off till you'd find a radiant lady with droves of bullocks on the plains of Meath, and herself bedizened in the diamond jewelries of Pharaoh's ma. That'd be your match, Shaneen. So God save you now! (*She retreats behind* CHRISTY.)

SHAWN. Won't you hear me telling you . . . ?

CHRISTY (*with ferocity*). Take yourself from this, young fellow, or I'll maybe add a murder to my deeds to-day.

MICHAEL (*springing up with a shriek*). Murder is it? Is it mad yous are? Would you go making murder in this place, and it piled with poteen for our drink to-night? Go on to the foreshore if it's fighting you want, where the rising tide will wash all traces from the memory of man. (*Pushing* SHAWN *towards* CHRISTY.)

SHAWN (*shaking himself free, and getting behind* MICHAEL). I'll not fight him, Michael James. I'd liefer live a bachelor, simmering in passions to the end of time, than face a lepping savage the like of him has descended from the Lord knows where. Strike him yourself, Michael James, or you'll lose my drift of heifers and my blue bull from Sneem.

MICHAEL. Is it me fight him, when it's father-slaying he's bred to now? (*Pushing* SHAWN) Go on you fool and fight him now.

SHAWN (*coming forward a little*). Will I strike him with my hand?

MICHAEL. Take the loy is on your western side.

SHAWN. I'd be afeard of the gallows if I struck him with that.

CHRISTY (*taking up the loy*). Then I'll make you face the gallows or quit off from this.

(SHAWN *flies out of the door.*)

CHRISTY. Well, fine weather be after him, (*going to* MICHAEL, *coaxingly*) and I'm thinking you wouldn't wish to have that quaking blackguard in your house at all. Let you give us your blessing and hear her swear her faith to me, for I'm mounted on the springtide of the stars of luck, the way it'll be good for any to have me in the house.

PEGEEN (*at the other side of* MICHAEL). Bless us now, for I swear to God I'll wed him, and I'll not renege.

MICHAEL (*standing up in the centre, holding on to both of them*). It's the will of God, I'm thinking, that all should win an easy or a cruel end, and it's the will of God that all should rear up lengthy families for the nurture of the earth. What's a single man, I ask you, eating a bit in one house and drinking a sup in another, and he with no place of his own, like an old braying jackass strayed upon the rocks? (*To* CHRISTY) It's many would be in dread to bring your like into their house for to end them, maybe, with a sudden end; but I'm a decent man of Ireland, and I liefer face the grave untimely and I seeing a score of grandsons growing up little gallant swearers by the name of God, than go peopling my bedside with puny weeds the like of what you'd breed, I'm thinking, out of Shaneen Keogh. (*He joins their hands*) A daring fellow is the jewel of the world, and a man did split his father's middle with a single clout, should have the bravery of ten, so may God and Mary and St. Patrick bless you, and increase you from this mortal day.

CHRISTY AND PEGEEN. Amen, O Lord!

(*Hubbub outside.*)

(OLD MAHON *rushes in, followed by all the crowd, and* WIDOW QUIN. *He makes a rush at* CHRISTY, *knocks him down, and begins to beat him.*)

PEGEEN (*dragging back his arm*). Stop that, will you? Who are you at all?

MAHON. His father, God forgive me!

PEGEEN (*drawing back*). Is it rose from the dead?

MAHON. Do you think I look so easy quenched with the tap of a loy? (*Beats* CHRISTY *again.*)

PEGEEN (*glaring at* CHRISTY). And it's lies you told, letting on you had him slitted, and you nothing at all.

CHRISTY (*catching* MAHON's *stick*). He's not my father. He's a raving maniac would scare the world. (*Pointing to* WIDOW QUIN) Herself knows it is true.

CROWD. You're fooling Pegeen! The Widow Quin seen him this day, and you likely knew! You're a liar!

CHRISTY (*dumbfounded*). It's himself was a liar, lying stretched out with an open head on him, letting on he was dead.

MAHON. Weren't you off racing the hills before I got my breath with the start I had seeing you turn on me at all?

PEGEEN. And to think of the coaxing glory we had given him, and he after doing nothing but hitting a soft blow and chasing northward in a sweat of fear. Quit off from this.

CHRISTY (*piteously*). You've seen my doings this day, and let you save me from the old man; for why would you be in such a scorch of haste to spur me to destruction now?

PEGEEN. It's there your treachery is spurring me, till I'm hard set to think you're the one I'm after lacing in my heart-strings half-an-hour gone by. (*To* MAHON) Take him on from this, for I think bad the world should see me raging for a Munster liar, and the fool of men.

MAHON. Rise up now to retribution, and come on with me.

CROWD (*jeeringly*). There's the playboy! There's the lad thought he'd rule the roost in Mayo. Slate him now, mister.

CHRISTY (*getting up in shy terror*). What is it drives you to torment me here, when I'd asked the thunders of the might of God to blast me if I ever did hurt to any saving only that one single blow.

MAHON (*loudly*). If you didn't, you're a poor good-for-nothing, and isn't it by the like of you the sins of the whole world are committed?

CHRISTY (*raising his hands*). In the name of the Almighty God. . . .

MAHON. Leave troubling the Lord God. Would you have him sending down droughts, and fevers, and the old hen and the cholera morbus?

CHRISTY (*to* WIDOW QUIN) Will you come between us and protect me now?

WIDOW QUIN. I've tried a lot, God help me, and my share is done.

CHRISTY (*looking round in desperation*). And I must go back into my torment is it, or run off like a vagabond straying through the Unions with the dusts of August making mud-stains in the gullet of my throat, or the winds of March blowing on me till I'd take an oath I felt them making whistles of my ribs within?

SARA. Ask Pegeen to aid you. Her like does often change.

CHRISTY. I will not then, for there's torment in the splendour of her like, and she a girl any moon of midnight would take pride to meet, facing southwards on the heaths of Keel. But what did I want crawling forward to scorch my understanding at her flaming brow?

PEGEEN (*to* MAHON, *vehemently, fearing she will break into tears*). Take him on from this or I'll set the young lads to destroy him here.

MAHON (*going to him, shaking his stick*). Come on now if you wouldn't have the company to see you skelped.

PEGEEN (*half laughing, through her tears*). That's it, now the world will see him pandied, and he an ugly liar was playing off the hero, and the fright of men.

CHRISTY (*to* MAHON, *very sharply*). Leave me go!

CROWD. That's it. Now, Christy. If them two set fighting, it will lick the world.

MAHON (*making a grab at* CHRISTY). Come here to me.

CHRISTY (*more threateningly*). Leave me go, I'm saying.

MAHON. I will maybe, when your legs is limping, and your back is blue.

CROWD. Keep it up, the two of you. I'll back the old one. Now the playboy.

CHRISTY (*in low and intense voice*). Shut your yelling, for if you're after making a mighty man of me this day by the power of a lie, you're setting me now to think if it's a poor thing to be lonesome, it's worse maybe to go mixing with the fools of earth.

(MAHON *makes a movement towards him.*)

CHRISTY (*almost shouting*). Keep off . . . lest I do show a blow unto the lot of you would set the guardian angels winking in the clouds above. (*He swings round with a sudden rapid movement and picks up a loy.*)

CROWD (*half frightened, half amused*). He's going mad! Mind yourselves! Run from the idiot!

CHRISTY. If I am an idiot, I'm after hearing my voice this day saying words would raise the topknot on a poet in a merchant's town. I've won your racing, your lepping, and . . .

MAHON. Shut your gullet and come on with me.

CHRISTY. I'm going, but I'll stretch you first.

(*He runs at old* MAHON *with the loy, chases him out of the door, followed by crowd and* WIDOW QUIN. *There is a great noise outside, then a yell, and dead silence for a moment.* CHRISTY *comes in, half dazed, and goes to fire.*)

WIDOW QUIN (*coming in, hurriedly, and going to him*). They're turning again you. Come on, or you'll be hanged, indeed.

CHRISTY. I'm thinking, from this out, Pegeen'll be giving me praises the same as in the hours gone by.

WIDOW QUIN (*impatiently*). Come by the back-door. I'd think bad to have you stifled on the gallows tree.

CHRISTY (*indignantly*). I will not, then. What good'd be my life-time, if I left Pegeen?

WIDOW QUIN. Come on, and you'll be no worse than you were last night; and you with a double murder this time to be telling to the girls.

CHRISTY. I'll not leave Pegeen Mike.

WIDOW QUIN (*impatiently*). Isn't there the match of her in every parish public, from Binghamstown unto the plain of Meath? Come on, I tell you, and I'll find you finer sweethearts at each waning moon.

CHRISTY. It's Pegeen I'm seeking only, and what'd I care if you brought me a drift of chosen females, standing in their shifts itself, maybe, from this place to the Eastern World?

SARA (*runs in, pulling off one of her petticoats*). They're going to hang him. (*Holding out petticoat and shawl*) Fit these upon him, and let him run off to the east.

WIDOW QUIN. He's raving now; but we'll fit them on him, and I'll take him, in the ferry, to the Achill boat.

CHRISTY (*struggling feebly*). Leave me go, will you? when I'm thinking of my luck to-day, for she will wed me surely, and I a proven hero in the end of all.

(*They try to fasten petticoat round him.*)

WIDOW QUIN. Take his left hand, and we'll pull him now. Come on, young fellow.

CHRISTY (*suddenly starting up*). You'll be taking me from her? You're jealous, is it, of her wedding me? Go on from this. (*He snatches up a stool, and threatens them with it.*)

WIDOW QUIN (*going*). It's in the mad-house they should put him, not in jail, at all. We'll go by the back-door, to call the doctor, and we'll save him so.

(*She goes out, with SARA, through inner room. Men crowd in the doorway. CHRISTY sits down again by the fire.*)

MICHAEL (*in a terrified whisper*). Is the old lad killed surely?

PHILLY. I'm after feeling the last gasps quitting his heart.

(*They peer in at CHRISTY.*)

MICHAEL (*with a rope*). Look at the way he is. Twist a hangman's knot on it, and slip it over his head, while he's not minding at all.

PHILLY. Let you take it, Shaneen. You're the soberest of all that's here.

SHAWN. Is it me to go near him, and he the wickedest and worst with me? Let you take it, Pegeen Mike.

PEGEEN. Come on, so.

(*She goes forward with the others, and they drop the double hitch over his head.*)

CHRISTY. What ails you?

SHAWN (*triumphantly, as they pull the rope tight on his arms*). Come on to the peelers, till they stretch you now.

CHRISTY. Me!

MICHAEL. If we took pity on you, the Lord God would, maybe, bring us ruin from the law to-day, so you'd best come easy, for hanging is an easy and a speedy end.

CHRISTY. I'll not stir. (*To* PEGEEN) And what is it you'll say to me, and I after doing it this time in the face of all?

PEGEEN. I'll say, a strange man is a marvel, with his mighty talk; but what's a squabble in your back-yard, and the blow of a loy, have taught me that there's a great gap between a gallous story and a dirty deed. (*To* MEN) Take him on from this, or the lot of us will be likely put on trial for his deed to-day.

CHRISTY (*with horror in his voice*). And it's yourself will send me off, to have a horny-fingered hangman hitching his bloody slip-knots at the butt of my ear.

MEN (*pulling rope*). Come on, will you?

(*He is pulled down on the floor.*)

CHRISTY (*twisting his legs round the table*). Cut the rope, Pegeen, and I'll quit the lot of you, and live from this out, like the madmen of Keel, eating muck and green weeds, on the faces of the cliffs.

PEGEEN. And leave us to hang, is it, for a saucy liar, the like of you? (*To* MEN) Take him on, out from this.

SHAWN. Pull a twist on his neck, and squeeze him so.

PHILLY. Twist yourself. Sure he cannot hurt you, if you keep your distance from his teeth alone.

SHAWN. I'm afeard of him. (*To* PEGEEN) Lift a lighted sod, will you, and scorch his leg.

PEGEEN (*blowing the fire, with a bellows*). Leave go now, young fellow, or I'll scorch your shins.

CHRISTY. You're blowing for to torture me. (*His voice rising and growing stronger*) That's your kind, is it? Then let the lot of you be wary, for, if I've to face the gallows, I'll have a gay march down, I tell you, and shed the blood of some of you before I die.

SHAWN (*in terror*). Keep a good hold, Philly. Be wary, for the love of God. For I'm thinking he would liefest wreak his pains on me.

CHRISTY (*almost gaily*). If I do lay my hands on you, it's the way you'll be at the fall of night, hanging as a scarecrow for the fowls of hell. Ah, you'll have a gallous jaunt I'm saying, coaching out through Limbo with my father's ghost.

SHAWN (*to* PEGEEN). Make haste, will you? Oh, isn't he a holy terror, and isn't it true for Father Reilly, that all drink's a curse that has the lot of you so shaky and uncertain now?

CHRISTY. If I can wring a neck among you, I'll have a royal judgment looking on the trembling jury in the courts of law. And won't there be crying out in Mayo the day I'm stretched upon the rope with ladies in their silks and satins snivelling in their lacy kerchiefs, and they rhyming songs and ballads on the terror of my fate? (*He squirms round on the floor and bites* SHAWN's *leg.*)

SHAWN (*shrieking*). My leg's bit on me. He's the like of a mad dog, I'm thinking, the way that I will surely die.

CHRISTY (*delighted with himself*). You will then, the way you can shake out hell's flags of welcome for my coming in two weeks or three, for I'm thinking Satan hasn't many have killed their da in Kerry, and in Mayo too.

(OLD MAHON *comes in behind on all fours and looks on unnoticed.*)

MEN (*to* PEGEEN). Bring the sod, will you?

PEGEEN (*coming over*). God help him so. (*Burns his leg.*)

CHRISTY (*kicking and screaming*). O, glory be to God!

(*He kicks loose from the table, and they all drag him towards the door.*)

JIMMY (*seeing old* MAHON). Will you look what's come in?

(*They all drop* CHRISTY *and run left.*)

CHRISTY (*scrambling on his knees face to face with old* MAHON). Are you coming to be killed a third time, or what ails you now?

MAHON. For what is it they have you tied?

CHRISTY. They're taking me to the peelers to have me hanged for slaying you.

MICHAEL (*apologetically*). It is the will of God that all should guard their little cabins from the treachery of law, and what would my daughter be doing if I was ruined or was hanged itself?

MAHON (*grimly, loosening* CHRISTY). It's little I care if you put a bag on her back, and went picking cockles till the hour of death; but my son and myself will be going our own way, and we'll have great times from this out telling stories of the vil-

lainy of Mayo, and the fools is here. (*To* CHRISTY, *who is freed*)
Come on now.

CHRISTY. Go with you, is it? I will then, like a gallant captain
with his heathen slave. Go on now and I'll see you from this day
stewing my oatmeal and washing my spuds, for I'm master of
all fights from now. (*Pushing* MAHON) Go on, I'm saying.

MAHON. Is it me?

CHRISTY. Not a word out of you. Go on from this.

MAHON (*walking out and looking back at* CHRISTY *over his
shoulder*). Glory be to God! (*With a broad smile*) I am crazy
again! (*Goes.*)

CHRISTY. Ten thousand blessings upon all that's here, for you've
turned me a likely gaffer in the end of all, the way I'll go
romancing through a romping lifetime from this hour to the
dawning of the judgment day. (*He goes out.*)

MICHAEL. By the will of God, we'll have peace now for our
drinks. Will you draw the porter, Pegeen?

SHAWN (*going up to her*). It's a miracle Father Reilly can wed
us in the end of all, and we'll have none to trouble us when his
vicious bite is healed.

PEGEEN (*hitting him a box on the ear*). Quit my sight. (*Putting
her shawl over her head and breaking out into wild lamenta-
tions*) Oh my grief, I've lost him surely. I've lost the only Playboy of the Western World.

CURTAIN

Juno and the Paycock

A TRAGEDY IN THREE ACTS

BY SEAN O'CASEY

CHARACTERS

"CAPTAIN" JACK BOYLE
JUNO BOYLE, *his wife*
JOHNNY BOYLE } *their children*
MARY BOYLE
"JOXER" DALY   *Residents in*
MRS. MAISIE MADIGAN   *the Tenement*
"NEEDLE" NUGENT, *a tailor*
MRS. TANCRED

JERRY DEVINE
CHARLIE BENTHAM, *a school teacher*
AN IRREGULAR MOBILIZER
TWO IRREGULARS
A COAL-BLOCK VENDOR
A SEWING MACHINE MAN
TWO FURNITURE REMOVAL MEN
TWO NEIGHBOURS

SCENE

ACT I.—The living apartment of a two-roomed tenancy of the Boyle family, in a tenement house in Dublin.

ACT II.—The same.

ACT III.—The same.

A few days elapse between Acts I and II, and two months between Acts II and III.

During Act III the curtain is lowered for a few minutes to denote the lapse of one hour.

Period of the play, 1922.

Juno and the Paycock

ACT ONE

The living room of a two-room tenancy occupied by the BOYLE *family in a tenement house in Dublin. Left, a door leading to another part of the house; left of door a window looking into the street; at back a dresser; farther to right at back, a window looking into the back of the house. Between the window and the dresser is a picture of the Virgin; below the picture, on a bracket, is a crimson bowl in which a floating votive light is burning. Farther to the right is a small bed partly concealed by cretonne hangings strung on a twine. To the right is the fireplace; near the fireplace is a door leading to the other room. Beside the fireplace is a box containing coal. On the mantelshelf is an alarm clock lying on its face. In a corner near the window looking into the back is a galvanized bath. A table and some chairs. On the table are breakfast things for one. A teapot is on the hob and a frying-pan stands inside the fender. There are a few books on the dresser and one on the table. Leaning against the dresser is a long-handled shovel—the kind invariably used by labourers when turning concrete or mixing mortar.* JOHNNY BOYLE *is sitting crouched beside the fire.* MARY *with her jumper off—it is lying on the back of a chair—is arranging her hair before a tiny mirror perched on the table. Beside the mirror is stretched out the morning paper, which she looks at when she isn't gazing into the mirror. She is a well-made and good-looking girl of twenty-two. Two forces are working in her mind—one, through the circumstances of her life, pulling her back; the other, through the influence of books she has read, pushing her forward. The opposing forces are apparent in her speech and her manners, both of which are degraded by her environment, and improved by her acquaintance —slight though it be—with literature. The time is early forenoon.*

MARY (*looking at the paper*). On a little bye-road, out beyant Finglas, he was found.

(MRS. BOYLE *enters by door on right; she has been shopping and carries a small parcel in her hand. She is forty-five years of age, and twenty years ago she must have been a pretty woman; but her face has now assumed that look which ultimately settles down upon the faces of the women of the working-class; a look of listless monotony and harassed anxiety, blending with an expression of mechanical resistance. Were circumstances favourable, she would probably be a handsome, active and clever woman.*)

MRS. BOYLE. Isn't he come in yet?

MARY. No, mother.

MRS. BOYLE. Oh, he'll come in when he likes; struttin' about the town like a paycock with Joxer, I suppose. I hear all about Mrs. Tancred's son is in this mornin's paper.

MARY. The full details are in it this mornin'; seven wounds he had—one entherin' the neck, with an exit wound beneath the left shoulder-blade; another in the left breast penethratin' the heart, an' . . .

JOHNNY (*springing up from the fire*). Oh, quit that readin', for God's sake! Are yous losin' all your feelin's? It'll soon be that none of yous'll read anythin' that's not about butcherin'! (*He goes quickly into the room on left.*)

MARY. He's gettin' very sensitive, all of a sudden!

MRS. BOYLE. I'll read it myself, Mary, by an' by, when I come home. Everybody's sayin' that he was a die-hard—thanks be to God that Johnny had nothin' to do with him this long time. . . . (*Opening the parcel and taking out some sausages, which she places on a plate*) Ah, then, if that father o' yours doesn't come in soon for his breakfast, he may go without any; I'll not wait much longer for him.

MARY. Can't you let him get it himself when he comes in?

MRS. BOYLE. Yes, an' let him bring in Joxer Daly along with him? Ay, that's what he'd like, an' that's what he's waitin' for— till he thinks I'm gone to work, an' then sail in with the boul' Joxer, to burn all the coal an' dhrink all the tea in the place, to show them what a good Samaritan he is! But I'll stop here till he comes in, if I have to wait till to-morrow mornin'.

VOICE OF JOHNNY INSIDE. Mother!

MRS. BOYLE. Yis?

VOICE OF JOHNNY. Bring us in a dhrink o' wather.

MRS. BOYLE. Bring in that fella a dhrink o' wather, for God's sake, Mary.

MARY. Isn't he big an' able enough to come out an' get it himself?

MRS. BOYLE. If you weren't well yourself you'd like somebody to bring you in a dhrink o' wather. (*She brings in drink and returns.*)

MRS BOYLE. Isn't it terrible to have to be waitin' this way! You'd think he was bringin' twenty poun's a week into the house the way he's goin' on. He wore out the Health Insurance long ago, he's afther wearin' out the unemployment dole, an', now, he's thryin' to wear out me! An' constantly singin', no less, when he ought always to be on his knees offerin' up a Novena for a job!

MARY (*tying a ribbon, fillet-wise around her head*). I don't like this ribbon, ma; I think I'll wear the green—it looks betther than the blue.

MRS. BOYLE. Ah, wear whatever ribbon you like, girl, only don't be botherin' me. I don't know what a girl on strike wants to be wearin' a ribbon round her head for or silk stockin's on her legs either; it's wearin' them things that make the employers think they're givin' yous too much money.

MARY. The hour is past now when we'll ask the employers' permission to wear what we like.

MRS. BOYLE. I don't know why you wanted to walk out for Jennie Claffey; up to this you never had a good word for her.

MARY. What's the use of belongin' to a Trades Union if you won't stand up for your principles? Why did they sack her? It was a clear case of victimization. We couldn't let her walk the streets, could we?

MRS. BOYLE. No, of course yous couldn't—yous wanted to keep her company. Wan victim wasn't enough. When the employers sacrifice wan victim, the Trades Unions go wan betther be sacrificin' a hundred.

MARY. It doesn't matther what you say, ma—a principle's a principle.

MRS. BOYLE. Yis; an' when I go into oul' Murphy's to-morrow, an' he gets to know that, instead o' payin' all, I'm goin' to borry more, what'll he say when I tell him a principle's a principle? What'll we do if he refuses to give us any more on tick?

MARY. He daren't refuse—if he does, can't you tell him he's paid?

MRS. BOYLE. It's lookin' as if he was paid, whether he refuses or no.

(JOHNNY *appears at the door on left. He can be plainly seen now; he is a thin delicate fellow, something younger than* MARY. *He has evidently gone through a rough time. His face is pale and drawn; there is a tremulous look of indefinite fear in his eyes. The left sleeve of his coat is empty, and he walks with a slight halt.*)

JOHNNY. I was lyin' down; I thought yous were gone. Oul' Simon Mackay is thrampin' about like a horse over me head, an' I can't sleep with him—they're like thunder-claps in me brain! The curse o'—God forgive me for goin' to curse!

MRS. BOYLE. There, now; go back an' lie down agan, an' I'll bring you in a nice cup o' tay.

JOHNNY. Tay, tay, tay! You're always thinkin' o' tay. If a man was dyin', you'd thry to make him swally a cup o' tay! (*He goes back.*)

MRS. BOYLE. I don't know what's goin' to be done with him. The bullet he got in the hip in Easter Week was bad enough.

but the bomb that shatthered his arm in the fight in O'Connell Street put the finishin' touch on him. I knew he was makin' a fool of himself. God knows I went down on me bended knees to him not to go agen the Free State.

MARY. He stuck to his principles, an', no matther how you may argue, ma, a principle's a principle.

VOICE OF JOHNNY. Is Mary goin' to stay here?

MARY. No, I'm not goin' to stay here; you can't expect me to be always at your beck an' call, can you?

VOICE OF JOHNNY. I won't stop here be meself!

MRS. BOYLE. Amn't I nicely handicapped with the whole o' yous! I don't know what any o' yous ud do without your ma. (*To* JOHNNY) Your father'll be here in a minute, an' if you want anythin', he'll get it for you.

JOHNNY. I hate assin' him for anythin'. . . . He hates to be assed to stir. . . . Is the light lightin' before the picture o' the Virgin?

MRS. BOYLE. Yis, yis! The wan inside to St. Anthony isn't enough, but he must have another wan to the Virgin here!

(JERRY DEVINE *enters hastily. He is about twenty-five, well set, active and earnest. He is a type, becoming very common now in the Labour Movement, of a mind knowing enough to make the mass of his associates, who know less, a power, and too little to broaden that power for the benefit of all.* MARY *seizes her jumper and runs hastily into room left.*)

JERRY (*breathless*). Where's the Captain, Mrs. Boyle; where's the Captain?

MRS. BOYLE. You may well ass a body that: he's wherever Joxer Daly is—dhrinkin' in some snug or another.

JERRY. Father Farrell is just afther stoppin' to tell me to run up an' get him to go to the new job that's goin' on in Rathmines; his cousin is foreman o' the job, an' Father Farrell was speakin' to him about poor Johnny an' his father bein' idle so long, an' the foreman told Father Farrell to send the Captain up an' he'd give him a start—I wondher where I'd find him?

MRS. BOYLE. You'll find he's ayther in Ryan's or Foley's.

JERRY. I'll run round to Ryan's—I know it's a great house o' Joxer's. (*He rushes out.*)

MRS. BOYLE (*piteously*). There now, he'll miss that job, or I know for what! If he gets win' o' the word, he'll not come back till evenin', so that it'll be too late. There'll never be any good got out o' him so long as he goes with that shouldher-shruggin' Joxer. I killin' meself workin', an' he sthruttin' about from mornin' till night like a paycock!

(*The steps of two persons are heard coming up a flight of stairs. They are the footsteps of* CAPTAIN BOYLE *and* JOXER. CAPTAIN BOYLE *is singing in a deep, sonorous, self-honouring voice.*)

THE CAPTAIN. Sweet Spirit, hear me prayer! Hear . . . oh . . . hear . . . me prayer . . . hear, oh, hear . . . Oh, he . . . ar . . . oh, he . . . ar . . . me . . . pray . . . er!

JOXER (*outside*). Ah, that's a darlin' song, a daaarlin' song!

MRS. BOYLE (*viciously*). Sweet spirit hear his prayer! Oh, then, I'll take me solemn affeydavey, it's not for a job he's prayin'!

(*She sits down on the bed so that the cretonne hangings hide her from the view of those entering.*)

(THE CAPTAIN *comes slowly in. He is a man of about sixty; stout, grey-haired and stocky. His neck is short, and his head looks like a stone ball that one sometimes sees on top of a gate-post. His cheeks, reddish-purple, are puffed out, as if he were always repressing an almost irrepressible ejaculation. On his upper lip is a crisp, tightly cropped moustache; he carries himself with the upper part of his body slightly thrown back, and his stomach slightly thrust forward. His walk is a slow, consequential strut. His clothes are dingy, and he wears a faded seaman's cap with a glazed peak.*)

BOYLE (*to* JOXER, *who is still outside*). Come on, come on in, Joxer; she's gone out long ago, man. If there's nothing else to be got, we'll furrage out a cup o' tay, anyway. It's the only bit I get in comfort when she's away. 'Tisn't Juno should be her pet name at all, but Deirdre of the Sorras, for she's always grousin'.

(JOXER *steps cautiously into the room. He may be younger than* THE CAPTAIN *but he looks a lot older. His face is like a bundle of crinkled paper; his eyes have a cunning twinkle; he is spare and loosely built; he has a habit of constantly shrugging his shoulders with a peculiar twitching movement, meant to be ingratiating. His face is invariably ornamented with a grin.*)

JOXER. It's a terrible thing to be tied to a woman that's always grousin'. I don't know how you stick it—it ud put years on me. It's a good job she has to be so ofen away, for (*with a shrug*) when the cat's away, the mice can play!

BOYLE (*with a commanding and complacent gesture*). Pull over to the fire, Joxer, an' we'll have a cup o' tay in a minute.

JOXER. Ah, a cup o' tay's a darlin' thing, a daaarlin' thing—the cup that cheers but doesn't . . .

(JOXER's *rhapsody is cut short by the sight of* JUNO *coming forward and confronting the two cronies. Both are stupefied.*)

MRS. BOYLE (*with sweet irony—poking the fire, and turning her head to glare at* JOXER). Pull over to the fire, Joxer Daly, an' we'll have a cup o' tay in a minute! Are you sure, now, you wouldn't like an egg?

JOXER. I can't stop, Mrs. Boyle; I'm in a desperate hurry, a desperate hurry.

MRS. BOYLE. Pull over to the fire, Joxer Daly; people is always far more comfortabler here than they are in their own place.

(JOXER *makes hastily for the door.* BOYLE *stirs to follow him; thinks of something to relieve the situation—stops, and says suddenly*):

Joxer!

JOXER (*at door ready to bolt*). Yis?

BOYLE. You know the foreman o' that job that's goin' on down in Killesther, don't you, Joxer?

JOXER (*puzzled*). Foreman—Killesther?

BOYLE (*with a meaning look*). He's a butty o' yours, isn't he?

JOXER (*the truth dawning on him*). The foreman at Killesther —oh, yis, yis. He's an oul' butty o' mine—oh, he's a darlin' man, a daarlin' man.

BOYLE. Oh, then, it's a sure thing. It's a pity we didn't go down at breakfast first thing this mornin'—we might ha' been working now; but you didn't know it then.

JOXER (*with a shrug*). It's betther late than never.

BOYLE. It's nearly time we got a start, anyhow; I'm fed up knockin' round, doin' nothin'. He promised you—gave you the straight tip?

JOXER. Yis. "Come down on the blow o' dinner," says he, "an' I'll start you, an' any friend you like to brin' with you." Ah, says I, you're a darlin' man, a daaarlin' man.

BOYLE. Well, it couldn't come at a betther time—we're a long time waitin' for it.

JOXER. Indeed we were; but it's a long lane that has no turnin'.

BOYLE. The blow up for dinner is at one—wait till I see what time it 'tis. (*He goes over to the mantelpiece, and gingerly lifts the clock.*)

MRS. BOYLE. Min' now, how you go on fiddlin' with that clock—you know the least little thing sets it asthray.

BOYLE. The job couldn't come at a betther time; I'm feelin' in great fettle, Joxer. I'd hardly believe I ever had a pain in me legs, an' last week I was nearly crippled with them.

JOXER. That's betther and betther; ah, God never shut wan door but he opened another!

BOYLE. It's only eleven o'clock; we've lashins o' time. I'll slip on me oul' moleskins afther breakfast, an' we can saunther down at our ayse. (*Putting his hand on the shovel*) I think, Joxer, we'd betther bring our shovels?

JOXER. Yis, Captain, yis; it's betther to go fully prepared 'an ready for all eventualities. You bring your long-tailed shovel, an' I'll bring me navvy. We mighten' want them, an', then agen, we might: for want of a nail the shoe was lost, for want of a shoe the horse was lost, an' for want of a horse the man was lost—aw, that's a darlin' proverb, a daarlin' . . .

(*As* JOXER *is finishing his sentence,* MRS. BOYLE *approaches the door and* JOXER *retreats hurriedly. She shuts the door with a bang.*)

BOYLE (*suggestively*). We won't be long pullin' ourselves together agen when I'm working for a few weeks.

(MRS. BOYLE *takes no notice.*)

BOYLE. The foreman on the job is an oul' butty o' Joxer's; I have an idea that I know him meself. (*Silence*) . . . There's a button off the back o' me moleskin trousers. . . . If you leave out a needle an' thread I'll sew it on meself. . . . Thanks be to God, the pains in me legs is gone, anyhow!

MRS. BOYLE (*with a burst*). Look here, Mr. Jacky Boyle, them yarns won't go down with Juno. I know you an' Joxer Daly of an oul' date, an', if you think you're able to come it over me with them fairy tales, you're in the wrong shop.

BOYLE (*coughing subduedly to relieve the tenseness of the situation*). U-u-u-ugh.

MRS. BOYLE. Butty o' Joxer's! Oh, you'll do a lot o' good as long as you continue to be a butty o' Joxer's!

BOYLE. U-u-u-ugh.

MRS. BOYLE. Shovel! Ah, then, me boyo, you'd do far more work with a knife an' fork than ever you'll do with a shovel! If there was e'er a genuine job goin' you'd be dh'other way about— not able to lift your arms with the pains in your legs! Your poor wife slavin' to keep the bit in your mouth, an' you galli-vantin' about all the day like a paycock!

BOYLE. It ud be betther for a man to be dead, betther for a man to be dead.

MRS. BOYLE (*ignoring the interruption*). Everybody callin' you "Captain," an' you only wanst on the wather, in an oul' collier from here to Liverpool, when anybody, to listen or look at you, ud take you for a second Christo For Columbus!

BOYLE. Are you never goin' to give us a rest?

MRS. BOYLE. Oh, you're never tired o' lookin' for a rest.

BOYLE. D'ye want to dhrive me out o' the house?

MRS. BOYLE. It ud be easier to dhrive you out o' the house than to dhrive you into a job. Here, sit down an' take your break-fast—it may be the last you'll get, for I don't know where the next is goin' to come from.

BOYLE. If I get this job we'll be all right.

MRS. BOYLE. Did ye see Jerry Devine?

BOYLE (*testily*). No, I didn't see him.

MRS. BOYLE. No, but you seen Joxer. Well, he was here lookin' for you.

BOYLE. Well, let him look!

MRS. BOYLE. Oh, indeed, he may well look, for it ud be hard for him to see you, an' you stuck in Ryan's snug.

BOYLE. I wasn't in Ryan's snug—I don't go into Ryan's.

MRS. BOYLE. Oh, is there a mad dog there? Well, if you weren't in Ryan's you were in Foley's.

BOYLE. I'm telling you for the last three weeks I haven't tasted a dhrop of intoxicatin' liquor. I wasn't in ayther wan snug or dh'other—I could swear that on a prayer-book—I'm as innocent as the child unborn!

MRS. BOYLE. Well, if you'd been in for your breakfast you'd ha' seen him.

BOYLE (*suspiciously*). What does he want me for?

MRS. BOYLE. He'll be back any minute an' then you'll soon know.

BOYLE. I'll dhrop out an' see if I can meet him.

MRS. BOYLE. You'll sit down an' take your breakfast, an' let me go to me work, for I'm an hour late already waitin' for you.

BOYLE. You needn't ha' waited, for I'll take no breakfast—I've a little spirit left in me still!

MRS. BOYLE. Are you goin' to have your breakfast—yes or no?

BOYLE (*too proud to yield*). I'll have no breakfast—yous can keep your breakfast. (*Plaintively*) I'll knock out a bit somewhere, never fear.

MRS. BOYLE. Nobody's goin' to coax you—don't think that. (*She vigorously replaces the pan and the sausages in the press.*)

BOYLE. I've a little spirit left in me still.

(JERRY DEVINE *enters hastily.*)

JERRY. Oh, here you are at last! I've been searchin' for you everywhere. The foreman in Foley's told me you hadn't left the snug with Joxer ten minutes before I went in.

MRS. BOYLE. An' he swearin' on the holy prayer-book that he wasn't in no snug!

BOYLE (*to* JERRY). What business is it o' yours whether I was in a snug or no? What do you want to be gallopin' about afther me for? Is a man not to be allowed to leave his house for a minute without havin' a pack o' spies, pimps an' informers cantherin' at his heels?

JERRY. Oh, you're takin' a wrong view of it, Mr. Boyle; I simply was anxious to do you a good turn. I have a message for you from Father Farrell: he says that if you go to the job that's on in Rathmines, an' ask for Foreman Mangan, you'll get a start.

BOYLE. That's all right, but I don't want the motions of me body to be watched the way an asthronomer ud watch a star. If you're folleyin' Mary aself, you've no pereeogative to be folleyin' me. (*Suddenly catching his thigh*) U-ugh, I'm afther gettin' a terrible twinge in me right leg!

MRS. BOYLE. Oh, it won't be very long now till it travels into your left wan. It's miraculous that whenever he scents a job in front of him, his legs begin to fail him! Then, me bucko, if you lose this chance, you may go an' furrage for yourself!

JERRY. This job'll last for some time, too, Captain, an' as soon as the foundations are in, it'll be cushy enough.

BOYLE. Won't it be a climbin' job? How d'ye expect me to be able to go up a ladder with these legs? An', if I get up aself, how am I goin' to get down agen?

MRS. BOYLE (*viciously*). Get wan o' the labourers to carry you down in a hod! You can't climb a laddher, but you can skip like a goat into a snug!

JERRY. I wouldn't let meself be let down that easy, Mr. Boyle; a little exercise, now, might do you all the good in the world.

BOYLE. It's a docthor you should have been, Devine—maybe you know more about the pains in me legs than meself that has them?

JERRY (*irritated*). Oh, I know nothin' about the pains in your legs; I've brought the message that Father Farrell gave me, an' that's all I can do.

MRS. BOYLE. Here, sit down an' take your breakfast, an' go an' get ready; an' don't be actin' as if you couldn't pull a wing out of a dead bee.

BOYLE. I want no breakfast, I tell you; it ud choke me afther all that's been said. I've a little spirit left in me still.

MRS. BOYLE. Well, let's see your spirit, then, an' go in at wanst an' put on your moleskin trousers!

BOYLE (*moving towards the door on left*). It ud be betther for a man to be dead! U-ugh! There's another twinge in me other leg! Nobody but meself knows the sufferin' I'm goin' through with the pains in these legs o' mine! (*He goes into the room on left as* MARY *comes out with her hat in her hand*.)

MRS. BOYLE. I'll have to push off now, for I'm terrible late already, but I was determined to stay an' hunt that Joxer this time. (*She goes off*.)

JERRY. Are you going out, Mary?

MARY. It looks like it when I'm putting on my hat, doesn't it?

JERRY. The bitther word agen, Mary.

MARY. You won't allow me to be friendly with you; if I thry, you deliberately misundherstand it.

JERRY. I didn't always misundherstand it; you were ofen delighted to have the arms of Jerry around you.

MARY. If you go on talkin' like this, Jerry Devine, you'll make me hate you!

JERRY. Well, let it be either a weddin' or a wake! Listen, Mary, I'm standin' for the Secretaryship of our Union. There's only one opposin' me; I'm popular with all the men, an' a good speaker—all are sayin' that I'll get elected.

MARY. Well?

JERRY. The job's worth three hundred an' fifty pounds a year, Mary. You an' I could live nice an' cosily on that; it would lift you out o' this place an'. . .

MARY. I haven't time to listen to you now—I have to go. (*She is going out when* JERRY *bars the way.*)

JERRY (*appealingly*). Mary, what's come over you with me for the last few weeks? You hardly speak to me, an' then only a word with a face o' bittherness on it. Have you forgotten, Mary, all the happy evenin's that were as sweet as the scented hawthorn that sheltered the sides o' the road as we saunthered through the country?

MARY. That's all over now. When you get your new job, Jerry, you won't be long findin' a girl far bether than I am for your sweetheart.

JERRY. Never, never, Mary! No matther what happens you'll always be the same to me.

MARY. I must be off; please let me go, Jerry.

JERRY. I'll go a bit o' the way with you.

MARY. You needn't, thanks; I want to be by meself.

JERRY (*catching her arm*). You're goin' to meet another fella; you've clicked with some one else, me lady!

MARY. That's no concern o' yours, Jerry Devine; let me go!

JERRY. I saw yous comin' out o' the Cornflower Dance Class, an' you hangin' on his arm—a thin, lanky strip of a Micky Dazzler, with a walkin'-stick an' gloves!

VOICE OF JOHNNY (*loudly*). What are you doin' there—pullin' about everything!

VOICE OF BOYLE (*loudly and viciously*). I'm puttin' on me mole-skin trousers!

MARY. You're hurtin' me arm! Let me go, or I'll scream, an' then you'll have the oul' fella out on top of us!

JERRY. Don't be so hard on a fella, Mary, don't be so hard.

BOYLE (*appearing at the door*). What's the meanin' of all this hillabaloo?

MARY. Let me go, let me go!

BOYLE. D'ye hear me—what's all this hillabaloo about?

JERRY (*plaintively*). Will you not give us one kind word, one kind word, Mary?

BOYLE. D'ye hear me talkin' to yous? What's all this hillabaloo for?

JERRY. Let me kiss your hand, your little, tiny, white hand!

BOYLE. Your little, tiny, white hand—are you takin' leave o' your senses, man?

(MARY *breaks away and rushes out.*)

BOYLE. This is nice goin's on in front of her father!

JERRY. Ah, dhry up, for God's sake! (*He follows* MARY.)

BOYLE. Chiselurs don't care a damn now about their parents, they're bringin' their fathers' grey hairs down with sorra to the grave, an' laughin' at it, laughin' at it. Ah, I suppose it's just the same everywhere—the whole worl's in a state o' chassis! (*He sits by the fire*) Breakfast! Well, they can keep their breakfast for me. Not if they went down on their bended knees would I take it—I'll show them I've a little spirit left in me still! (*He goes over to the press, takes out a plate and looks at it*) Sassige! Well, let her keep her sassige. (*He returns to the fire, takes up the teapot and gives it a gentle shake*) The tay's wet right enough. (*A pause; he rises, goes to the press, takes out the sausage, puts it on the pan, and puts both on the fire. He attends the sausage with a fork.*)

BOYLE (*singing*):
When the robins nest agen,
And the flowers are in bloom,
When the Springtime's sunny smile seems to banish all sorrow
       an' gloom;
Then me bonny blue-ey'd lad, if me heart be true till then—

He's promised he'll come back to me,
When the robins nest agen!

(*He lifts his head at the high note, and then drops his eyes
to the pan.*)

BOYLE (*singing*):

When the . . .

(*Steps are heard approaching; he whips the pan off the fire
and puts it under the bed, then sits down at the fire. The door
opens and a bearded man looking in says*):

You don't happen to want a sewin' machine?

BOYLE (*furiously*). No, I don't want e'er a sewin' machine! (*He
returns the pan to the fire, and commences to sing again.*)

BOYLE (*singing*):

When the robins nest agen,
And the flowers they are in bloom,
He's . . .

(*A thundering knock is heard at the street door.*)

BOYLE. There's a terrible tatheraraa—that's a stranger—that's
nobody belongin' to the house. (*Another loud knock.*)

JOXER (*sticking his head in at the door*). Did ye hear them
tatherarahs?

BOYLE. Well, Joxer, I'm not deaf.

JOHNNY (*appearing in his shirt and trousers at the door on left;
his face is anxious and his voice is tremulous*). Who's that at
the door; who's that at the door? Who gave that knock—d'ye
yous hear me—are yous deaf or dhrunk or what?

BOYLE (*to* JOHNNY). How the hell do I know who 'tis? Joxer, stick your head out o' the window an' see.

JOXER. An' mebbe get a bullet in the kisser? Ah, none o' them thricks for Joxer! It's betther to be a coward than a corpse!

BOYLE (*looking cautiously out of the window*). It's a fella in a thrench coat.

JOHNNY. Holy Mary, Mother o' God, I . . .

BOYLE. He's goin' away—he must ha' got tired knockin'.

(JOHNNY *returns to the room on left*.)

BOYLE. Sit down an' have a cup o' tay, Joxer.

JOXER. I'm afraid the missus ud pop in on us agen before we'd know where we are. Somethin's tellin' me to go at wanst.

BOYLE. Don't be superstitious, man; we're Dublin men, an' not boyos that's only afther comin' up from the bog o' Allen—though if she did come in, right enough, we'd be caught like rats in a thrap.

JOXER. An' you know the sort she is—she wouldn't listen to reason—an' wanse bitten twice shy.

BOYLE (*going over to the window at back*). If the worst came to the worst, you could dart out here, Joxer; it's only a dhrop of a few feet to the roof of the return room, an' the first minute she goes into dh'other room, I'll give you the bend, an' you can slip in an' away.

JOXER (*yielding to the temptation*). Ah, I won't stop very long anyhow. (*Picking up a book from the table*) Whose is the buk?

BOYLE. Aw, one o' Mary's; she's always readin' lately—nothin' but thrash, too. There's one I was lookin' at dh'other day: three stories, The Doll's House, Ghosts, an' The Wild Duck— buks only fit for chiselurs!

JOXER. Didja ever rade *Elizabeth, or Th' Exile o' Sibayria* . . . ah, it's a darlin' story, a daarlin' story!

BOYLE. You eat your sassige, an' never min' *Th' Exile o' Sibayria.*

   (*Both sit down;* BOYLE *fills out tea, pours gravy on* JOXER's *plate, and keeps the sausage for himself.*)

JOXER. What are you wearin' your moleskin trousers for?

BOYLE. I have to go to a job, Joxer. Just afther you'd gone, Devine kem runnin' in to tell us that Father Farrell said if I went down to the job that's goin' on in Rathmines I'd get a start.

JOXER. Be the holy, that's good news!

BOYLE. How is it good news? I wondher if you were in my con- dition, would you call it good news?

JOXER. I thought . . .

BOYLE. You thought! You think too sudden sometimes, Joxer. D'ye know, I'm hardly able to crawl with the pains in me legs!

JOXER. Yis, yis; I forgot the pains in your legs. I know you can do nothin' while they're at you.

BOYLE. You forgot; I don't think any of yous realize the state I'm in with the pains in me legs. What ud happen if I had to carry a bag o' cement?

JOXER. Ah, any man havin' the like of them pains id be down an' out, down an' out.

BOYLE. I wouldn't mind if he had said it to meself; but, no, oh

no, he rushes in an' shouts it out in front o' Juno, an' you
know what Juno is, Joxer. We all know Devine knows a little
more than the rest of us, but he doesn't act as if he did; he's a
good boy, sober, able to talk an' all that, but still . . .

JOXER. Oh ay; able to argufy, but still . . .

BOYLE. If he's runnin' afther Mary, aself, he's not goin' to be
runnin' afther me. Captain Boyle's able to take care of himself. Afther all, I'm not gettin' brought up on Virol. I never
heard him usin' a curse; I don't believe he was ever dhrunk in
his life—sure he's not like a Christian at all!

JOXER. You're afther takin' the word out o' me mouth—afther
all, a Christian's natural, but he's unnatural.

BOYLE. His oul' fella was just the same—a Wicklow man.

JOXER. A Wicklow man! That explains the whole thing. I've
met many a Wicklow man in me time, but I never met wan
that was any good.

BOYLE. "Father Farrell," says he, "sent me down to tell you."
Father Farrell! . . . D'ye know, Joxer, I never like to be be-
holden to any o' the clergy.

JOXER. It's dangerous, right enough.

BOYLE. If they do anything for you, they'd want you to be livin'
in the Chapel. . . . I'm goin' to tell you somethin', Joxer, that
I wouldn't tell to anybody else—the clergy always had too much
power over the people in this unfortunate country.

JOXER. You could sing that if you had an air to it!

BOYLE (becoming enthusiastic). Didn't they prevent the people
in '47 from seizin' the corn, an' they starvin'; didn't they down

Parnell; didn't they say that hell wasn't hot enough nor eternity long enough to punish the Fenians? We don't forget, we don't forget them things, Joxer. If they've taken everything else from us, Joxer, they've left us our memory.

JOXER (*emotionally*). For mem'ry's the only friend that grief can call its own, that grief . . . can . . . call . . . its own!

BOYLE. Father Farrell's beginnin' to take a great intherest in Captain Boyle; because of what Johnny did for his country, says he to me wan day. It's a curious way to reward Johnny be makin' his poor oul' father work. But, that's what the clergy want, Joxer—work, work, work for me an' you; havin' us mulin' from mornin' till night, so that they may be in betther fettle when they come hoppin' round for their dues! Job! Well, let him give his job to wan of his hymn-singin', prayer-spoutin', craw-thumpin' Confraternity men!

(*The voice of a coal-block vendor is heard chanting in the street.*)

VOICE OF COAL VENDOR. Blocks . . . coal-blocks! Blocks . . . coal-blocks!

JOXER. God be with the young days when you were steppin' the deck of a manly ship, with the win' blowin' a hurricane through the masts, an' the only sound you'd hear was, "Port your helm!" an' the only answer, "Port it is, sir!"

BOYLE. Them was days, Joxer, them was days. Nothin' was too hot or too heavy for me then. Sailin' from the Gulf o' Mexico to the Antarctic Ocean. I seen things, I seen things, Joxer, that no mortal man should speak about that knows his Catechism. Ofen, an' ofen, when I was fixed to the wheel with a marlin-spike, an' the win's blowin' fierce an' the waves lashin' an' lashin', till you'd think every minute was goin' to be your last, an' it blowed, an' blowed—blew is the right word, Joxer, but blowed is what the sailors use. . . .

JOXER. Aw, it's a darlin' word, a daarlin' word.

BOYLE. An', as it blowed an' blowed, I ofen looked up at the sky an' assed meself the question—what is the stars, what is the stars?

VOICE OF COAL VENDOR. Any blocks, coal-blocks; blocks, coal-blocks!

JOXER. Ah, that's the question, that's the question—what is the stars?

BOYLE. An' then, I'd have another look, an' I'd ass meself—what is the moon?

JOXER. Ah, that's the question—what is the moon, what is the moon?

(*Rapid steps are heard coming towards the door.* BOYLE *makes desperate efforts to hide everything;* JOXER *rushes to the window in a frantic effort to get out;* BOYLE *begins to innocently lilt—* "Oh, me darlin' Jennie, I will be thrue to thee," *when the door is opened, and the black face of the* COAL VENDOR *appears.*)

THE COAL VENDOR. D'yes want any blocks?

BOYLE (*with a roar*). No, we don't want any blocks!

JOXER (*coming back with a sigh of relief*). That's afther puttin' the heart across me—I could ha' sworn it was Juno. I'd betther be goin', Captain; you couldn't tell the minute Juno'd hop in on us.

BOYLE. Let her hop in; we may as well have it out first as at

last. I've made up me mind—I'm not goin' to do only what she
damn well likes.

JOXER. Them sentiments does you credit, Captain; I don't like
to say anything as between man an' wife, but I say as a butty,
as a butty, Captain, that you've stuck it too long, an' that it's
about time you showed a little spunk.

> How can a man die betther than facin' fearful odds,
> For th' ashes of his fathers an' the temples of his gods.

BOYLE. She has her rights—there's no one denyin' it, but haven't
I me rights too?

JOXER. Of course you have—the sacred rights o' man!

BOYLE. To-day, Joxer, there's goin' to be issued a proclamation
be me, establishin' an independent Republic, an' Juno'll have to
take an oath of allegiance.

JOXER. Be firm, be firm, Captain; the first few minutes'll be
the worst:—if you gently touch a nettle it'll sting you for your
pains; grasp it like a lad of mettle, an's as soft as silk remains!

VOICE OF JUNO OUTSIDE. Can't stop, Mrs. Madigan—I haven't
a minute!

JOXER (*flying out of the window*). Holy God, here she is!

BOYLE (*packing the things away with a rush in the press*). I
knew that fella ud stop till she was in on top of us! (*He sits
down by the fire.*)

(JUNO *enters hastily; she is flurried and excited.*)

JUNO. Oh, you're in—you must have been only afther comin'
in?

BOYLE. No, I never went out.

JUNO. It's curious, then, you never heard the knockin'. (*She puts her coat and hat on bed.*)

BOYLE. Knockin'? Of course I heard the knockin'.

JUNO. An' why didn't you open the door, then? I suppose you were so busy with Joxer that you hadn't time.

BOYLE. I haven't seen Joxer since I seen him before. Joxer! What ud bring Joxer here?

JUNO. D'ye mean to tell me that the pair of yous wasn't collogin' together here when me back was turned?

BOYLE. What ud we be collogin' together about? I have somethin' else to think of besides collogin' with Joxer. I can swear on all the holy prayer-books . . .

MRS. BOYLE. That you weren't in no snug! Go on in at wanst now, an' take aff that moleskin trousers o' yours, an' put on a collar an' tie to smarten yourself up a bit. There's a visitor comin' with Mary in a minute, an' he has great news for you.

BOYLE. A job, I suppose; let us get wan first before we start lookin' for another.

MRS. BOYLE. That's the thing that's able to put the win' up you. Well, it's no job, but news that'll give you the chance o' your life.

BOYLE. What's all the mysthery about?

MRS. BOYLE. G'win an' take off the moleskin trousers when you're told!

(BOYLE *goes into room on left.* MRS. BOYLE *tidies up the room, puts the shovel under the bed, and goes to the press.*)

MRS. BOYLE. Oh, God bless us, looka the way everythin's thrun about! Oh, Joxer was here, Joxer was here!

(MARY *enters with* CHARLIE BENTHAM; *he is a young man of twenty-five, tall, good-looking, with a very high opinion of himself generally. He is dressed in a brown coat, brown knee-breeches, grey stockings, a brown sweater, with a deep blue tie; he carries gloves and a walking-stick.*)

MRS. BOYLE (*fussing round*). Come in, Mr. Bentham; sit down, Mr. Bentham, in this chair; it's more comfortabler than that, Mr. Bentham. Himself'll be here in a minute; he's just takin' off his trousers.

MARY. Mother!

BENTHAM. Please don't put yourself to any trouble, Mrs. Boyle —I'm quite all right here, thank you.

MRS. BOYLE. An' to think of you knowin' Mary, an' she knowin' the news you had for us, an' wouldn't let on; but it's all the more welcomer now, for we were on our last lap!

VOICE OF JOHNNY INSIDE. What are you kickin' up all the racket for?

BOYLE (*roughly*). I'm takin' off me moleskin trousers!

JOHNNY. Can't you do it, then, without lettin' th' whole house know you're takin' off your trousers? What d'ye want puttin' them on an' takin' them off again?

BOYLE. Will you let me alone, will you let me alone? Am I never goin' to be done thryin' to please th' whole o' yous?

MRS. BOYLE (*to* BENTHAM). You must excuse th' state o' th' place, Mr. Bentham; th' minute I turn me back that man o' mine always makes a litther o' th' place, a litther o' th' place.

BENTHAM. Don't worry, Mrs. Boyle; it's all right, I assure . . .

BOYLE (*inside*). Where's me braces; where in th' name o' God did I leave me braces. . . . Ay, did you see where I put me braces?

JOHNNY (*inside, calling out*). Ma, will you come in here an' take da away ou' o' this or he'll dhrive me mad.

MRS. BOYLE (*going towards door*). Dear, dear, dear, that man'll be lookin' for somethin' on th' day o' Judgement. (*Looking into room and calling to* BOYLE) Look at your braces, man, hangin' round your neck!

BOYLE (*inside*). Aw, Holy God!

MRS. BOYLE (*calling*). Johnny, Johnny, come out here for a minute.

JOHNNY. Oh, leave Johnny alone, an' don't be annoyin' him!

MRS. BOYLE. Come on, Johnny, till I inthroduce you to Mr. Bentham. (*To* BENTHAM) Me son, Mr. Bentham; he's afther goin' through the mill. He was only a chiselur of a Boy Scout in Easter Week, when he got hit in the hip; and his arm was blew off in the fight in O'Connell Street. (JOHNNY *comes in.*) Here he is, Mr. Bentham; Mr. Bentham, Johnny. None can deny he done his bit for Irelan', if that's going to do him any good.

JOHNNY (*boastfully*). I'd do it agen, ma, I'd do it agen; for a principle's a principle.

MRS. BOYLE. Ah, you lost your best principle, me boy, when you lost your arm; them's the only sort o' principles that's any good to a workin' man.

JOHNNY. Ireland only half free'll never be at peace while she has a son left to pull a trigger.

MRS. BOYLE. To be sure, to be sure—no bread's a lot betther than half a loaf. (*Calling loudly in to* BOYLE) Will you hurry up there?

(BOYLE *enters in his best trousers, which aren't too good, and looks very uncomfortable in his collar and tie.*)

MRS. BOYLE. This is me husband; Mr. Boyle, Mr. Bentham.

BENTHAM. Ah, very glad to know you, Mr. Boyle. How are you?

BOYLE. Ah, I'm not too well at all; I suffer terrible with pains in me legs. Juno can tell you there what . . .

MRS. BOYLE. You won't have many pains in your legs when you hear what Mr. Bentham has to tell you.

BENTHAM. Juno! What an interesting name! It reminds one of Homer's glorious story of ancient gods and heroes.

BOYLE. Yis, doesn't it? You see, Juno was born an' christened in June; I met her in June; we were married in June, an' Johnny was born in June, so wan day I says to her, "You should ha' been called Juno," an' the name stuck to her ever since.

MRS. BOYLE. Here, we can talk o' them things agen; let Mr. Bentham say what he has to say now.

BENTHAM. Well, Mr. Boyle, I suppose you'll remember a Mr. Ellison of Santry—he's a relative of yours, I think.

BOYLE (*viciously*). Is it that prognosticator an' procrastinator! Of course I remember him.

BENTHAM. Well, he's dead, Mr. Boyle . . .

BOYLE. Sorra many'll go into mournin' for him.

MRS. BOYLE. Wait till you hear what Mr. Bentham has to say, an' then, maybe, you'll change your opinion.

BENTHAM. A week before he died he sent for me to write his will for him. He told me that there were two only that he wished to leave his property to: his second cousin Michael Finnegan of Santry, and John Boyle, his first cousin of Dublin.

BOYLE (*excitedly*). Me, is it me, me?

BENTHAM. You, Mr. Boyle; I'll read a copy of the will that I have here with me, which has been duly filed in the Court of Probate. (*He takes a paper from his pocket and reads*):

6th February 1922.

This is the last Will and Testament of William Ellison, of Santry, in the County of Dublin. I hereby order and wish my property to be sold and divided as follows:—

£20 to the St. Vincent De Paul Society.

£60 for Masses for the repose of my soul (5s. for Each Mass).

The rest of my property to be divided between my first and second cousins.

I hereby appoint Timothy Buckly, of Santry, and Hugh Brierly, of Coolock, to be my Executors.

(*Signed*)   WILLIAM ELLISON.
                HUGH BRIERLY.
                TIMOTHY BUCKLY.
                CHARLES BENTHAM, N.T.

BOYLE (*eagerly*). An' how much'll be comin' out of it, Mr. Bentham?

BENTHAM. The Executors told me that half of the property would be anything between £1500 and £2000.

MARY. A fortune, father, a fortune!

JOHNNY. We'll be able to get out o' this place now, an' go somewhere we're not known.

MRS. BOYLE. You won't have to trouble about a job for a while, Jack.

BOYLE (*fervently*). I'll never doubt the goodness o' God agen.

BENTHAM. I congratulate you, Mr. Boyle. (*They shake hands.*)

BOYLE. An' now, Mr. Bentham, you'll have to have a wet.

BENTHAM. A wet?

BOYLE. A wet—a jar—a boul!

MRS. BOYLE. Jack, you're speakin' to Mr. Bentham, an' not to Joxer.

BOYLE (*solemnly*). Juno . . . Mary . . . Johnny . . . we'll have to go into mournin' at wanst. . . . I never expected that poor Bill ud die so sudden. . . . Well, we all have to die some day . . . you, Juno, to-day . . . an' me, maybe, to-morrow. . . . It's sad, but it can't be helped. . . . Requiescat in pace . . . or, usin' our oul' tongue like St. Patrick or St. Briget, Guh sayeree jeea ayera!

MARY. Oh, father, that's not Rest in Peace; that's God save Ireland.

BOYLE. U-u-ugh, it's all the same—isn't it a prayer? . . . Juno, I'm done with Joxer; he's nothin' but a prognosticator an' a . . .

JOXER (*climbing angrily through the window and bounding into the room*). You're done with Joxer, are you? Maybe you thought I'd stop on the roof all the night for you! Joxer out on the roof with the win' blowin' through him was nothin' to you an' your friend with the collar an' tie!

MRS. BOYLE. What in the name o' God brought you out on the roof; what were you doin' there?

JOXER (*ironically*). I was dhreamin' I was standin' on the bridge of a ship, an' she sailin' the Antarctic Ocean, an' it blowed, an' blowed, an' I lookin' up at the sky an' sayin', what is the stars, what is the stars?

MRS. BOYLE (*opening the door and standing at it*). Here, get ou' o' this, Joxer Daly; I was always thinkin' you had a slate off.

JOXER (*moving to the door*). I have to laugh every time I look at the deep sea sailor; an' a row on a river ud make him sea-sick!

BOYLE. Get ou' o' this before I take the law into me own hands!

JOXER (*going out*). Say aw rewaeawr, but not good-bye. Lookin' for work, an' prayin' to God he won't get it! (*He goes.*)

MRS. BOYLE. I'm tired tellin' you what Joxer was; maybe now you see yourself the kind he is.

BOYLE. He'll never blow the froth off a pint o' mine agen, that's a sure thing. Johnny . . . Mary . . . you're to keep yourselves to yourselves for the future. Juno, I'm done with Joxer. . . . I'm a new man from this out. . . . (*Clasping* JUNO's *hand, and singing emotionally*):

> Oh, me darlin' Juno, I will be thrue to thee;
> Me own, me darlin' Juno, you're all the world to me.

CURTAIN

ACT TWO

SCENE. *The same, but the furniture is more plentiful, and of a vulgar nature. A glaringly upholstered arm-chair and lounge; cheap pictures and photos everywhere. Every available spot is ornamented with huge vases filled with artificial flowers. Crossed festoons of coloured paper chains stretch from end to end of ceiling. On the table is an old attaché case. It is about six in the evening, and two days after the First Act.* BOYLE, *in his shirt sleeves, is voluptuously stretched on the sofa; he is smoking a clay pipe. He is half asleep. A lamp is lighting on the table. After a few moments' pause the voice of* JOXER *is heard singing softly outside at the door—"Me pipe I'll smoke, as I dhrive me moke—are you there, Mor . . . ee . . . ar . . . i . . teeel"*

BOYLE (*leaping up, takes a pen in his hand and busies himself with papers*). Come along, Joxer, me son, come along.

JOXER (*putting his head in*). Are you be yourself?

BOYLE. Come on, come on; that doesn't matther; I'm masther now, an' I'm goin' to remain masther.

(JOXER *comes in.*)

JOXER. How d'ye feel now, as a man o' money?

BOYLE (*solemnly*). It's a responsibility, Joxer, a great responsibility.

JOXER. I suppose 'tis now, though you wouldn't think it.

BOYLE. Joxer, han' me over that attackey case on the table there.

119

(JOXER *hands the case*) Ever since the Will was passed I've run hundhreds o' dockyments through me han's—I tell you, you have to keep your wits about you. (*He busies himself with papers.*)

JOXER. Well, I won't disturb you; I'll dhrop in when . . .

BOYLE (*hastily*). It's all right, Joxer, this is the last one to be signed to-day. (*He signs a paper, puts it into the case, which he shuts with a snap, and sits back pompously in the chair.*) Now, Joxer, you want to see me; I'm at your service—what can I do for you, me man?

JOXER. I've just dhropped in with the £3 : 5s. that Mrs. Madigan riz on the blankets an' table for you, and she says you're to be in no hurry payin' it back.

BOYLE. She won't be long without it; I expect the first cheque for a couple o' hundhred any day. There's the five bob for yourself—go on, take it, man; it'll not be the last you'll get from the Captain. Now an' agen we have our differ, but we're there together all the time.

JOXER. Me for you, an' you for me, like the two Musketeers.

BOYLE. Father Farrell stopped me to-day an' tole me how glad he was I fell in for the money.

JOXER. He'll be stoppin' you ofen enough now; I suppose it was "Mr." Boyle with him?

BOYLE. He shuk me be the han'. . . .

JOXER (*ironically*). I met with Napper Tandy, an' he shuk me be the han'!

BOYLE. You're seldom asthray, Joxer, but you're wrong shipped this time. What you're sayin' of Father Farrell is very near to blasfeemey. I don't like any one to talk disrespectful of Father Farrell.

JOXER. You're takin' me up wrong, Captain; I wouldn't let a word be said agen Father Farrell—the heart o' the rowl, that's what he is; I always said he was a darlin' man, a daarlin' man.

BOYLE. Comin' up the stairs who did I meet but that bummer, Nugent. "I seen you talkin' to Father Farrell," says he, with a grin on him. "He'll be folleyin' you," says he, "like a Guardian Angel from this out"—all the time the oul' grin on him, Joxer.

JOXER. I never seen him yet but he had that oul' grin on him!

BOYLE. "Mr. Nugent," says I, "Father Farrell is a man o' the people, an', as far as I know the History o' me country, the priests was always in the van of the fight for Irelan's freedom."

JOXER (*fervently*):

> Who was it led the van, Soggart Aroon?
> Since the fight first began, Soggart Aroon?

BOYLE. "Who are you tellin'?" says he. "Didn't they let down the Fenians, an' didn't they do in Parnell? An' now . . ." "You ought to be ashamed o' yourself," says I, interruptin' him, "not to know the History o' your country." An' I left him gawkin' where he was.

JOXER. Where ignorance 's bliss 'tis folly to be wise; I wondher did he ever read the Story o' Irelan'.

BOYLE. Be J. L. Sullivan? Don't you know he didn't?

JOXER. Ah, it's a darlin' buk, a daarlin' buk!

BOYLE. You'd betther be goin', now, Joxer, his Majesty, Bentham, 'll be here any minute, now.

JOXER. Be the way things is lookin', it'll be a match between him an' Mary. She's thrun over Jerry altogether. Well, I hope it will, for he's a darlin' man.

BOYLE. I'm glad you think so—I don't. (*Irritably*) What's darlin' about him?

JOXER (*nonplussed*). I only seen him twiced; if you want to know me, come an' live with me.

BOYLE. He's too ignified for me—to hear him talk you'd think he knew as much as a Boney's Oraculum. He's given up his job as teacher, an' is goin' to become a solicitor in Dublin—he's been studyin' law. I suppose he thinks I'll set him up, but he's wrong shipped. An' th' other fella—Jerry's as bad. The two o' them ud give you a pain in your face, listenin' to them; Jerry believin' in nothin', an' Bentham believin' in everythin'. One that says all is God an' no man; an' th' other that says all is man an' no God!

JOXER. Well, I'll be off now.

BOYLE. Don't forget to dhrop down afther a while; we'll have a quiet jar, an' a song or two.

JOXER. Never fear.

BOYLE. An' tell Mrs. Madigan that I hope we'll have the pleasure of her organization at our little enthertainment.

JOXER. Righto; we'll come down together. (*He goes out.*)

(JOHNNY *comes from room on left, and sits down moodily at the fire.* BOYLE *looks at him for a few moments, and shakes his head. He fills his pipe.*)

VOICE OF JUNO AT THE DOOR. Open the door, Jack; this thing has me nearly kilt with the weight.

(BOYLE *opens the door.* JUNO *enters carrying the box of a gramophone, followed by* MARY *carrying the horn, and some parcels.* JUNO *leaves the box on the table and flops into a chair.*)

JUNO. Carryin' that from Henry Street was no joke.

BOYLE. U-u-ugh, that's a grand lookin' insthrument—how much was it?

JUNO. Pound down, an' five to be paid at two shillin's a week.

BOYLE. That's reasonable enough.

JUNO. I'm afraid we're runnin' into too much debt; first the furniture, an' now this.

BOYLE. The whole lot won't be much out of £2000.

MARY. I don't know what you wanted a gramophone for—I know Charlie hates them; he says they're destructive of real music.

BOYLE. Desthructive of music—that fella ud give you a pain in your face. All a gramophone wants is to be properly played; its thrue wondher is only felt when everythin's quiet—what a gramophone wants is dead silence!

MARY. But, father, Jerry says the same; afther all, you can only appreciate music when your ear is properly trained.

BOYLE. That's another fella ud give you a pain in your face. Properly thrained! I suppose you couldn't appreciate football unless your fut was properly thrained.

MRS. BOYLE (*to* MARY). Go on in ower that an' dress, or Charlie 'll be in on you, an' tay nor nothin' 'll be ready.

(MARY *goes into room left.*)

MRS. BOYLE (*arranging table for tea*). You didn't look at our new gramophone, Johnny?

JOHNNY. 'Tisn't gramophones I'm thinking of.

MRS. BOYLE. An' what is it you're thinkin' of, allanna?

JOHNNY. Nothin', nothin', nothin'.

MRS. BOYLE. Sure, you must be thinkin' of somethin'; it's yourself that has yourself the way y'are; sleepin' wan night in me sisther's, an' the nex' in your father's brother's—you'll get no rest goin' on that way.

JOHNNY. I can rest nowhere, nowhere, nowhere.

MRS. BOYLE. Sure, you're not thryin' to rest anywhere.

JOHNNY. Let me alone, let me alone, let me alone, for God's sake.

(*A knock at street door.*)

MRS. BOYLE (*in a flutter*). Here he is; here's Mr. Bentham!

BOYLE. Well, there's room for him; it's a pity there's not a brass band to play him in.

MRS. BOYLE. We'll han' the tay round, an' not be clusthered round the table, as if we never seen nothin'.

(Steps are heard approaching, and JUNO, *opening the door, allows* BENTHAM *to enter.)*

JUNO. Give your hat an' stick to Jack, there . . . sit down, Mr. Bentham . . . no, not there . . . in th' easy chair be the fire . . . there, that's betther. Mary'll be out to you in a minute.

BOYLE *(solemnly)*. I seen be the paper this mornin' that Consols was down half per cent. That's serious, min' you, an' shows the whole counthry's in a state o' chassis.

MRS. BOYLE. What's Consols, Jack?

BOYLE. Consols? Oh, Consols is—oh, there's no use tellin' women what Consols is—th' wouldn't undherstand.

BENTHAM. It's just as you were saying, Mr. Boyle . . .

*(*MARY *enters charmingly dressed.)*

BENTHAM. Oh, good evening, Mary; how pretty you're looking!

MARY *(archly)*. Am I?

BOYLE. We were just talkin' when you kem in, Mary, I was tellin' Mr. Bentham that the whole counthry's in a state o' chassis.

MARY *(to* BENTHAM*)*. Would you prefer the green or the blue ribbon round me hair, Charlie?

MRS. BOYLE. Mary, your father's speakin'.

BOYLE *(rapidly)*. I was jus' tellin' Mr. Bentham that the whole counthry's in a state o' chassis.

MARY. I'm sure you're frettin', da, whether it is or no.

MRS. BOYLE. With all our churches an' religions, the worl's not a bit the betther.

BOYLE (*with a commanding gesture*). Tay!

(MARY *and* MRS. BOYLE *dispense the tea.*)

MRS. BOYLE. An' Irelan's takin' a leaf out o' the worl's buk; when we got the makin' of our own laws I thought we'd never stop to look behind us, but instead of that we never stopped to look before us! If the people ud folley up their religion betther there'd be a betther chance for us—what do you think, Mr. Bentham?

BENTHAM. I'm afraid I can't venture to express an opinion on that point, Mrs. Boyle; dogma has no attraction for me.

MRS. BOYLE. I forgot you didn't hold with us: what's this you said you were?

BENTHAM. A Theosophist, Mrs. Boyle.

MRS. BOYLE. An' what in the name o' God's a Theosophist?

BOYLE. A Theosophist, Juno, 's a—tell her, Mr. Bentham, tell her.

BENTHAM. It's hard to explain in a few words: Theosophy's founded on The Vedas, the religious books of the East. Its central theme is the existence of an all-pervading Spirit—the Life-Breath. Nothing really exists but this one Universal Life-Breath. And whatever even seems to exist separately from this Life-Breath, doesn't really exist at all. It is all vital force in man, in all animals, and in all vegetation. This Life-Breath is called the Prawna.

MRS. BOYLE. The Prawna! What a comical name!

BOYLE. Prawna; yis, the Prawna. (*Blowing gently through his lips*) That's the Prawna!

MRS. BOYLE. Whist, whist, Jack.

BENTHAM. The happiness of man depends upon his sympathy with this Spirit. Men who have reached a high state of excellence are called Yogi. Some men become Yogi in a short time, it may take others millions of years.

BOYLE. Yogi! I seen hundhreds of them in the streets o' San Francisco.

BENTHAM. It is said by these Yogi that if we practise certain mental exercises that we would have powers denied to others—for instance, the faculty of seeing things that happen miles and miles away.

MRS. BOYLE. I wouldn't care to meddle with that sort o' belief; it's a very curious religion, altogether.

BOYLE. What's curious about it? Isn't all religions curious? If they weren't, you wouldn't get any one to believe them. But religions is passin' away—they've had their day like everything else. Take the real Dublin people, f'rinstance: they know more about Charlie Chaplin an' Tommy Mix than they do about SS. Peter an' Paul!

MRS. BOYLE. You don't believe in ghosts, Mr. Bentham?

MARY. Don't you know he doesn't, mother?

BENTHAM. I don't know, that, Mary. Scientists are beginning to think that what we call ghosts are sometimes seen by persons of a certain nature. They say that sensational actions, such as the killing of a person, demand great energy, and that that energy

lingers in the place where the action occurred. People may live
in the place and see nothing, when some one may come along
whose personality has some peculiar connection with the energy
of the place, and, in a flash, the person sees the whole affair.

JOHNNY (*rising swiftly, pale and affected*). What sort o' talk is
this to be goin' on with? Is there nothin' bether to be talkin'
about but the killin' o' people? My God, isn't it bad enough for
these things to happen without talkin' about them! (*He hurriedly goes into the room on left.*)

BENTHAM. Oh, I'm very sorry, Mrs. Boyle; I never thought . . .

MRS. BOYLE (*apologetically*). Never mind, Mr. Bentham, he's
very touchy. (*A frightened scream is heard from* JOHNNY *inside.*)

MRS. BOYLE. Mother of God? What's that?

  (*He rushes out again, his face pale, his lips twitching, his
limbs trembling.*)

JOHNNY. Shut the door, shut the door, quick, for God's sake!
Great God, have mercy on me! Blessed Mother o' God, shelter
me, shelter your son!

MRS. BOYLE (*catching him in her arms*). What's wrong with you?
What ails you? Sit down, sit down, here, on the bed . . . there
now . . . there now.

MARY. Johnny, Johnny, what ails you?

JOHNNY. I seen him, I seen him . . . kneelin' in front o' the
statue . . . merciful Jesus, have pity on me!

MRS. BOYLE (*to* BOYLE). Get him a glass o' whisky . . . quick,
man, an' don't stand gawkin'.

(BOYLE *gets the whisky.*)

JOHNNY. Sit here, sit here, mother . . . between me an' the door.

MRS. BOYLE. I'll sit beside you as long as you like, only tell me what was it came across you at all?

JOHNNY (*after taking some drink*). I seen him. . . . I seen Robbie Tancred kneelin' down before the statue . . . an' the red light shinin' on him . . . an' when I went in . . . he turned an' looked at me . . . an' I seen the woun's bleedin' in his breast. . . . Oh, why did he look at me like that . . . it wasn't my fault that he was done in. . . . Mother o' God, keep him away from me!

MRS. BOYLE. There, there, child, you've imagined it all. There was nothin' there at all—it was the red light you seen, an' the talk we had put all the rest into your head. Here, dhrink more o' this—it'll do you good. . . . An', now, stretch yourself down on the bed for a little. (*To* BOYLE) Go in, Jack, an' show him it was only in his own head it was.

BOYLE (*making no move*). E-e-e-eh; it's all nonsense; it was only a shadda he saw.

MARY. Mother o' God, he made me heart lep!

BENTHAM. It was simply due to an overwrought imagination— we all get that way at times.

MRS. BOYLE. There, dear, lie down in the bed, an' I'll put the quilt across you . . . e-e-e-eh, that's it . . . you'll be as right as the mail in a few minutes.

JOHNNY. Mother, go into the room an' see if the light's lightin' before the statue.

MRS. BOYLE (*to* BOYLE). Jack, run in, an' see if the light's lightin' before the statue.

BOYLE (*to* MARY). Mary, slip in an' see if the light's lightin' before the statue.

(MARY *hesitates to go in.*)

BENTHAM. It's all right; Mary, I'll go. (*He goes into the room; remains for a few moments, and returns.*)

BENTHAM. Everything's just as it was—the light burning bravely before the statue.

BOYLE. Of course; I knew it was all nonsense.

(*A knock at the door.*)

BOYLE (*going to open the door*). E-e-e-e-eh. (*He opens it, and* JOXER, *followed by* MRS. MADIGAN, *enters.* MRS. MADIGAN *is a strong, dapper little woman of about forty-five; her face is almost always a widespread smile of complacency. She is a woman who, in manner at least, can mourn with them that mourn, and rejoice with them that do rejoice. When she is feeling comfortable, she is inclined to be reminiscent; when others say anything, or following a statement made by herself, she has a habit of putting her head a little to one side, and nodding it rapidly several times in succession, like a bird pecking at a hard berry. Indeed, she has a good deal of the bird in her, but the bird instinct is by no means a melodious one. She is ignorant, vulgar and forward, but her heart is generous withal. For instance, she would help a neighbour's sick child; she would probably kill the child, but her intentions would be to cure it; she would be more at home helping a drayman to lift a fallen horse. She is dressed in a rather soiled grey dress and a vivid purple blouse; in her hair is a huge comb, ornamented with huge coloured beads. She enters with a gliding step, beaming smile and nodding head.* BOYLE *receives them effusively.*)

BOYLE. Come on in, Mrs. Madigan; come on in; I was afraid you weren't comin'. . . . (*Slyly*) There's some people able to dhress, ay, Joxer?

JOXER. Fair as the blossoms that bloom in the May, an' sweet as the scent of the new mown hay. . . . Ah, well she may wear them.

MRS. MADIGAN (*looking at* MARY). I know some as are as sweet as the blossoms that bloom in the May—oh, no names, no pack dhrill!

BOYLE. An', now, I'll inthroduce the pair o' yous to Mary's intended: Mr. Bentham, this is Mrs. Madigan, an oul' back-parlour neighbour, that, if she could help it at all, ud never see a body shuk!

BENTHAM (*rising, and tentatively shaking the hand of* MRS. MADIGAN). I'm sure, it's a great pleasure to know you, Mrs. Madigan.

MRS. MADIGAN. An' I'm goin' to tell you, Mr. Bentham, you're goin' to get as nice a bit o' skirt in Mary, there, as ever you seen in your puff. Not like some of the dhressed up dolls that's knockin' about lookin' for men when it's a skelpin' they want. I remember as well as I remember yesterday, the day she was born—of a Tuesday, the 25th o' June, in the year 1901, at thirty-three minutes past wan in the day be Foley's clock, the pub at the corner o' the street. A cowld day it was too, for the season o' the year, an' I remember sayin' to Joxer, there, who I met comin' up th' stairs, that the new arrival in Boyle's ud grow up a hardy chiselur if it lived, an' that she'd be somethin' one o' these days that nobody suspected, an' so signs on it, here she is to-day, goin' to be married to a young man lookin' as if he'd be fit to com-mensurate in any position in life it ud please God to call him!

BOYLE (*effusively*). Sit down, Mrs. Madigan, sit down, me oul' sport. (*To* BENTHAM) This is Joxer Daly, Past Chief Ranger of the Dear Little Shamrock Branch of the Irish National For-esters, an oul' front-top neighbour, that never despaired, even in the darkest days of Ireland's sorra.

JOXER. Nil desperandum, Captain, nil desperandum.

BOYLE. Sit down, Joxer, sit down. The two of us was ofen in a tight corner.

MRS. BOYLE. Ay, in Foley's snug!

JOXER. An' we kem out of it flyin', we kem out of it flyin', Cap-tain.

BOYLE. An', now, for a dhrink—I know yous won't refuse an oul' friend.

MRS. MADIGAN (*to* JUNO). Is Johnny not well, Mrs. . . .

MRS. BOYLE (*warningly*). S-s-s-sh.

MRS. MADIGAN. Oh, the poor darlin'

BOYLE. Well, Mrs. Madigan, is it tay or what?

MRS. MADIGAN. Well, speakin' for meself, I jus' had me tea a minute ago, an' I'm afraid to dhrink any more—I'm never the same when I dhrink too much tay. Thanks, all the same, Mr. Boyle.

BOYLE. Well, what about a bottle o' stout or a dhrop o' whisky?

MRS. MADIGAN. A bottle o' stout ud be a little too heavy for me stummock afther me tay. . . . A-a-ah, I'll thry the ball o' malt.

(BOYLE *prepares the whisky.*)

MRS. MADIGAN. There's nothin' like a ball o' malt occasional like —too much of it isn't good. (*To* BOYLE, *who is adding water*) Ah, God, Johnny, don't put too much wather on it! (*She drinks*) I suppose yous'll be lavin' this place.

BOYLE. I'm looking for a place near the sea; I'd like the place that you might say was me cradle, to be me grave as well. The sea is always callin' me.

JOXER. She is callin', callin', callin', in the win' an' on the sea.

BOYLE. Another dhrop o' whisky, Mrs. Madigan?

MRS. MADIGAN. Well, now, it ud be hard to refuse seein' the suspicious times that's in it.

BOYLE (*with a commanding gesture*). Song! . . . Juno . . . Mary . . . "Home to Our Mount'ins"!

MRS. MADIGAN (*enthusiastically*). Hear, hear!

JOXER. Oh, tha's a darlin' song, a daarlin' song!

MARY (*bashfully*). Ah, no, da; I'm not in a singin' humour.

MRS. MADIGAN. Gawn with you, child, an' you only goin' to be marrid; I remember as well as I remember yesterday,—it was on a lovely August evenin', exactly, accordin' to date, fifteen years ago, come the Tuesday folleyin' the nex' that's comin' on, when me own man (*the Lord be good to him*) an' me was sit-tin' shy together in a doty little nook on a counthry road, adja-cent to The Stiles. "That'll scratch your lovely, little white neck," says he, ketchin' hould of a danglin' bramble branch, holdin' clusters of the loveliest flowers you ever seen, an' breakin' it off, so that his arm fell, accidental like, roun' me waist, an' as I felt it tightenin', an' tightenin', an' tightenin', I thought me buzzum was every minute goin' to burst out into a roystherin' song about

> The little green leaves that were shakin' on the threes,
> The gallivantin' butterflies, an' buzzin' o' the bees!

BOYLE. Ordher for the song!

JUNO. Come on, Mary—we'll do our best. (JUNO *and* MARY *stand up, and choosing a suitable position, sing simply "Home to Our Mountains."*)

(*They bow to company, and return to their places.*)

BOYLE (*emotionally, at the end of the song*). Lull . . . me . . . to . . . rest!

JOXER (*clapping his hands*). Bravo, bravo! Darlin' girulls, darlin' girulls!

MRS. MADIGAN. Juno, I never seen you in betther form.

BENTHAM. Very nicely rendered indeed.

MRS. MADIGAN. A noble call, a noble call!

MRS. BOYLE. What about yourself, Mrs. Madigan? (*After some coaxing,* MRS. MADIGAN *rises, and in a quavering voice sings the following verse*):

> If I were a blackbird I'd whistle and sing;
> I'd follow the ship that my thrue love was in;
> An' on the top riggin', I'd there build me nest,
> An' at night I would sleep on me Willie's white breast!

(*Becoming husky, amid applause, she sits down.*)

MRS. MADIGAN. Ah, me voice is too husky now, Juno; though I remember the time when Maisie Madigan could sing like a nightingale at matin' time. I remember as well as I remember yestherday, at a party given to celebrate the comin' of the first chiselur to Annie an' Benny Jimeson—who was the barber, yous may remember, in Henrietta Street, that, afther Easter Week, hung out a green, white an' orange pole, an', then, when the Tans started their Jazz dancin', whipped it in agen, an' stuck out a red, white an' blue wan instead, given as an excuse that a barber's pole was strictly non-political—singin' "An' You'll Remember Me," with the top notes quiverin' in a dead hush of pethrified attention, folleyed by a clappin' o' han's that shuk the tumblers on the table, an' capped be Jimeson, the barber, sayin' that it was the best rendherin' of "You'll Remember Me" he ever heard in his natural!

BOYLE (*peremptorily*). Ordher for Joxer's song!

JOXER. Ah, no, I couldn't; don't ass me, Captain.

BOYLE. Joxer's song, Joxer's song—give us wan of your shut-eyed wans. (JOXER *settles himself in his chair; takes a drink; clears his throat; solemnly closes his eyes, and begins to sing in a very querulous voice*):

She is far from the lan' where her young hero sleeps,
An' lovers around her are sighing (*He hesitates*)
An' lovers around her are sighin' . . . sighin' . . . sighin' . . .
(*A pause.*)

BOYLE (*imitating* JOXER):

      And lovers around her are sighing!

What's the use of you thryin' to sing the song if you don't know it?

MARY. Thry another one, Mr. Daly—maybe you'd be more fortunate.

MRS. MADIGAN. Gawn, Joxer, thry another wan.

JOXER (*starting again*):

I have heard the mavis singin' his love song to the morn;
I have seen the dew-dhrop clingin' to the rose jus' newly born;
    but . . . but . . . (*frantically*) to the rose jus' newly born
    . . . newly born . . . born.

JOHNNY. Mother, put on the gramophone, for God's sake, an' stop Joxer's bawlin'.

BOYLE (*commandingly*). Gramophone! . . . I hate to see fellas thryin' to do what they're not able to do. (BOYLE *arranges the gramophone, and is about to start it, when voices are heard of persons descending the stairs.*)

MRS. BOYLE (*warningly*). Whisht, Jack, don't put it on, don't put it on yet; this must be poor Mrs. Tancred comin' down to go to the hospital—I forgot all about them bringin' the body to the church to-night. Open the door, Mary, an' give them a bit o' light.

(MARY *opens the door, and* MRS. TANCRED—*a very old woman, obviously shaken by the death of her son—appears, accompanied by several neighbours. The first few phrases are spoken before they appear.*)

FIRST NEIGHBOUR. It's a sad journey we're goin' on, but God's good, an' the Republicans won't be always down.

MRS. TANCRED. Ah, what good is that to me now? Whether they're up or down—it won't bring me darlin' boy from the grave.

MRS. BOYLE. Come in an' have a hot cup o' tay, Mrs. Tancred, before you go.

MRS. TANCRED. Ah, I can take nothin' now, Mrs. Boyle—I won't be long afther him.

FIRST NEIGHBOUR. Still an' all, he died a noble death, an' we'll bury him like a king.

MRS. TANCRED. An' I'll go on livin' like a pauper. Ah, what's the pains I suffered bringin' him into the world to carry him to his cradle, to the pains I'm sufferin' now, carryin' him out o' the world to bring him to his grave!

MARY. It would be better for you not to go at all, Mrs. Tancred, but to stay at home beside the fire with some o' the neighbours.

MRS. TANCRED. I seen the first of him, an' I'll see the last of him.

MRS. BOYLE. You'd want a shawl, Mrs. Tancred; it's a cowld night, an' the win's blowin' sharp.

MRS. MADIGAN (*rushing out*). I've a shawl above.

MRS. TANCRED. Me home is gone, now; he was me only child, an' to think that he was lyin' for a whole night stretched out on the side of a lonely counthry lane, with his head, his darlin' head, that I ofen kissed an' fondled, half hidden in the wather of a runnin' brook. An' I'm told he was the leadher of the ambush where me nex' door neighbour, Mrs. Mannin', lost her Free State soldier son. An' now here's the two of us oul' women, standin' one on each side of a scales o' sorra, balanced be the bodies of our two dead darlin' sons. (MRS. MADIGAN *returns, and wraps a shawl around her*) God bless you, Mrs. Madigan. . . . (*She moves slowly towards the door*) Mother o' God, Mother o' God, have pity on the pair of us! . . . O Blessed Virgin, where were you when me darlin' son was riddled with bullets, when me darlin' son was riddled with bullets! . . . Sacred Heart of the Crucified Jesus, take away our hearts o' stone . . . an' give us hearts o' flesh! . . . Take away this murdherin' hate . . . an' give us Thine own eternal love! (*They pass out of the room.*)

MRS. BOYLE (*explanatorily to* BENTHAM). That was Mrs. Tancred of the two-pair back; her son was found, e'er yestherday, lyin' out beyant Finglas riddled with bullets. A die-hard he was, be all accounts. He was a nice quiet boy, but lattherly he went to hell, with his Republic first, an' Republic last an' Republic over all. He ofen took tea with us here, in the oul' days, an' Johnny, there, an' him used to be always together.

JOHNNY. Am I always to be havin' to tell you that he was no friend o' mine? I never cared for him, an' he could never stick me. It's not because he was Commandant of the Battalion that I was Quarther-Masther of, that we were friends.

MRS. BOYLE. He's gone, now—the Lord be good to him! God help his poor oul' creature of a mother, for no matther whose friend or enemy he was, he was her poor son.

BENTHAM. The whole thing is terrible, Mrs. Boyle; but the only way to deal with a mad dog is to destroy him.

MRS. BOYLE. An' to think of me forgettin' about him bein' brought to the church to-night, an' we singin' an' all, but it was well we hadn't the gramophone goin', anyhow.

BOYLE. Even if we had aself. We've nothin' to do with these things, one way or t'other. That's the Government's business, an' let them do what we're payin' them for doin'.

MRS. BOYLE. I'd like to know how a body's not to mind these things; look at the way they're afther leavin' the people in this very house. Hasn't the whole house, nearly, been massacreed? There's young Mrs. Dougherty's husband with his leg off; Mrs. Travers that had her son blew up be a mine in Inchegeela, in Co. Cork; Mrs. Mannin' that lost wan of her sons in an ambush a few weeks ago, an' now, poor Mrs. Tancred's only child gone West with his body made a collandher of. Sure, if it's not our business, I don't know whose business it is.

BOYLE. Here, there, that's enough about them things; they don't affect us, an' we needn't give a damn. If they want a wake, well, let them have a wake. When I was a sailor, I was always re-signed to meet with a wathery grave; an', if they want to be soldiers, well, there's no use o' them squealin' when they meet a soldier's fate.

JOXER. Let me like a soldier fall—me breast expandin' to th' ball!

MRS. BOYLE. In wan way, she deserves all she got; for lately, she let th' die-hards make an open house of th' place; an' for th' last couple of months, either when th' sun was risin', or when th' sun was settin', you had C.I.D. men burstin' into your room, assin' you where were you born, where were you christened, where were you married, an' where would you be buried!

JOHNNY. For God's sake, let us have no more o' this talk.

MRS. MADIGAN. What about Mr. Boyle's song before we start th' gramophone?

MARY (*getting her hat, and putting it on*). Mother, Charlie and I are goin' out for a little sthroll.

MRS. BOYLE. All right, darlin'.

BENTHAM (*going out with* MARY). We won't be long away, Mrs. Boyle.

MRS. MADIGAN. Gwan, Captain, gwan.

BOYLE. E-e-e-e-eh, I'd want to have a few more jars in me, before I'd be in fettle for singin'.

JOXER. Give us that poem you writ t'other day. (*To the rest*) Aw, it's a darlin' poem, a daarlin' poem.

MRS. BOYLE. God bless us, is he startin' to write poetry!

BOYLE (*rising to his feet*). E-e-e-e-eh. (*He recites in an emotional, consequential manner the following verses*):

Shawn an' I were friends, sir, to me he was all in all.
His work was very heavy and his wages were very small.
None betther on th' beach as Docker, I'll go bail,
'Tis now I'm feelin' lonely, for to-day he lies in jail.
He was not what some call pious—seldom at church or prayer;
For the greatest scoundrels I know, sir, goes every Sunday there.
Fond of his pint—well, rather, but hated the Boss by creed
But never refused a copper to comfort a pal in need.

E-e-e-e-eh. (*He sits down.*)

MRS. MADIGAN. Grand, grand; you should folley that up, you should folley that up.

JOXER. It's a daarlin' poem!

BOYLE (*delightedly*). E-e-e-e-eh.

JOHNNY. Are yous goin' to put on th' gramophone to-night, or are yous not?

MRS. BOYLE. Gwan, Jack, put on a record.

MRS. MADIGAN. Gwan, Captain, gwan.

BOYLE. Well, yous'll want to keep a dead silence. (*He sets a record, starts the machine, and it begins to play "If you're Irish, come into the Parlour." As the tune is in full blare, the door is suddenly opened by a brisk, little bald-headed man, dressed circumspectly in a black suit; he glares fiercely at all in the room; he is "*NEEDLE NUGENT,*" a tailor. He carries his hat in his hands.*)

NUGENT (*loudly, above the noise of the gramophone*). Are yous goin' to have that thing bawlin' an' the funeral of Mrs. Tancred's son passin' the house? Have none of yous any respect for the Irish people's National regard for the dead?

(BOYLE *stops the gramophone.*)

MRS. BOYLE. Maybe, Needle Nugent, it's nearly time we had a little less respect for the dead, an' a little more regard for the livin'.

MRS. MADIGAN. We don't want you, Mr. Nugent, to teach us what we learned at our mother's knee. You don't look yourself as if you were dyin' of grief; if y'ass Maisie Madigan anything, I'd call you a real thrue die-hard an' live-soft Republican, attendin' Republican funerals in the day, an' stoppin' up half the night makin' suits for the Civic Guards! (*Persons are heard running down to the street, some saying, "Here it is, here it is." NUGENT withdraws, and the rest, except JOHNNY, go to the window look-*

ing into the street, and look out. Sounds of a crowd coming nearer are heard; portion are singing):

> To Jesus' Heart all burning
> With fervent love for men,
> My heart with fondest yearning
> Shall raise its joyful strain.
> While ages course along,
> Blest be with loudest song,
> The Sacred Heart of Jesus
> By every heart and tongue.

MRS. BOYLE. Here's the hearse, here's the hearse!

BOYLE. There's t'oul' mother walkin' behin' the coffin.

MRS. MADIGAN. You can hardly see the coffin with the wreaths.

JOXER. Oh, it's a darlin' funeral, a daarlin' funeral!

MRS. MADIGAN. We'd have a betther view from the street.

BOYLE. Yes—this place ud give you a crick in your neck. (*They leave the room, and go down.* JOHNNY *sits moodily by the fire.*)

(*A young man enters; he looks at* JOHNNY *for a moment.*)

THE YOUNG MAN. Quarther-Masther Boyle.

JOHNNY (*with a start*). The Mobilizer!

THE YOUNG MAN. You're not at the funeral?

JOHNNY. I'm not well.

THE YOUNG MAN. I'm glad I've found you; you were stoppin' at your aunt's; I called there but you'd gone. I've to give you an ordher to attend a Battalion Staff meetin' the night afther to-morrow.

JOHNNY. Where?

THE YOUNG MAN. I don't know; you're to meet me at the Pillar at eight o'clock; then we're to go to a place I'll be told of to-night; there we'll meet a mothor that'll bring us to the meeting. They think you might be able to know somethin' about them that gave the bend where Commandant Tancred was shelterin'.

JOHNNY. I'm not goin', then. I know nothing about Tancred.

THE YOUNG MAN (*at the door*). You'd betther come for your own sake—remember your oath.

JOHNNY (*passionately*). I won't go! Haven't I done enough for Ireland! I've lost me arm, an' me hip's desthroyed so that I'll never be able to walk right agen! Good God, haven't I done enough for Ireland?

THE YOUNG MAN. Boyle, no man can do enough for Ireland! (*He goes.*)

(*Faintly in the distance the crowd is heard saying*:)

Hail, Mary, full of grace, the Lord is with Thee;
Blessed art Thou amongst women, and blessed, etc.

CURTAIN

ACT THREE

SCENE. *The same as Act Two. It is about half-past six on a No-*
vember evening; a bright fire is burning in the grate; MARY,
dressed to go out, is sitting on a chair by the fire, leaning for-
ward, her hands under her chin, her elbows on her knees. A
look of dejection, mingled with uncertain anxiety, is on her
face. A lamp, turned low, is lighting on the table. The votive
light under the picture of the Virgin, gleams more redly than
ever. MRS. BOYLE *is putting on her hat and coat. It is two months*
later.

MRS. BOYLE. An' has Bentham never even written to vou since—
not one line for the past month?

MARY (*tonelessly*). Not even a line, mother.

MRS. BOYLE. That's very curious. . . . What came between the
two of yous at all? To leave you so sudden, an' yous so great
together. . . . To go away t' England, an' not to even leave you
his address. . . . The way he was always bringin' you to dances,
I thought he was mad afther you. Are you sure you said nothin'
to him?

MARY. No, mother—at least nothing that could possibly explain
his givin' me up.

MRS. BOYLE. You know you're a bit hasty at times, Mary, an' say
things you shouldn't say.

MARY. I never said to him what I shouldn't say, I'm sure of that.

MRS. BOYLE. How are you sure of it?

MARY. Because I love him with all my heart and soul, mother. Why, I don't know; I often thought to myself that he wasn't the man poor Jerry was, but I couldn't help loving him, all the same.

MRS. BOYLE. But you shouldn't be frettin' the way you are; when a woman loses a man, she never knows what she's afther losin', to be sure, but, then, she never knows what she's afther gainin', either. You're not the one girl of a month ago—you look like one pinin' away. It's long ago I had a right to bring you to the doctor, instead of waitin' till to-night.

MARY. There's no necessity, really, mother, to go to the doctor; nothing serious is wrong with me—I'm run down and disappointed, that's all.

MRS. BOYLE. I'll not wait another minute; I don't like the look of you at all. . . . I'm afraid we made a mistake in throwin' over poor Jerry. . . . He'd have been betther for you than that Bentham.

MARY. Mother, the best man for a woman is the one for whom she has the most love, and Charlie had it all.

MRS. BOYLE. Well, there's one thing to be said for him—he couldn't have been thinkin' of the money, or he wouldn't ha' left you . . . it must ha' been somethin' else.

MARY (*wearily*). I don't know . . . I don't know, mother . . . only I think . . .

MRS. BOYLE. What d'ye think?

MARY. I imagine . . . he thought . . . we weren't . . . good enough for him.

MRS. BOYLE. An' what was he himself, only a school teacher? Though I don't blame him for fightin' shy of people like that Joxer fella an' that oul' Madigan wan—nice sort o' people for your father to inthroduce to a man like Mr. Bentham. You might have told me all about this before now, Mary; I don't know why you like to hide everything from your mother; you knew Bentham, an' I'd ha' known nothin' about it if it hadn't bin for the Will; an' it was only to-day, afther long coaxin', that you let out that he'd left you.

MARY. It would have been useless to tell you—you wouldn't understand.

MRS. BOYLE (*hurt*). Maybe not. . . . Maybe I wouldn't understand. . . . Well, we'll be off now. (*She goes over to the door left, and speaks to* BOYLE *inside.*)

MRS. BOYLE. We're goin' now to the doctor's. Are you goin' to get up this evenin'?

BOYLE (*from inside*). The pains in me legs is terrible! It's me should be poppin' off to the doctor instead o' Mary, the way I feel.

MRS. BOYLE. Sorra mend you! A nice way you were in last night —carried in a frog's march, dead to the world. If that's the way you'll go on when you get the money it'll be the grave for you, an asylum for me and the Poorhouse for Johnny.

BOYLE. I thought you were goin'?

MRS. BOYLE. That's what has you as you are—you can't bear to be spoken to. Knowin' the way we are, up to our ears in debt, it's a wondher you wouldn't ha' got up to go to th' solicitor's an' see if we could ha' gettin' a little o' the money even.

BOYLE (*shouting*). I can't be goin' up there night, noon an' mornin', can I? He can't give the money till he gets it, can he? I can't get blood out of a turnip, can I?

MRS. BOYLE. It's nearly two months since we heard of the Will, an' the money seems as far off as ever. . . . I suppose you know we owe twenty poun's to oul' Murphy?

BOYLE. I've a faint recollection of you tellin' me that before.

MRS. BOYLE. Well, you'll go over to the shop yourself for the things in future—I'll face him no more.

BOYLE. I thought you said you were goin'?

MRS. BOYLE. I'm goin' now; come on, Mary.

BOYLE. Ey, Juno, ey!

MRS. BOYLE. Well, what d'ye want now?

BOYLE. Is there e'er a bottle o' stout left?

MRS. BOYLE. There's two o' them here still.

BOYLE. Show us in one o' them an' leave t'other there till I get up. An' throw us in the paper that's on the table, an' the bottle o' Sloan's Liniment that's in th' drawer.

MRS. BOYLE (*getting the liniment and the stout*). What paper is it you want—the *Messenger*?

BOYLE. *Messenger! The News o' the World!*

(MRS. BOYLE *brings in the things asked for and comes out again.*)

MRS. BOYLE (*at door*). Mind the candle, now, an' don't burn the house over our heads. I left t'other bottle o' stout on the table.

(*She puts bottle of stout on table. She goes out with* MARY. *A cork is heard popping inside.*)

   (*A pause; then outside the door is heard the voice of* JOXER *lilting softly: "Me pipe I'll smoke, as I dhrive me moke . . . are you . . . there . . . More . . . aar . . . i . . . tee!" A gentle knock is heard and, after a pause, the door opens, and* JOXER, *followed by* NUGENT, *enters.*)

JOXER. Be God, they must all be out; I was thinkin' there was somethin' up when he didn't answer the signal. We seen Juno an' Mary goin', but I didn't see him, an' it's very seldom he escapes me.

NUGENT. He's not goin' to escape me—he's not goin' to be let go to the fair altogether.

JOXER. Sure, the house couldn't hould them lately; an' he goin' about like a mastherpiece of the Free State counthry; forgettin' their friends; forgettin' God—wouldn't even lift his hat passin' a chapel! Sure they were bound to get a dhrop! An' you really think there's no money comin' to him afther all?

NUGENT. Not as much as a red rex, man; I've been a bit anxious this long time over me money, an' I went up to the solicitor's to find out all I could—ah, man, they were goin' to throw me down the stairs. They toul' me that the oul' cock himself had the stairs worn away comin' up afther it, an' they black in the face tellin' him he'd get nothin'. Some way or another that the Will is writ he won't be entitled to get as much as a make!

JOXER. Ah, I thought there was somethin' curious about the whole thing; I've bin havin' sthrange dreams for the last couple o' weeks. An' I notice that that Bentham fella doesn't be comin' here now—there must be somethin' on the mat there too. Anyhow, who, in the name o' God, ud leave anythin' to that oul' bummer? Sure it ud be unnatural. An' the way Juno an' him's been throwin' their weight about for the last few months! Ah, him that goes a borrowin' goes a sorrowin'!

NUGENT. Well, he's not goin' to throw his weight about in the suit I made for him much longer. I'm tellin' you seven poun's aren't to be found growin' on the bushes these days.

JOXER. An' there isn't hardly a neighbour in the whole street that hasn't lent him money on the strength of what he was goin' to get, but they're after backing the wrong horse. Wasn't it a mercy o' God that I'd nothin' to give him! The softy I am, you know, I'd ha' lent him me last juice! I must have had somebody's good prayers. Ah, afther all, an honest man's the noblest work o' God!

(BOYLE *coughs inside.*)

JOXER. Whisht, damn it, he must be inside in bed.

NUGENT. Inside o' bed or outside of it he's goin' to pay me for that suit, or give it back—he'll not climb up my back as easily as he thinks.

JOXER. Gwan in at wanst, man, an' get it off him, an' don't be a fool.

NUGENT (*going to the door left, opening it and looking in*). Ah, don't disturb yourself, Mr. Boyle; I hope you're not sick?

BOYLE. Th' oul' legs, Mr. Nugent, the oul' legs.

NUGENT. I just called over to see if you could let me have anything off the suit?

BOYLE. E-e-e-eh, how much is this it is?

NUGENT. It's the same as it was at the start—seven poun's.

BOYLE. I'm glad you kem, Mr. Nugent; I want a good heavy top-coat—Irish frieze, if you have it. How much would a top-coat like that be now?

NUGENT. About six poun's.

BOYLE. Six poun's—six an' seven, six an' seven is thirteen—that'll be thirteen poun's I'll owe you.

(JOXER *slips the bottle of stout that is on the table into his pocket.* NUGENT *rushes into the room, and returns with the suit on his arm; he pauses at the door.*)

NUGENT. You'll owe me no thirteen poun's. Maybe you think you're betther able to owe it than pay it!

BOYLE (*frantically*). Here, come back to hell ower that—where're you goin' with them clothes o' mine?

NUGENT. Where am I goin' with them clothes o' yours? Well, I like your damn cheek!

BOYLE. Here, what am I going to dhress meself in when I'm goin' out?

NUGENT. What do I care what you dhress yourself in? You can put yourself in a bolsther cover, if you like. (*He goes towards the other door, followed by* JOXER.)

JOXER. What'll he dhress himself in! Gentleman Jack an' his frieze coat!

(*They go out.*)

BOYLE (*inside*). Ey, Nugent, ey, Mr. Nugent, Mr. Nugent! (*After a pause* BOYLE *enters hastily, buttoning the braces of his*

moleskin trousers; his coat and vest are on his arm; he throws
these on a chair and hurries to the door on right.)

BOYLE. Ey, Mr. Nugent, Mr. Nugent!

JOXER (*meeting him at the door*). What's up, what's wrong,
Captain?

BOYLE. Nugent's been here an' took away me suit—the only
things I had to go out in!

JOXER. Tuk your suit—for God's sake! An' what were you doin'
while he was takin' them?

BOYLE. I was in bed when he stole in like a thief in the night,
an' before I knew even what he was thinkin' of, he whipped them
from the chair, an' was off like a redshank!

JOXER. An' what, in the name o' God, did he do that for?

BOYLE. What did he do it for? How the hell do I know what he
done it for? Jealousy an' spite, I suppose.

JOXER. Did he not say what he done it for?

BOYLE. Amn't I afther tellin' you that he had them whipped up
an' was gone before I could open me mouth?

JOXER. That was a very sudden thing to do; there mus' be somethin' behin' it. Did he hear anythin', I wondher?

BOYLE. Did he hear anythin'?—you talk very queer, Joxer—
what could he hear?

JOXER. About you not gettin' the money, in some way or t'other?

BOYLE. An' what ud prevent me from gettin' th' money?

JOXER. That's jus' what I was thinkin'—what ud prevent you
from gettin' the money—nothin', as far as I can see.

BOYLE (*looking round for bottle of stout with an exclamation*). Aw, holy God!

JOXER. What's up, Jack?

BOYLE. He must have afther lifted the bottle o' stout that Juno left on the table!

JOXER (*horrified*). Ah, no, ah, no! He wouldn't be afther doin' that, now.

BOYLE. An' who done it then? Juno left a bottle o' stout here, an' it's gone—it didn't walk, did it?

JOXER. Oh, that's shockin'; ah, man's inhumanity to man makes countless thousands mourn!

MRS. MADIGAN (*appearing at the door*). I hope I'm not disturbin' you in any discussion on your forthcomin' legacy—if I may use the word—an' that you'll let me have a barny for a minute or two with you, Mr. Boyle.

BOYLE (*uneasily*). To be sure, Mrs. Madigan—an oul' friend's always welcome.

JOXER. Come in the evenin', come in th' mornin'; come when you're assed, or come without warnin', Mrs. Madigan.

BOYLE. Sit down, Mrs. Madigan.

MRS. MADIGAN (*ominously*). Th' few words I have to say can be said standin'. Puttin' aside all formularies, I suppose you remember me lendin' you some time ago three poun's that I raised on blankets an' furniture in me uncle's?

BOYLE. I remember it well. I have it recorded in me book—three poun's five shillin's from Maisie Madigan, raised on ar-

ticles pawned; an', item: fourpence, given to make up the price
of a pint, on th' principle that no bird ever flew on wan wing;
all to be repaid at par, when the ship comes home.

MRS. MADIGAN. Well, ever since I shoved in the blankets I've been
perishing with th' cowld, an' I've decided, if I'll be too hot in th'
nex' world aself, I'm not goin' to be too cowld in this wan; an'
consequently, I want me three poun's, if you please.

BOYLE. This is a very sudden demand, Mrs. Madigan, an' can't
be met; but I'm willin' to give you a receipt in full, in full.

MRS. MADIGAN. Come on, out with th' money, an' don't be jack-
actin'.

BOYLE. You can't get blood out of a turnip, can you?

MRS. MADIGAN (*rushing over and shaking him*). Gimme me
money, y'oul' reprobate, or I'll shake the worth of it out of you!

BOYLE. Ey, houl' on, there; houl' on, there! You'll wait for your
money now, me lassie!

MRS. MADIGAN (*looking around the room and seeing the gramophone*). I'll wait for it, will I? Well, I'll not wait long; if I can't
get th' cash, I'll get th' worth of it. (*She catches up the gramophone.*)

BOYLE. Ey, ey, there, wher'r you goin' with that?

MRS. MADIGAN. I'm goin' to th' pawn to get me three quid five
shillin's; I'll bring you th' ticket, an' then you can do what you
like, me bucko.

BOYLE. You can't touch that, you can't touch that! It's not my
property, an' it's not ped for yet!

MRS. MADIGAN. So much th' betther. It'll be an ayse to me conscience, for I'm takin' what doesn't belong to you. You're not goin' to be swankin' it like a paycock with Maisie Madigan's money—I'll pull some o' the gorgeous feathers out o' your tail! (*She goes off with the gramophone.*)

BOYLE. What's th' world comin' to at all? I ass you, Joxer Daly, is there any morality left anywhere?

JOXER. I wouldn't ha' believed it, only I seen it with me own two eyes. I didn't think Maisie Madigan was that sort of a woman; she has either a sup taken, or she's heard somethin'.

BOYLE. Heard somethin'—about what, if it's not any harm to ass you?

JOXER. She must ha' heard some rumour or other that you weren't goin' to get th' money.

BOYLE. Who says I'm not goin' to get th' money?

JOXER. Sure, I know—I was only sayin'.

BOYLE. Only sayin' what?

JOXER. Nothin'.

BOYLE. You were goin' to say somethin', don't be a twisther.

JOXER (*angrily*). Who's a twisther?

BOYLE. Why don't you speak your mind, then?

JOXER. You never twisted yourself—no, you wouldn't know how!

BOYLE. Did you ever know me to twist; did you ever know me to twist?

JOXER (*fiercely*). Did you ever do anythin' else! Sure, you can't believe a word that comes out o' your mouth.

BOYLE. Here, get out, ower o' this; I always knew you were a prognosticator an' a procrastinator!

JOXER (*going out as* JOHNNY *comes in*). The anchor's weighed, farewell, re . . . mem . . . ber . . . me. Jacky Boyle, Esquire, infernal rogue an' damned liar!

JOHNNY. Joxer an' you at it agen?—when are you goin' to have a little respect for yourself, an' not be always makin' a show of us all?

BOYLE. Are you goin' to lecture me now?

JOHNNY. Is mother back from the doctor yet, with Mary?

(MRS. BOYLE *enters; it is apparent from the serious look on her face that something has happened. She takes off her hat and coat without a word and puts them by. She then sits down near the fire, and there is a few moments' pause.*)

BOYLE. Well, what did the doctor say about Mary?

MRS. BOYLE (*in an earnest manner and with suppressed agitation*). Sit down here, Jack; I've something to say to you . . . about Mary.

BOYLE (*awed by her manner*). About . . . Mary?

MRS. BOYLE. Close that door there and sit down here.

BOYLE (*closing the door*). More throuble in our native land, is it? (*He sits down*) Well, what is it?

MRS. BOYLE. It's about Mary.

BOYLE. Well, what about Mary—there's nothin' wrong with her, is there?

MRS. BOYLE. I'm sorry to say there's a gradle wrong with her.

BOYLE. A gradle wrong with her! (*Peevishly*) First Johnny an' now Mary; is the whole house goin' to become an hospital! It's not consumption, is it?

MRS. BOYLE. No . . . it's not consumption . . . it's worse.

JOHNNY. Worse! Well, we'll have to get her into some place ower this, there's no one here to mind her.

MRS. BOYLE. We'll all have to mind her now. You might as well know now, Johnny, as another time. (*To* BOYLE) D'ye know what the doctor said to me about her, Jack?

BOYLE. How ud I know—I wasn't there, was I?

MRS. BOYLE. He told me to get her married at wanst.

BOYLE. Married at wanst! An' why did he say the like o' that?

MRS. BOYLE. Because Mary's goin' to have a baby in a short time.

BOYLE. Goin' to have a baby!—my God, what'll Bentham say when he hears that?

MRS. BOYLE. Are you blind, man, that you can't see that it was Bentham that has done this wrong to her?

BOYLE (*passionately*). Then he'll marry her, he'll have to marry her!

MRS. BOYLE. You know he's gone to England, an' God knows where he is now.

BOYLE. I'll folley him, I'll folley him, an' bring him back, an' make him do her justice. The scoundrel, I might ha' known what he was, with his yogees an' his prawna!

MRS. BOYLE. We'll have to keep it quiet till we see what we can do.

BOYLE. Oh, isn't this a nice thing to come on top o' me, an' the state I'm in! A pretty show I'll be to Joxer an' to that oul' wan, Madigan! Amn't I afther goin' through enough without havin' to go through this!

MRS. BOYLE. What you an' I'll have to go through'll be nothin' to what poor Mary'll have to go through; for you an' me is middlin' old, an' most of our years is spent; but Mary'll have maybe forty years to face an' handle, an' every wan of them'll be tainted with a bitther memory.

BOYLE. Where is she? Where is she till I tell her off? I'm tellin' you when I'm done with her she'll be a sorry girl!

MRS. BOYLE. I left her in me sisther's till I came to speak to you. You'll say nothin' to her, Jack; ever since she left school she's earned her livin', an' your fatherly care never throubled the poor girl.

BOYLE. Gwan, take her part agen her father! But I'll let you see whether I'll say nothin' to her or no! Her an' her readin'! That's more o' th' blasted nonsense that has the house fallin' down on top of us! What did th' likes of her, born in a tenement house, want with readin'? Her readin's afther bringin' her to a nice pass—oh, it's madnin', madnin', madnin'!

MRS. BOYLE. When she comes back say nothin' to her, Jack, or she'll leave this place.

BOYLE. Leave this place! Ay, she'll leave this place, an' quick too!

MRS. BOYLE. If Mary goes, I'll go with her.

BOYLE. Well, go with her! Well, go, th' pair o' yous! I lived before I seen yous, an' I can live when yous are gone. Isn't this a nice thing to come rollin' in on top o' me afther all your prayin' to St. Anthony an' The Little Flower. An' she's a child o' Mary, too—I wonder what'll the nuns think of her now? An' it'll be bellows'd all over th' disthrict before you could say Jack Robinson; an' whenever I'm seen they'll whisper, "That's th' father of Mary Boyle that had th' kid be th' swank she used to go with; d'ye know, d'ye know?" To be sure they'll know—more about it than I will meself!

JOHNNY. She should be dhriven out o' th' house she's brought disgrace on!

MRS. BOYLE. Hush, you, Johnny. We needn't let it be bellows'd all over the place; all we've got to do is to leave this place quietly an' go somewhere where we're not known, an' nobody'll be the wiser.

BOYLE. You're talkin' like a two-year-oul', woman. Where'll we get a place ou' o' this?—places aren't that easily got.

MRS. BOYLE. But, Jack, when we get the money . . .

BOYLE. Money—what money?

MRS. BOYLE. Why, oul' Ellison's money, of course.

BOYLE. There's no money comin' from oul' Ellison, or any one else. Since you heard of wan throuble, you might as well hear of another. There's no money comin' to us at all—the Will's a wash out!

MRS. BOYLE. What are you sayin', man—no money?

JOHNNY. How could it be a wash out?

BOYLE. The boyo that's afther doin' it to Mary done it to me as well. The thick made out the Will wrong; he said in th' Will, only first cousin an' second cousin, instead of mentionin' our names, an' now any one that thinks he's a first cousin or second cousin t'oul' Ellison can claim the money as well as me, an' they're springin' up in hundreds, an' comin' from America an' Australia, thinkin' to get their whack out of it, while all the time the lawyers is gobblin' it up, till there's not as much as ud buy a stockin' for your lovely daughter's baby!

MRS. BOYLE. I don't believe it, I don't believe it, I don't believe it!

JOHNNY. Why did you say nothin' about this before?

MRS. BOYLE. You're not serious, Jack; you're not serious!

BOYLE. I'm tellin' you the scholar, Bentham, made a banjax o' th' Will; instead o' sayin', "th' rest o' me property to be divided between me first cousin, Jack Boyle, an' me second cousin, Mick Finnegan, o' Santhry," he writ down only, "me first an' second cousins," an' the world an' his wife are afther th' property now.

MRS. BOYLE. Now, I know why Bentham left poor Mary in th' lurch; I can see it all now—oh, is there not even a middlin' honest man left in th' world?

JOHNNY (to BOYLE). An' you let us run into debt, an' you borreyed money from everybody to fill yourself with beer! An' now, you tell us the whole thing's a wash out! Oh, if it's thrue, I'm done with you, for you're worse than me sisther Mary!

BOYLE. You hole your tongue, d'ye hear? I'll not take any lip from you. Go an' get Bentham if you want satisfaction for all that's afther happenin' us.

JOHNNY. I won't hole me tongue, I won't hole me tongue! I'll

tell you what I think of you, father an' all as you are . . .
you . . .

MRS. BOYLE. Johnny, Johnny, Johnny, for God's sake, be quiet!

JOHNNY. I'll not be quiet, I'll not be quiet; he's a nice father,
isn't he? Is it any wondher Mary went asthray, when . . .

MRS. BOYLE. Johnny, Johnny, for my sake be quiet—for your
mother's sake!

BOYLE. I'm goin' out now to have a few dhrinks with th' last
few makes I have, an' tell that lassie o' yours not to be here when
I come back; for if I lay me eyes on her, I'll lay me han's on her,
an' if I lay me han's on her, I won't be accountable for me
actions!

JOHNNY. Take care somebody doesn't lay his han's on you—
y'oul' . . .

MRS. BOYLE. Johnny, Johnny!

BOYLE (*at door, about to go out*). Oh, a nice son, an' a nicer
daughter, I have. (*Calling loudly upstairs*) Joxer, Joxer, are you
there?

JOXER (*from a distance*). I'm here, More . . . ee . . . aar . . .
i . . . tee!

BOYLE. I'm goin' down to Foley's—are you comin'?

JOXER. Come with you? With that sweet call me heart is stirred;
I'm only waiting for the word, an' I'll be with you, like a bird!

   (BOYLE *and* JOXER *pass the door going out.*)

JOHNNY (*throwing himself on the bed*). I've a nice sisther, an'
a nice father, there's no bettin' on it. I wish to God a bullet or

a bomb had whipped me ou' o' this long ago! Not one o' yous, not one o' yous, have any thought for me!

MRS. BOYLE (*with passionate remonstrance*). If you don't whisht, Johnny, you'll drive me mad. Who has kep' th' home together for the past few years—only me. An' who'll have to bear th' big-gest part o' this throuble but me—but whinin' an' whingin' isn't going to do any good.

JOHNNY. You're to blame yourself for a gradle of it—givin' him his own way in everything, an' never assin' to check him, no matther what he done. Why didn't you look afther th' money? why . . .

(*There is a knock at the door;* MRS. BOYLE *opens it;* JOHNNY *rises on his elbow to look and listen; two men enter.*)

FIRST MAN. We've been sent up be th' Manager of the Hibernian Furnishing Co., Mrs. Boyle, to take back the furniture that was got a while ago.

MRS. BOYLE. Yous'll touch nothin' here—how do I know who yous are?

FIRST MAN (*showing a paper*). There's the ordher, ma'am. (*Reading*) A chest o' drawers, a table, wan easy an' two ordi-nary chairs; wan mirror; wan chesterfield divan, an' a ward-robe an' two vases. (*To his comrade*) Come on, Bill, it's afther knockin' off time already.

JOHNNY. For God's sake, mother, run down to Foley's an' bring father back, or we'll be left without a stick.

(*The men carry out the table.*)

MRS. BOYLE. What good would it be? You heard what he said before he went out.

162 SEAN O'CASEY

JOHNNY. Can't you thry? He ought to be here, an' the like of this goin' on.

(MRS. BOYLE *puts a shawl around her, as* MARY *enters.*)

MARY. What's up, mother? I met men carryin' away the table, an' everybody's talking about us not gettin' the money after all.

MRS. BOYLE. Everythin's gone wrong, Mary, everythin'. We're not gettin' a penny out o' the Will, not a penny—I'll tell you all when I come back; I'm goin' for your father. (*She runs out.*)

JOHNNY (*to* MARY, *who has sat down by the fire*). It's a wondher you're not ashamed to show your face here, afther what has happened.

(JERRY *enters slowly; there is a look of earnest hope on his face. He looks at* MARY *for a few moments.*)

JERRY (*softly*). Mary!

(MARY *does not answer.*)

JERRY. Mary, I want to speak to you for a few moments, may I?

(MARY *remains silent;* JOHNNY *goes slowly into room on left.*)

JERRY. Your mother has told me everything, Mary, and I have come to you. . . . I have come to tell you, Mary, that my love for you is greater and deeper than ever. . . .

MARY (*with a sob*). Oh, Jerry, Jerry, say no more; all that is over now; anything like that is impossible now!

JERRY. Impossible? Why do you talk like that, Mary?

MARY. After all that has happened.

JERRY. What does it matter what has happened? We are young enough to be able to forget all those things. (*He catches her hand*) Mary, Mary, I am pleading for your love. With Labour, Mary, humanity is above everything; we are the Leaders in the fight for a new life. I want to forget Bentham, I want to forget that you left me—even for a while.

MARY. Oh, Jerry, Jerry, you haven't the bitter word of scorn for me after all.

JERRY (*passionately*). Scorn! I love you, love you, Mary!

MARY (*rising, and looking him in the eyes*). Even though . . .

JERRY. Even though you threw me over for another man; even though you gave me many a bitter word!

MARY. Yes, yes, I know; but you love me, even though . . . even though . . . I'm . . . goin' . . . goin' . . . (*He looks at her questioningly, and fear gathers in his eyes*) Ah, I was thinkin' so. . . . You don't know everything!

JERRY (*poignantly*). Surely to God, Mary, you don't mean that . . . that . . . that . . .

MARY. Now you know all, Jerry; now you know all!

JERRY. My God, Mary, have you fallen as low as that?

MARY. Yes, Jerry, as you say, I have fallen as low as that.

JERRY. I didn't mean it that way, Mary . . . it came on me so sudden, that I didn't mind what I was sayin'. . . . I never expected this—your mother never told me. . . . I'm sorry . . . God knows, I'm sorry for you, Mary.

MARY. Let us say no more, Jerry; I don't blame you for thinkin' it's terrible. . . . I suppose it is. . . . Everybody'll think the same. . . . It's only as I expected—your humanity is just as narrow as the humanity of the others.

JERRY. I'm sorry, all the same. . . . I shouldn't have troubled you. . . . I wouldn't if I'd known . . . if I can do anything for you . . . Mary . . . I will. (*He turns to go, and halts at the door.*)

MARY. Do you remember, Jerry, the verses you read when you gave the lecture in the Socialist Rooms some time ago, on Humanity's Strife with Nature?

JERRY. The verses—no; I don't remember them.

MARY. I do. They're runnin' in me head now—

> An' we felt the power that fashion'd
> All the lovely things we saw,
> That created all the murmur
> Of an everlasting law,
> Was a hand of force an' beauty,
> With an eagle's tearin' claw.
>
> Then we saw our globe of beauty
> Was an ugly thing as well,
> A hymn divine whose chorus
> Was an agonizin' yell;
> Like the story of a demon,
> That an angel had to tell.
>
> Like a glowin' picture by a
> Hand unsteady, brought to ruin;
> Like her craters, if their deadness
> Could give life unto the moon;
> Like the agonizing horror
> Of a violin out of tune.

(*There is a pause, and* DEVINE *goes slowly out.*)

JOHNNY (*returning*). Is he gone?

MARY. Yes.

(*The two men re-enter.*)

FIRST MAN. We can't wait any longer for t'oul' fella—sorry, Miss, but we have to live as well as th' nex' man.

(*They carry out some things.*)

JOHNNY. Oh, isn't this terrible! . . . I suppose you told him everything . . . couldn't you have waited for a few days . . . he'd have stopped th' takin' of the things, if you'd kep' your mouth shut. Are you burnin' to tell every one of the shame you've brought on us?

MARY (*snatching up her hat and coat*). Oh, this is unbearable! (*She rushes out.*)

FIRST MAN (*re-entering*). We'll take the chest o' drawers next— it's the heaviest.

(*The votive light flickers for a moment, and goes out.*)

JOHNNY (*in a cry of fear*). Mother o' God, the light's afther goin' out!

FIRST MAN. You put the win' up me the way you bawled that time. The oil's all gone, that's all.

JOHNNY (*with an agonizing cry*). Mother o' God, there's a shot I'm afther gettin'!

FIRST MAN. What's wrong with you, man? Is it a fit you're takin'?

JOHNNY. I'm afther feelin' a pain in me breast, like the tearin' by of a bullet!

FIRST MAN. He's goin' mad—it's a wondher they'd leave a chap like that here be himself.

(*Two* IRREGULARS *enter swiftly; they carry revolvers; one goes over to* JOHNNY; *the other covers the two furniture men.*)

FIRST IRREGULAR (*to the men, quietly and incisively*). Who are you—what are yous doin' here—quick!

FIRST MAN. Removin' furniture that's not paid for.

IRREGULAR. Get over to the other end of the room an' turn your faces to the wall—quick.

(*The two men turn their faces to the wall, with their hands up.*)

SECOND IRREGULAR (*to* JOHNNY). Come on, Sean Boyle, you're wanted; some of us have a word to say to you.

JOHNNY. I'm sick, I can't—what do you want with me?

SECOND IRREGULAR. Come on, come on; we've a distance to go, an' haven't much time—come on.

JOHNNY. I'm an oul' comrade—yous wouldn't shoot an oul' comrade.

SECOND IRREGULAR. Poor Tancred was an oul' comrade o' yours, but you didn't think o' that when you gave him away to the gang that sent him to his grave. But we've no time to waste; come on—here, Dermot, ketch his arm. (*To* JOHNNY) Have you your beads?

JOHNNY. Me beads! Why do you ass me that, why do you ass me that?

SECOND IRREGULAR. Go on, go on, march!

JOHNNY. Are yous goin' to do in a comrade—look at me arm, I lost it for Ireland.

SECOND IRREGULAR. Commandant Tancred lost his life for Ireland.

JOHNNY. Sacred Heart of Jesus, have mercy on me! Mother o' God, pray for me—be with me now in the agonies o' death! . . . Hail, Mary, full o' grace . . . the Lord is . . . with Thee.

(*They drag out* JOHNNY BOYLE, *and the curtain falls. When it rises again the most of the furniture is gone.* MARY *and* MRS. BOYLE, *one on each side, are sitting in a darkened room, by the fire; it is an hour later.*)

MRS. BOYLE. I'll not wait much longer . . . what did they bring him away in the mothor for? Nugent says he thinks they had guns . . . is me throubles never goin' to be over? . . . If anything ud happen to poor Johnny, I think I'd lost me mind . . . I'll go to the Police Station, surely they ought to be able to do somethin'.

(*Below is heard the sound of voices.*)

MRS. BOYLE. Whisht, is that something? Maybe, it's your father, though when I left him in Foley's he was hardly able to lift his head. Whisht!

(*A knock at the door, and the voice of* MRS. MADIGAN, *speaking very softly:*)

Mrs. Boyle, Mrs. Boyle. (MRS. BOYLE *opens the door.*)

MRS. MADIGAN. Oh, Mrs. Boyle, God an' His Blessed Mother be with you this night!

MRS. BOYLE (*calmly*). What is it, Mrs. Madigan? It's Johnny—something about Johnny.

MRS. MADIGAN. God send it's not. God send it's not Johnny!

MRS. BOYLE. Don't keep me waitin', Mrs. Madigan; I've gone through so much lately that I feel able for anything.

MRS. MADIGAN. Two polismen below wantin' you.

MRS. BOYLE. Wantin' me; an' why do they want me?

MRS. MADIGAN. Some poor fella's been found, an' they think it's, it's . . .

MRS. BOYLE. Johnny, Johnny!

MARY (*with her arms round her mother*). Oh, mother, mother, me poor, darlin' mother.

MRS. BOYLE. Hush, hush, darlin'; you'll shortly have your own throuble to bear. (*To* MRS. MADIGAN) An' why do the polis think it's Johnny, Mrs. Madigan?

MRS. MADIGAN. Because one o' the doctors knew him when he was attendin' with his poor arm.

MRS. BOYLE. Oh, it's thrue, then; it's Johnny, it's me son, me own son!

MARY. Oh, it's thrue, it's thrue what Jerry Devine says—there isn't a God, there isn't a God; if there was He wouldn't let these things happen!

MRS. BOYLE. Mary, Mary, you mustn't say them things. We'll

want all the help we can get from God an' His Blessed Mother now! These things have nothin' to do with the Will o' God. Ah, what can God do agen the stupidity o' men!

MRS. MADIGAN. The polis want you to go with them to the hospital to see the poor body—they're waitin' below.

MRS. BOYLE. We'll go. Come, Mary, an' we'll never come back here agen. Let your father furrage for himself now; I've done all I could an' it was all no use—he'll be hopeless till the end of his days. I've got a little room in me sisther's where we'll stop till your throuble is over, an' then we'll work together for the sake of the baby.

MARY. My poor little child that'll have no father!

MRS. BOYLE. It'll have what's far betther—it'll have two mothers.

(*A rough voice shouting from below:*)

Are yous goin' to keep us waitin' for yous all night?

MRS. MADIGAN (*going to the door, and shouting down*). Take your hour, there, take your hour! If yous are in such a hurry, skip off, then. for nobody wants you here—if they did yous wouldn't be found. For you're the same as yous were undher the British Government—never where yous are wanted! As far as I can see, the Polis as Polis, in this city, is Null an' Void!

MRS. BOYLE. We'll go, Mary, we'll go; you to see your poor dead brother, an' me to see me poor dead son!

MARY. I dhread it, mother, I dhread it!

MRS. BOYLE. I forgot, Mary, I forgot; your poor oul' selfish mother was only thinkin' of herself. No, no, you mustn't come—it

wouldn't be good for you. You go on to me sisther's an' I'll face
th' ordeal meself. Maybe I didn't feel sorry enough for Mrs.
Tancred when her poor son was found as Johnny's been found
now—because he was a Die-hard! Ah, why didn't I remember
that then he wasn't a Die-hard or a Stater, but only a poor dead
son! It's well I remember all that she said—an' it's my turn to
say it now: What was the pain I suffered, Johnny, bringin' you
into the world to carry you to your cradle to the pains I'll suffer
carryin' you out o' the world to bring you to your grave! Mother
o' God, Mother o' God, have pity on us all! Blessed Virgin,
where were you when me darlin' son was riddled with bullets,
when me darlin' son was riddled with bullets? Sacred Heart o'
Jesus, take away our hearts o' stone, and give us hearts o' flesh!
Take away this murdherin' hate, an' give us Thine own eternal
love!

(*They all go slowly out.*)

(*There is a pause; then a sound of shuffling steps on the stairs
outside. The door opens and* BOYLE *and* JOXER, *both of them very
drunk, enter.*)

BOYLE. I'm able to go no farther. . . . Two polis, ey . . . what
were they doin' here, I wondher? . . . Up to no good, anyhow
. . . an' Juno an' that lovely daughter o' mine with them. (*Taking a sixpence from his pocket and looking at it*) Wan single,
solitary tanner left out of all I borreyed. . . . (*He lets it fall*)
The last o' the Mohicans. . . . The blinds is down, Joxer, the
blinds is down!

JOXER (*walking unsteadily across the room, and anchoring at
the bed*). Put all . . . your throubles . . . in your oul' kit bag
. . . an' smile . . . smile . . . smile!

BOYLE. The counthry'll have to steady itself . . . it's goin' . . . to hell. . . . Where'r all . . . the chairs . . . gone to . . . steady itself, Joxer. . . . Chairs'll . . . have to . . . steady themselves. . . . No matther . . . what any one may . . . say . . . Irelan's sober . . . is Irelan' . . . free.

JOXER (*stretching himself on the bed*). Chains . . . an' . . . slaveree . . . that's a darlin' motto . . . a daaarlin' . . . motto!

BOYLE. If th' worst comes . . . to th' worse . . . I can join a . . . flyin' . . . column. . . . I done . . . me bit . . . in Eas-ther Week . . . had no business . . . to . . . be . . . there . . . but Captain Boyle's Captain Boyle!

JOXER. Breathes there a man with soul . . . so . . . de . . . ad . . . this . . . me . . . o . . . wn, me nat . . . ive l . . . an'!

BOYLE (*subsiding into a sitting posture on the floor*). Com-mandant Kelly died . . . in them . . . arms . . . Joxer. . . . Tell me Volunteer Butties . . . says he . . . that . . . I died for . . . Irelan'!

JOXER. D'jever rade Willie . . . Reilly . . . an' his . . . own . . . Colleen . . . Bawn? It's a darlin' story, a daarlin' story!

BOYLE. I'm telling you . . . Joxer . . . th' whole worl's . . . in a terr . . . ible state o' . . . chassis!

CURTAIN

Riders to the Sea

A PLAY IN ONE ACT

BY JOHN M. SYNGE

CHARACTERS

MAURYA (*an old woman*)

BARTLEY (*her son*)

CATHLEEN (*her daughter*)

NORA (*a younger daughter*)

MEN and WOMEN

Riders to the Sea

SCENE. *An Island off the West of Ireland.*
(*Cottage kitchen, with nets, oil-skins, spinning-wheel, some new boards standing by the wall, etc.* CATHLEEN, *a girl of about twenty, finishes kneading cake, and puts it down in the pot-oven by the fire; then wipes her hands, and begins to spin at the wheel.* NORA, *a young girl, puts her head in at the door.*)

NORA (*in a low voice*). Where is she?

CATHLEEN. She's lying down, God help her, and may be sleeping, if she's able.

(NORA *comes in softly, and takes a bundle from under her shawl.*)

CATHLEEN (*spinning the wheel rapidly*). What is it you have?

NORA. The young priest is after bringing them. It's a shirt and a plain stocking were got off a drowned man in Donegal.

(CATHLEEN *stops her wheel with a sudden movement, and leans out to listen.*)

NORA. We're to find out if it's Michael's they are, some time herself will be down looking by the sea.

CATHLEEN. How would they be Michael's, Nora. How would he go the length of that way to the far north?

NORA. The young priest says he's known the like of it. "If it's Michael's they are," says he, "you can tell herself he's got a clean burial by the grace of God, and if they're not his, let no one say a word about them, for she'll be getting her death," says he, "with crying and lamenting."

(*The door which* NORA *half closed is blown open by a gust of wind.*)

CATHLEEN (*looking out anxiously*). Did you ask him would he stop Bartley going this day with the horses to the Galway fair?

NORA. "I won't stop him," says he, "but let you not be afraid. Herself does be saying prayers half through the night, and the Almighty God won't leave her destitute," says he, "with no son living."

CATHLEEN. Is the sea bad by the white rocks, Nora?

NORA. Middling bad, God help us. There's a great roaring in the west, and it's worse it'll be getting when the tide's turned to the wind. (*She goes over to the table with the bundle*) Shall I open it now?

CATHLEEN. Maybe she'd wake up on us, and come in before we'd done. (*Coming to the table*) It's a long time we'll be, and the two of us crying.

NORA (*goes to the inner door and listens*). She's moving about on the bed. She'll be coming in a minute.

CATHLEEN. Give me the ladder, and I'll put them up in the turf-loft, the way she won't know of them at all, and maybe when the tide turns she'll be going down to see would he be floating from the east.

(*They put the ladder against the gable of the chimney;* CATHLEEN *goes up a few steps and hides the bundle in the turf-loft.* MAURYA *comes from the inner room.*)

MAURYA (*looking up at* CATHLEEN *and speaking querulously*). Isn't it turf enough you have for this day and evening?

CATHLEEN. There's a cake baking at the fire for a short space (*throwing down the turf*) and Bartley will want it when the tide turns if he goes to Connemara.

(NORA *picks up the turf and puts it round the pot-oven.*)

MAURYA (*sitting down on a stool at the fire*). He won't go this day with the wind rising from the south and west. He won't go this day, for the young priest will stop him surely.

NORA. He'll not stop him, mother, and I heard Eamon Simon and Stephen Pheety and Colum Shawn saying he would go.

MAURYA. Where is he itself?

NORA. He went down to see would there be another boat sailing in the week, and I'm thinking it won't be long till he's here now, for the tide's turning at the green head, and the hooker's tacking from the east.

CATHLEEN. I hear some one passing the big stones.

NORA (*looking out*). He's coming now, and he in a hurry.

BARTLEY (*comes in and looks round the room. Speaking sadly and quietly*). Where is the bit of new rope, Cathleen, was bought in Connemara?

CATHLEEN (*coming down*). Give it to him, Nora; it's on a nail by the white boards. I hung it up this morning, for the pig with the black feet was eating it.

NORA. (*giving him a rope*). Is that it, Bartley?

MAURYA. You'd do right to leave that rope, Bartley, hanging by the boards. (BARTLEY *takes the rope*) It will be wanting in this place, I'm telling you, if Michael is washed up to-morrow morning, or the next morning, or any morning in the week, for it's a deep grave we'll make him by the grace of God.

BARTLEY (*beginning to work with the rope*). I've no halter the way I can ride down on the mare, and I must go now quickly. This is the one boat going for two weeks or beyond it, and the fair will be a good fair for horses I heard them saying below.

MAURYA. It's a hard thing they'll be saying below if the body is washed up and there's no man in it to make the coffin, and I after giving a big price for the finest white boards you'd find in Connemara. (*She looks round at the boards.*)

BARTLEY. How would it be washed up, and we after looking each day for nine days, and a strong wind blowing a while back from the west and south?

MAURYA. If it wasn't found itself, that wind is raising the sea, and there was a star up against the moon, and it rising in the night. If it was a hundred horses, or a thousand horses you had itself, what is the price of a thousand horses against a son where there is one son only?

BARTLEY (*working at the halter, to* CATHLEEN). Let you go down each day, and see the sheep aren't jumping in on the rye, and if the jobber comes you can sell the pig with the black feet if there is a good price going.

MAURYA. How would the like of her get a good price for a pig?

BARTLEY (*to* CATHLEEN). If the west wind holds with the last bit of the moon let you and Nora get up weed enough for another cock for the kelp. It's hard set we'll be from this day with no one in it but one man to work.

MAURYA. It's hard set we'll be surely the day you're drown'd with the rest. What way will I live and the girls with me, and I an old woman looking for the grave?

(BARTLEY *lays down the halter, takes off his old coat, and puts on a newer one of the same flannel.*)

BARTLEY (*to* NORA). Is she coming to the pier?

NORA (*looking out*). She's passing the green head and letting fall her sails.

BARTLEY (*getting his purse and tobacco*). I'll have half an hour to go down, and you'll see me coming again in two days, or in three days, or maybe in four days if the wind is bad.

MAURYA (*turning round to the fire, and putting her shawl over her head*). Isn't it a hard and cruel man won't hear a word from an old woman, and she holding him from the sea?

CATHLEEN. It's the life of a young man to be going on the sea, and who would listen to an old woman with one thing and she saying it over?

BARTLEY (*taking the halter*). I must go now quickly. I'll ride down on the red mare, and the gray pony'll run behind me. . . . The blessing of God on you. (*He goes out.*)

MAURYA (*crying out as he is in the door*). He's gone now, God spare us, and we'll not see him again. He's gone now, and when the black night is falling I'll have no son left me in the world.

CATHLEEN. Why wouldn't you give him your blessing and he

looking round in the door? Isn't it sorrow enough is on every one in this house without your sending him out with an unlucky word behind him, and a hard word in his ear?

(MAURYA *takes up the tongs and begins raking the fire aimlessly without looking round.*)

NORA (*turning towards her*). You're taking away the turf from the cake.

CATHLEEN (*crying out*). The Son of God forgive us, Nora, we're after forgetting his bit of bread. (*She comes over to the fire.*)

NORA. And it's destroyed he'll be going till dark night, and he after eating nothing since the sun went up.

CATHLEEN (*turning the cake out of the oven*). It's destroyed he'll be, surely. There's no sense left on any person in a house where an old woman will be talking for ever.

(MAURYA *sways herself on her stool.*)

CATHLEEN (*cutting off some of the bread and rolling it in a cloth; to* MAURYA). Let you go down now to the spring well and give him this and he passing. You'll see him then and the dark word will be broken, and you can say "God speed you," the way he'll be easy in his mind.

MAURYA (*taking the bread*). Will I be in it as soon as himself?

CATHLEEN. If you go now quickly.

MAURYA (*standing up unsteadily*). It's hard set I am to walk.

CATHLEEN (*looking at her anxiously*). Give her the stick, Nora, or maybe she'll slip on the big stones.

NORA. What stick?

CATHLEEN. The stick Michael brought from Connemara.

MAURYA (*taking a stick* NORA *gives her*). In the big world the old people do be leaving things after them for their sons and children, but in this place it is the young men do be leaving things behind for them that do be old. (*She goes out slowly.* NORA *goes over to the ladder.*)

CATHLEEN. Wait, Nora, maybe she'd turn back quickly. She's that sorry, God help her, you wouldn't know the thing she'd do.

NORA. Is she gone round by the bush?

CATHLEEN (*looking out*). She's gone now. Throw it down quickly, for the Lord knows when she'll be out of it again.

NORA (*getting the bundle from the loft*). The young priest said he'd be passing to-morrow, and we might go down and speak to him below if it's Michael's they are surely.

CATHLEEN (*taking the bundle*). Did he say what way they were found?

NORA (*coming down*). "There were two men," says he, "and they rowing round with poteen before the cocks crowed, and the oar of one of them caught the body, and they passing the black cliffs of the north."

CATHLEEN (*trying to open the bundle*). Give me a knife, Nora, the string's perished with the salt water, and there's a black knot on it you wouldn't loosen in a week.

NORA (*giving her a knife*). I've heard tell it was a long way to Donegal.

CATHLEEN (*cutting the string*). It is surely. There was a man in here a while ago—the man sold us that knife—and he said if you set off walking from the rocks beyond, it would be seven days you'd be in Donegal.

NORA. And what time would a man take, and he floating?

(CATHLEEN *opens the bundle and takes out a bit of a stocking. They look at them eagerly.*)

CATHLEEN (*in a low voice*). The Lord spare us, Nora! isn't it a queer hard thing to say if it's his they are surely?

NORA. I'll get his shirt off the hook the way we can put the one flannel on the other. (*She looks through some clothes hanging in the corner*) It's not with them, Cathleen, and where will it be?

CATHLEEN. I'm thinking Bartley put it on him in the morning, for his own shirt was heavy with the salt in it (*pointing to the corner*). There's a bit of a sleeve was of the same stuff. Give me that and it will do.

(NORA *brings it to her and they compare the flannel.*)

CATHLEEN. It's the same stuff, Nora; but if it is itself aren't there great rolls of it in the shops of Galway, and isn't it many another man may have a shirt of it as well as Michael himself?

NORA (*who has taken up the stocking and counted the stitches, crying out*). It's Michael, Cathleen, it's Michael; God spare his soul, and what will herself say when she hears this story, and Bartley on the sea?

CATHLEEN (*taking the stocking*). It's a plain stocking.

NORA. It's the second one of the third pair I knitted, and I put up three score stitches, and I dropped four of them.

CATHLEEN (*counts the stitches*). It's that number is in it (*crying out*). Ah, Nora, isn't it a bitter thing to think of him floating that way to the far north, and no one to keen him but the black hags that do be flying on the sea?

NORA (*swinging herself round, and throwing out her arms on the clothes*). And isn't it a pitiful thing when there is nothing left of a man who was a great rower and fisher, but a bit of an old shirt and a plain stocking?

CATHLEEN (*after an instant*). Tell me is herself coming, Nora? I hear a little sound on the path.

NORA (*looking out*). She is, Cathleen. She's coming up to the door.

CATHLEEN. Put these things away before she'll come in. Maybe it's easier she'll be after giving her blessing to Bartley, and we won't let on we've heard anything the time he's on the sea.

NORA (*helping* CATHLEEN *to close the bundle*). We'll put them here in the corner.

(*They put them into a hole in the chimney corner.* CATHLEEN *goes back to the spinning-wheel.*)

NORA. Will she see it was crying I was?

CATHLEEN. Keep your back to the door the way the light'll not be on you.

(NORA *sits down at the chimney corner, with her back to the door.* MAURYA *comes in very slowly, without looking at the girls, and goes over to her stool at the other side of the fire. The cloth with the bread is still in her hand. The girls look at each other, and* NORA *points to the bundle of bread.*)

CATHLEEN (*after spinning for a moment*). You didn't give him his bit of bread?

(MAURYA *begins to keen softly, without turning round.*)

CATHLEEN. Did you see him riding down?

(MAURYA *goes on keening.*)

CATHLEEN (*a little impatiently*). God forgive you; isn't it a better thing to raise your voice and tell what you seen, than to be making lamentation for a thing that's done? Did you see Bartley, I'm saying to you.

MAURYA (*with a weak voice*). My heart's broken from this day.

CATHLEEN (*as before*). Did you see Bartley?

MAURYA. I seen the fearfulest thing.

CATHLEEN (*leaves her wheel and looks out*). God forgive you; he's riding the mare now over the green head, and the gray pony behind him.

MAURYA (*starts, so that her shawl falls back from her head and shows her white tossed hair. With a frightened voice*). The gray pony behind him.

CATHLEEN (*coming to the fire*). What is it ails you, at all?

MAURYA (*speaking very slowly*). I've seen the fearfulest thing any person has seen, since the day Bride Dara seen the dead man with the child in his arms.

CATHLEEN and NORA. Uah. (*They crouch down in front of the old woman at the fire.*)

NORA. Tell us what it is you seen.

MAURYA. I went down to the spring well, and I stood there saying a prayer to myself. Then Bartley came along, and he riding on the red mare with the gray pony behind him. (*She puts up her hands, as if to hide something from her eyes*) The Son of God spare us, Nora!

CATHLEEN. What is it you seen?

MAURYA. I seen Michael himself.

CATHLEEN (*speaking softly*). You did not, mother; it wasn't Michael you seen, for his body is after being found in the far north, and he's got a clean burial by the grace of God.

MAURYA (*a little defiantly*). I'm after seeing him this day, and he riding and galloping. Bartley came first on the red mare; and I tried to say "God speed you," but something choked the words in my throat. He went by quickly; and "the blessing of God on you," says he, and I could say nothing. I looked up then, and I crying, at the gray pony, and there was Michael upon it—with fine clothes on him, and new shoes on his feet.

CATHLEEN (*begins to keen*). It's destroyed we are from this day. It's destroyed, surely.

NORA. Didn't the young priest say the Almighty God wouldn't leave her destitute with no son living?

MAURYA (*in a low voice, but clearly*). It's little the like of him knows of the sea. . . . Bartley will be lost now, and let you call in Eamon and make me a good coffin out of the white boards, for I won't live after them. I've had a husband, and a husband's father, and six sons in this house—six fine men, though it was a hard birth I had with every one of them and they coming to the world—and some of them were found and some of them were not found, but they're gone now the lot of them. . . . There were Stephen, and Shawn, were lost in the great wind, and found after in the Bay of Gregory of the Golden Mouth, and carried up the two of them on the one plank, and in by that door. (*She pauses for a moment, the girls start as if they heard something through the door that is half open behind them.*)

NORA (*in a whisper*). Did you hear that, Cathleen? Did you hear a noise in the north-east?

CATHLEEN (*in a whisper*). There's some one after crying out by the seashore.

MAURYA (*continues without hearing anything*). There was Sheamus and his father, and his own father again, were lost in a dark night, and not a stick or sign was seen of them when the sun went up. There was Patch after was drowned out of a curragh that turned over. I was sitting here with Bartley, and he a baby, lying on my two knees, and I seen two women, and three women, and four women coming in, and they crossing themselves, and not saying a word. I looked out then, and there were men coming after them, and they holding a thing in the half of a red sail, and water dripping out of it—it was a dry day, Nora—and leaving a track to the door. (*She pauses again with her hand stretched out towards the door. It opens softly and old women begin to come in, crossing themselves on the threshold, and kneeling down in front of the stage with red petticoats over their heads.*)

MAURYA (*half in a dream, to* CATHLEEN). Is it Patch, or Michael, or what is it at all?

CATHLEEN. Michael is after being found in the far north, and when he is found there how could he be here in this place?

MAURYA. There does be a power of young men floating round in the sea, and what way would they know if it was Michael they had, or another man like him, for when a man is nine days in the sea, and the wind blowing, it's hard set his own mother would be to say what man was it.

CATHLEEN. It's Michael, God spare him, for they're after sending us a bit of his clothes from the far north. (*She reaches out and hands* MAURYA *the clothes that belonged to Michael.* MAURYA *stands up slowly and takes them in her hands.* NORA *looks out.*)

NORA. They're carrying a thing among them and there's water dripping out of it and leaving a track by the big stones.

CATHLEEN (*in a whisper to the women who have come in.*) Is it Bartley it is?

ONE OF THE WOMEN. It is surely, God rest his soul.

(*Two younger women come in and pull out the table. Then men carry in the body of Bartley, laid on a plank, with a bit of a sail over it, and lay it on the table.*)

CATHLEEN (*to the women, as they are doing so.*) What way was he drowned?

ONE OF THE WOMEN. The gray pony knocked him into the sea, and he was washed out where there is a great surf on the white rocks.

(MAURYA *has gone over and knelt down at the head of the table. The women are keening softly and swaying themselves with a slow movement.* CATHLEEN *and* NORA *kneel at the other end of the table. The men kneel near the door.*)

MAURYA (*raising her head and speaking as if she did not see the people around her*). They're all gone now, and there isn't anything more the sea can do to me. . . . I'll have no call now to be up crying and praying when the wind breaks from the south, and you can hear the surf is in the east, and the surf is in the west, making a great stir with the two noises, and they hitting one on the other. I'll have no call now to be going down and getting Holy Water in the dark nights after Samhain, and I won't care what way the sea is when the other women will be keening. (*To* NORA) Give me the Holy Water, Nora, there's a small sup still on the dresser.

(NORA *gives it to her.*)

MAURYA (*drops Michael's clothes across Bartley's feet, and sprinkles the Holy Water over him*). It isn't that I haven't prayed for you, Bartley, to the Almighty God. It isn't that I haven't said prayers in the dark night till you wouldn't know what I'd be saying; but it's a great rest I'll have now, and it's time surely. It's a great rest I'll have now, and great sleeping in the long nights after Samhain, if it's only a bit of wet flour we do have to eat, and maybe a fish that would be stinking. (*She kneels down again, crossing herself, and saying prayers under her breath.*)

CATHLEEN (*to an old man*). Maybe yourself and Eamon would make a coffin when the sun rises. We have fine white boards herself bought, God help her, thinking Michael would be found, and I have a new cake you can eat while you'll be working.

THE OLD MAN (*looking at the boards*). Are there nails with them?

CATHLEEN. There are not, Colum; we didn't think of the nails.

ANOTHER MAN. It's a great wonder she wouldn't think of the nails, and all the coffins she's seen made already.

CATHLEEN. It's getting old she is, and broken.

(MAURYA *stands up again very slowly and spreads out the pieces of Michael's clothes beside the body, sprinkling them with the last of the Holy Water.*)

NORA (*in a whisper to* CATHLEEN). She's quiet now and easy; but the day Michael was drowned you could hear her crying out from this to the spring well. It's fonder she was of Michael, and would any one have thought that?

CATHLEEN (*slowly and clearly*). An old woman will be soon tired with anything she will do, and isn't it nine days herself is after crying and keening, and making great sorrow in the house?

MAURYA (*puts the empty cup mouth downwards on the table, and lays her hands together on Bartley's feet*). They're all together this time, and the end is come. May the Almighty God have mercy on Bartley's soul, and on Michael's soul, and on the souls of Sheamus and Patch, and Stephen and Shawn (*bending her head*); and may He have mercy on my soul, Nora, and on the soul of every one is left living in the world. (*She pauses, and the keen rises a little more loudly from the women, then sinks away.*)

MAURYA (*continuing*). Michael has a clean burial in the far north, by the grace of the Almighty God. Bartley will have a fine coffin out of the white boards, and a deep grave surely. What more can we want than that? No man at all can be living for ever, and we must be satisfied. (*She kneels down again and the curtain falls slowly.*)

Spreading the News

A PLAY IN ONE ACT

BY LADY GREGORY

CHARACTERS

Bartley Fallon

Mrs. Fallon

Jack Smith

Shawn Early

Tim Casey

James Ryan

Mrs. Tarpey

Mrs. Tully

A Policeman (*Jo Muldoon*)

A Removable Magistrate

Spreading the News

SCENE: *The outskirts of a Fair. An Apple Stall.* MRS. TARPEY *sitting at it.* MAGISTRATE *and* POLICEMAN *enter.*

MAGISTRATE. So that is the Fair Green. Cattle and sheep and mud. No system. What a repulsive sight!

POLICEMAN. That is so, indeed.

MAGISTRATE. I suppose there is a good deal of disorder in this place?

POLICEMAN. There is.

MAGISTRATE. Common assault.

POLICEMAN. It's common enough.

MAGISTRATE. Agrarian crime, no doubt?

POLICEMAN. That is so.

MAGISTRATE. Boycotting? Maiming of cattle? Firing into houses?

POLICEMAN. There was one time, and there might be again.

MAGISTRATE. That is bad. Does it go any farther than that?

POLICEMAN. Far enough, indeed.

MAGISTRATE. Homicide, then! This district has been shamefully neglected! I will change all that. When I was in the Andaman Islands, my system never failed. Yes, yes, I will change all that. What has that woman on her stall?

POLICEMAN. Apples mostly—and sweets.

MAGISTRATE. Just see if there are any unlicensed goods underneath—spirits or the like. We had evasions of the salt tax in the Andaman Islands.

POLICEMAN (*sniffing cautiously and upsetting a heap of apples*). I see no spirits here—or salt.

MAGISTRATE (*to* MRS. TARPEY). Do you know this town well, my good woman?

MRS. TARPEY (*holding out some apples*). A penny the half-dozen, your honour.

POLICEMAN (*shouting*). The gentleman is asking do you know the town! He's the new magistrate!

MRS. TARPEY (*rising and ducking*). Do I know the town? I do, to be sure.

MAGISTRATE (*shouting*). What is its chief business?

MRS. TARPEY. Business, is it? What business would the people here have but to be minding one another's business?

MAGISTRATE. I mean what trade have they?

MRS. TARPEY. Not a trade. No trade at all but to be talking.

MAGISTRATE. I shall learn nothing here.

(*James Ryan comes in, pipe in mouth. Seeing* MAGISTRATE *he retreats quickly, taking pipe from mouth.*)

MAGISTRATE. The smoke from that man's pipe had a greenish look; he may be growing unlicensed tobacco at home. I wish I had brought my telescope to this district. Come to the post-office, I will telegraph for it. I found it very useful in the Andaman Islands.

(MAGISTRATE *and* POLICEMAN *go out left.*)

MRS. TARPEY. Bad luck to Jo Muldoon, knocking my apples this way and that way. (*Begins arranging them.*) Showing off he was to the new magistrate.

(*Enter* BARTLEY FALLON *and* MRS. FALLON.)

BARTLEY. Indeed it's a poor country and a scarce country to be living in. But I'm thinking if I went to America it's long ago the day I'd be dead!

MRS. FALLON. So you might, indeed. (*She puts her basket on a barrel and begins putting parcels in it, taking them from under her cloak.*)

BARTLEY. And it's a great expense for a poor man to be buried in America.

MRS. FALLON. Never fear, Bartley Fallon, but I'll give you a good burying the day you'll die.

BARTLEY. Maybe it's yourself will be buried in the graveyard of Cloonmara before me, Mary Fallon, and I myself that will be dying unbeknownst some night, and no one a-near me. And the cat itself may be gone straying through the country, and the mice squealing over the quilt.

MRS. FALLON. Leave off talking of dying. It might be twenty years you'll be living yet.

BARTLEY (*with a deep sigh*). I'm thinking if I'll be living at the end of twenty years, it's a very old man I'll be then!

MRS. TARPEY (*turns and sees them*). Good morrow, Bartley Fallon; good morrow, Mrs. Fallon. Well, Bartley, you'll find no cause for complaining to-day; they are all saying it was a good fair.

BARTLEY (*raising his voice*). It was not a good fair, Mrs. Tarpey. It was a scattered sort of a fair. If we didn't expect more, we got less. That's the way with me always; whatever I have to sell goes down and whatever I have to buy goes up. If there's ever any misfortune coming to this world, it's on myself it pitches, like a flock of crows on seed potatoes.

MRS. FALLON. Leave off talking of misfortunes, and listen to Jack Smith that is coming the way, and he singing.

(*Voice of* JACK SMITH *heard singing*):

>   I thought, my first love,
>   There'd be but one house between you and me,
>   And I thought I would find
>   Yourself coaxing my child on your knee.
>   Over the tide
>   I would leap with the leap of a swan,
>   Till I came to the side
>   Of the wife of the Red-haired man!

(JACK SMITH *comes in; he is a red-haired man, and is carrying a hayfork.*)

MRS. TARPEY. That should be a good song if I had my hearing.

MRS. FALLON (*shouting*). It's "The Red-haired Man's Wife."

MRS. TARPEY. I know it well. That's the song that has a skin on it! (*She turns her back to them and goes on arranging her apples.*)

MRS. FALLON. Where's herself, Jack Smith?

JACK SMITH. She was delayed with her washing; bleaching the clothes on the hedge she is, and she daren't leave them, with all the tinkers that do be passing to the fair. It isn't to the fair I came myself, but up to the Five Acre Meadow I'm going, where I have a contract for the hay. We'll get a share of it into tramps to-day. (*He lays down hayfork and lights his pipe.*)

BARTLEY. You will not get it into tramps to-day. The rain will be down on it by evening, and on myself too. It's seldom I ever started on a journey but the rain would come down on me before I'd find any place of shelter.

JACK SMITH. If it didn't itself, Bartley, it is my belief you would carry a leaky pail on your head in place of a hat, the way you'd not be without some cause for complaining.

(*A voice heard, "Go on, now, go on out o' that. Go on I say."*)

JACK SMITH. Look at that young mare of Pat Ryan's that is backing into Shaughnessy's bullocks with the dint of the crowd! Don't be daunted, Pat, I'll give you a hand with her. (*He goes out, leaving his hayfork.*)

MRS. FALLON. It's time for ourselves to be going home. I have all I bought put in the basket. Look at there, Jack Smith's hay-fork he left after him! He'll be wanting it. (*Calls*) Jack Smith! Jack Smith!—He's gone through the crowd—hurry after him, Bartley, he'll be wanting it.

BARTLEY. I'll do that. This is no safe place to be leaving it. (*He takes up fork awkwardly and upsets the basket*) Look at that now! If there is any basket in the fair upset, it must be our own basket! (*He goes out to right.*)

MRS. FALLON. Get out of that! It is your own fault, it is. Talk of misfortunes and misfortunes will come. Glory be! Look at my new egg-cups rolling in every part—and my two pound of sugar with the paper broke—

MRS. TARPEY (*turning from stall*). God help us, Mrs. Fallon, what happened to your basket?

MRS. FALLON. It's himself that knocked it down, bad manners to him. (*Putting things up.*) My grand sugar that's destroyed, and he'll not drink his tea without it. I had best go back to the shop for more, much good may it do him!

(*Enter* TIM CASEY.)

TIM CASEY. Where is Bartley Fallon, Mrs. Fallon? I want a word with him before he'll leave the fair. I was afraid he might have gone home by this, for he's a temperate man.

MRS. FALLON. I wish he did go home! It'd be best for me if he went home straight from the fair green, or if he never came with me at all! Where is he, is it? He's gone up the road (*jerks elbow*) following Jack Smith with a hayfork. (*She goes out to left.*)

TIM CASEY. Following Jack Smith with a hayfork! Did ever any one hear the like of that. (*Shouts*) Did you hear that news, Mrs. Tarpey?

MRS. TARPEY. I heard no news at all.

TIM CASEY. Some dispute I suppose it was that rose between Jack Smith and Bartley Fallon, and it seems Jack made off, and Bartley is following him with a hayfork!

MRS. TARPEY. Is he now? Well, that was quick work! It's not ten minutes since the two of them were here, Bartley going home and Jack going to the Five Acre Meadow; and I had my apples to settle up, that Jo Muldoon of the police had scattered, and when I looked round again Jack Smith was gone, and Bartley Fallon was gone, and Mrs. Fallon's basket upset, and all in it strewed upon the ground—the tea here—the two pound of sugar there—the egg-cups there—Look, now, what a great hardship the deafness puts upon me, that I didn't hear the commincement of the fight! Wait till I tell James Ryan that I see below; he is a neighbour of Bartley's, it would be a pity if he wouldn't hear the news!

(*She goes out. Enter* SHAWN EARLY *and* MRS. TULLY.)

TIM CASEY. Listen, Shawn Early! Listen, Mrs. Tully, to the news! Jack Smith and Bartley Fallon had a falling out, and Jack knocked Mrs. Fallon's basket into the road, and Bartley made an attack on him with a hayfork, and away with Jack, and Bartley after him. Look at the sugar here yet on the road!

SHAWN EARLY. Do you tell me so? Well, that's a queer thing, and Bartley Fallon so quiet a man!

MRS. TULLY. I wouldn't wonder at all. I would never think well of a man that would have that sort of a mouldering look. It's likely he has overtaken Jack by this.

(*Enter* JAMES RYAN *and* MRS. TARPEY.)

JAMES RYAN. That is great news Mrs. Tarpey was telling me! I suppose that's what brought the police and the magistrate up this way. I was wondering to see them in it a while ago.

SHAWN EARLY. The police after them? Bartley Fallon must have injured Jack so. They wouldn't meddle in a fight that was only for show!

MRS. TULLY. Why wouldn't he injure him? There was many a man killed with no more of a weapon than a hayfork.

JAMES RYAN. Wait till I run north as far as Kelly's bar to spread the news! (*He goes out.*)

TIM CASEY. I'll go tell Jack Smith's first cousin that is standing there south of the church after selling his lambs. (*Goes out.*)

MRS. TULLY. I'll go telling a few of the neighbours I see beyond to the west. (*Goes out.*)

SHAWN EARLY. I'll give word of it beyond at the east of the green. (*Is going out when* MRS. TARPEY *seizes hold of him.*)

MRS. TARPEY. Stop a minute, Shawn Early, and tell me did you see red Jack Smith's wife, Kitty Keary, in any place?

SHAWN EARLY. I did. At her own house she was, drying clothes on the hedge as I passed.

MRS. TARPEY. What did you say she was doing?

SHAWN EARLY (*breaking away*). Laying out a sheet on the hedge. (*He goes.*)

MRS. TARPEY. Laying out a sheet for the dead! The Lord have mercy on us! Jack Smith dead, and his wife laying out a sheet for his burying! (*Calls out*) Why didn't you tell me that before, Shawn Early? Isn't the deafness the great hardship? Half the world might be dead without me knowing of it or getting word of it at all! (*She sits down and rocks herself*) O my poor Jack Smith! To be going to his work so nice and so hearty, and to be left stretched on the ground in the full light of the day!

(*Enter* TIM CASEY.)

TIM CASEY. What is it, Mrs. Tarpey? What happened since?

MRS. TARPEY. O my poor Jack Smith!

TIM CASEY. Did Bartley overtake him?

MRS. TARPEY. O the poor man!

TIM CASEY. Is it killed he is?

MRS. TARPEY. Stretched in the Five Acre Meadow!

TIM CASEY. The Lord have mercy on us! Is that a fact?

MRS. TARPEY. Without the rites of the Church or a ha'porth!

TIM CASEY. Who was telling you?

MRS. TARPEY. And the wife laying out a sheet for his corpse. (*Sits up and wipes her eyes*) I suppose they'll wake him the same as another?

(*Enter* MRS. TULLY, SHAWN EARLY, *and* JAMES RYAN.)

MRS. TULLY. There is great talk about this work in every quarter of the fair.

MRS. TARPEY. Ochone! cold and dead. And myself maybe the last he was speaking to!

JAMES RYAN. The Lord save us! Is it dead he is?

TIM CASEY. Dead surely, and his wife getting provision for the wake.

SHAWN EARLY. Well, now, hadn't Bartley Fallon great venom in him?

MRS. TULLY. You may be sure he had some cause. Why would

he have made an end of him if he had not? (*To* MRS. TARPEY, *raising her voice*) What was it rose the dispute at all, Mrs Tarpey?

MRS. TARPEY. Not a one of me knows. The last I saw of them, Jack Smith was standing there, and Bartley Fallon was standing there, quiet and easy, and he listening to "The Red-haired Man's Wife."

MRS. TULLY. Do you hear that, Tim Casey? Do you hear that, Shawn Early and James Ryan? Bartley Fallon was here this morning listening to red Jack Smith's wife, Kitty Keary that was! Listening to her and whispering with her! It was she started the fight so!

SHAWN EARLY. She must have followed him from her own house. It is likely some person roused him.

TIM CASEY. I never knew, before, Bartley Fallon was great with Jack Smith's wife.

MRS. TULLY. How would you know it? Sure it's not in the streets they would be calling it. If Mrs. Fallon didn't know of it, and if I that have the next house to them didn't know of it, and if Jack Smith himself didn't know of it, it is not likely you would know of it, Tim Casey.

SHAWN EARLY. Let Bartley Fallon take charge of her from this out so, and let him provide for her. It is little pity she will get from any person in this parish.

TIM CASEY. How can he take charge of her? Sure he has a wife of his own. Sure you don't think he'd turn souper and marry her in a Protestant church?

JAMES RYAN. It would be easy for him to marry her if he brought her to America.

SHAWN EARLY. With or without Kitty Keary, believe me it is for America he's making at this minute. I saw the new magistrate and Jo Muldoon of the police going into the post-office as I came up—there was hurry on them—you may be sure it was to telegraph they went, the way he'll be stopped in the docks at Queenstown!

MRS. TULLY. It's likely Kitty Keary is gone with him, and not minding a sheet or a wake at all. The poor man, to be deserted by his own wife, and the breath hardly gone out yet from his body that is lying bloody in the field!

(*Enter* MRS. FALLON.)

MRS. FALLON. What is it the whole of the town is talking about? And what is it you yourselves are talking about? Is it about my man Bartley Fallon you are talking? Is it lies about him you are telling, saying that he went killing Jack Smith? My grief that ever he came into this place at all!

JAMES FALLON. Be easy now, Mrs. Fallon. Sure there is no one at all in the whole fair but is sorry for you!

MRS. FALLON. Sorry for me, is it? Why would any one be sorry for me? Let you be sorry for yourselves, and that there may be shame on you for ever and at the day of judgment, for the words you are saying and the lies you are telling to take away the character of my poor man, and to take the good name off of him, and to drive him to destruction! That is what you are doing!

SHAWN EARLY. Take comfort now, Mrs. Fallon. The police are

not so smart as they think. Sure he might give them the slip yet, the same as Lynchehaun.

MRS. TULLY. If they do get him, and if they do put a rope around his neck, there is no one can say he does not deserve it!

MRS. FALLON. Is that what you are saying, Bridget Tully, and is that what you think? I tell you it's too much talk you have, making yourself out to be such a great one, and to be running down every respectable person! A rope, is it? It isn't much of a rope was needed to tie up your own furniture the day you came into Martin Tully's house, and you never bringing as much as a blanket, or a penny, or a suit of clothes with you and I myself bringing seventy pounds and two feather beds. And now you are stiffer than a woman would have a hundred pounds! It is too much talk the whole of you have. A rope is it? I tell you the whole of this town is full of liars and schemers that would hang you up for half a glass of whiskey. (*Turning to go.*) People they are you wouldn't believe as much as daylight from without you'd get up to have a look at it yourself. Killing Jack Smith indeed! Where are you at all, Bartley, till I bring you out of this? My nice quiet little man! My decent comrade! He that is as kind and as harmless as an innocent beast of the field! He'll be doing no harm at all if he'll shed the blood of some of you after this day's work! That much would be no harm at all. (*Calls out*) Bartley! Bartley Fallon! Where are you? (*Going out*) Did any one see Bartley Fallon?

(*All turn to look after her.*)

JAMES RYAN. It is hard for her to believe any such a thing, God help her!

(*Enter* BARTLEY FALLON *from right, carrying hayfork.*)

BARTLEY. It is what I often said to myself, if there is ever any misfortune coming to this world it is on myself it is sure to come!

(*All turn round and face him.*)

BARTLEY. To be going about with this fork and to find no one to take it, and no place to leave it down, and I wanting to be gone out of this— Is that you, Shawn Early? (*Holds out fork*) It's well I met you. You have no call to be leaving the fair for a while the way I have, and how can I go till I'm rid of this fork? Will you take it and keep it until such time as Jack Smith—

SHAWN EARLY (*backing*). I will not take it, Bartley Fallon, I'm very thankful to you!

BARTLEY (*turning to apple stall*). Look at it now, Mrs. Tarpey, it was here I got it; let me thrust it in under the stall. It will lie there safe enough, and no one will take notice of it until such time as Jack Smith—

MRS. TARPEY. Take your fork out of that! Is it to put trouble on me and to destroy me you want? putting it there for the police to be rooting it out maybe. (*Thrusts him back.*)

BARTLEY. That is a very unneighbourly thing for you to do, Mrs. Tarpey. Hadn't I enough care on me with that fork before this, running up and down with it like the swinging of a clock, and afeard to lay it down in any place! I wish I never touched it or meddled with it at all!

JAMES RYAN. It is a pity, indeed, you ever did.

BARTLEY. Will you yourself take it, James Ryan? You were always a neighbourly man.

JAMES RYAN (*backing*). There is many a thing I would do for you, Bartley Fallon, but I won't do that!

SHAWN EARLY. I tell you there is no man will give you any help or any encouragement for this day's work. If it was something agrarian now—

BARTLEY. If no one at all will take it, maybe it's best to give it up to the police.

TIM CASEY. There'd be a welcome for it with them surely! (*Laughter*.)

MRS. TULLY. And it is to the police Kitty Keary herself will be brought.

MRS. TARPEY (*rocking to and fro*). I wonder now who will take the expense of the wake for poor Jack Smith?

BARTLEY. The wake for Jack Smith!

TIM CASEY. Why wouldn't he get a wake as well as another? Would you begrudge him that much?

BARTLEY. Red Jack Smith dead! Who was telling you?

SHAWN EARLY. The whole town knows of it by this.

BARTLEY. Do they say what way did he die?

JAMES RYAN. You don't know that yourself, I suppose, Bartley Fallon? You don't know he was followed and that he was laid dead with the stab of a hayfork?

BARTLEY. The stab of a hayfork!

SHAWN EARLY. You don't know, I suppose, that the body was found in the Five Acre Meadow?

BARTLEY. The Five Acre Meadow!

TIM CASEY. It is likely you don't know that the police are after the man that did it?

BARTLEY. The man that did it?

MRS. TULLY. You don't know, maybe, that he was made away with for the sake of Kitty Keary, his wife?

BARTLEY. Kitty Keary, his wife! (*Sits down bewildered.*)

MRS. TULLY. And what have you to say now, Bartley Fallon?

BARTLEY (*crossing himself*). I to bring that fork here, and to find that news before me! It is much if I can ever stir from this place at all, or reach as far as the road!

TIM CASEY. Look, boys, at the new magistrate, and Jo Muldoon along with him! It's best for us to quit this.

SHAWN EARLY. That is so. It is best not to be mixed in this business at all.

JAMES RYAN. Bad as he is, I wouldn't like to be an informer against any man.

(*All hurry away except* MRS. TARPEY, *who remains behind her stall. Enter* MAGISTRATE *and* POLICEMAN.)

MAGISTRATE. I knew the district was in a bad state, but I did not expect to be confronted with a murder at the first fair I came to.

POLICEMAN. I am sure you did not, indeed.

MAGISTRATE. It was well I had not gone home. I caught a few words here and there that roused my suspicions.

POLICEMAN. So they would, too.

MAGISTRATE. You heard the same story from everyone you asked?

POLICEMAN. The same story—or if it was not altogether the same, anyway it was no less than the first story.

MAGISTRATE. What is that man doing? He is sitting alone with a hayfork. He has a guilty look. The murder was done with a hayfork!

POLICEMAN (*in a whisper*). That's the very man they say did the act; Bartley Fallon himself!

MAGISTRATE. He must have found escape difficult—he is trying to brazen it out. A convict in the Andaman Islands tried the same game, but he could not escape my system! Stand aside—Don't go far—have the handcuffs ready. (*He walks up to Bartley, folds his arms, and stands before him.*) Here, my man, do you know anything of John Smith?

BARTLEY. Of John Smith! Who is he, now?

POLICEMAN. Jack Smith, sir—Red Jack Smith!

MAGISTRATE (*coming a step nearer and tapping him on the shoulder*). Where is Jack Smith?

BARTLEY (*with a deep sigh, and shaking his head slowly*). Where is he, indeed?

MAGISTRATE. What have you to tell?

BARTLEY. It is where he was this morning, standing in this spot, singing his share of songs—no, but lighting his pipe—scraping a match on the sole of his shoe—

MAGISTRATE. I ask you, for the third time, where is he?

BARTLEY. I wouldn't like to say that. It is a great mystery, and it is hard to say of any man, did he earn hatred or love.

MAGISTRATE. Tell me all you know.

BARTLEY. All that I know— Well, there are the three estates; there is Limbo, and there is Purgatory, and there is—

MAGISTRATE. Nonsense! This is trifling! Get to the point.

BARTLEY. Maybe you don't hold with the clergy so? That is the teaching of the clergy. Maybe you hold with the old people. It is what they do be saying, that the shadow goes wandering, and the soul is tired, and the body is taking a rest— The shadow! (*Starts up*) I was nearly sure I saw Jack Smith not ten minutes ago at the corner of the forge, and I lost him again— Was it his ghost I saw, do you think?

MAGISTRATE (*to policeman*). Conscience-struck! He will confess all now!

BARTLEY. His ghost to come before me! It is likely it was on account of the fork! I do have it and he to have no way to defend himself the time he met with his death!

MAGISTRATE (*to policeman*). I must note down his words. (*Takes out notebook.*) (*To* BARTLEY): I warn you that your words are being noted.

BARTLEY. If I had ha' run faster in the beginning, this terror would not be on me at the latter end! Maybe he will cast it up against me at the day of judgment— I wouldn't wonder at all at that.

MAGISTRATE (*writing*). At the day of judgment—

BARTLEY. It was soon for his ghost to appear to me—is it coming after me always by day it will be, and stripping the clothes off in the night time?— I wouldn't wonder at all at that, being as I am an unfortunate man!

MAGISTRATE (*sternly*). Tell me this truly. What was the motive of this crime?

BARTLEY. The motive, is it?

MAGISTRATE. Yes; the motive; the cause.

BARTLEY. I'd sooner not say that.

MAGISTRATE. You had better tell me truly. Was it money?

BARTLEY. Not at all! What did poor Jack Smith ever have in his pockets unless it might be his hands that would be in them?

MAGISTRATE. Any dispute about land?

BARTLEY (*indignantly*). Not at all! He never was a grabber or grabbed from any one!

MAGISTRATE. You will find it better for you if you tell me at once.

BARTLEY. I tell you I wouldn't for the whole world wish to say what it was—it is a thing I would not like to be talking about.

MAGISTRATE. There is no use in hiding it. It will be discovered in the end.

BARTLEY. Well, I suppose it will, seeing that mostly everybody knows it before. Whisper here now. I will tell no lie; where would be the use? (*Puts his hand to his mouth, and* MAGISTRATE *stoops*) Don't be putting the blame on the parish, for such a thing was never done in the parish before—it was done for the sake of Kitty Keary, Jack Smith's wife.

MAGISTRATE (*to policeman*). Put on the handcuffs. We have been saved some trouble. I knew he would confess if taken in the right way.

(*Policeman puts on handcuffs.*)

BARTLEY. Handcuffs now! Glory be! I always said, if there was ever any misfortune coming to this place it was on myself it would fall. I to be in handcuffs! There's no wonder at all in that.

(*Enter* MRS. FALLON, *followed by the rest. She is looking back at them as she speaks.*)

MRS. FALLON. Telling lies the whole of the people of this town are; telling lies, telling lies as fast as a dog will trot! Speaking against my poor respectable man! Saying he made an end of Jack Smith! My decent comrade! There is no better man and no kinder man in the whole of the five parishes! It's little annoyance he ever gave to any one! (*Turns and sees him*) What in the earthly world do I see before me? Bartley Fallon in charge of the police! Handcuffs on him! O Bartley, what did you do at all at all?

BARTLEY. O Mary, there has a great misfortune come upon me! It is what I always said, that if there is ever any misfortune—

MRS. FALLON. What did he do at all, or is it bewitched I am?

MAGISTRATE. This man has been arrested on a charge of murder.

MRS. FALLON. Whose charge is that? Don't believe them! They are all liars in this place! Give me back my man!

MAGISTRATE. It is natural that you should take his part, but you have no cause of complaint against your neighbours. He has been arrested for the murder of John Smith, on his own confession.

MRS. FALLON. The saints of heaven protect us! And what did he want killing Jack Smith?

MAGISTRATE. It is best you should know all. He did it on account of a love affair with the murdered man's wife.

MRS. FALLON (*sitting down*). With Jack Smith's wife! With Kitty Keary!—Ochone, the traitor!

THE CROWD. A great shame, indeed. He is a traitor, indeed.

MRS. TULLY. To America he was bringing her, Mrs. Fallon.

BARTLEY. What are you saying, Mary? I tell you—

MRS. FALLON. Don't say a word! I won't listen to any word you'll say! (*Stops her ears*). O, isn't he the treacherous villain? Ochone go deo!

BARTLEY. Be quiet till I speak! Listen to what I say!

MRS. FALLON. Sitting beside me on the ass car coming to the town, so quiet and so respectable, and treachery like that in his heart!

BARTLEY. Is it your wits you have lost or is it I myself that have lost my wits?

MRS. FALLON. And it's hard I earned you, slaving, slaving—and you grumbling, and sighing, and coughing, and discontented, and the priest wore out anointing you, with all the times you threatened to die!

BARTLEY. Let you be quiet till I tell you!

MRS. FALLON. You to bring such a disgrace into the parish. A thing that was never heard of before!

BARTLEY. Will you shut your mouth and hear me speaking?

MRS. FALLON. And if it was for any sort of a fine handsome woman, but for a little fistful of a woman like Kitty Keary, that's not four feet high hardly, and not three teeth in her head unless she got new ones! May God reward you, Bartley Fallon, for the black treachery in your heart and the wickedness in your mind, and the red blood of poor Jack Smith that is wet upon your hand!

(*Voice of Jack Smith heard singing*)

> The sea shall be dry.
>   The earth under mourning and ban!
>   Then loud shall he cry
>   For the wife of the red-haired man!

BARTLEY. It's Jack Smith's voice—I never knew a ghost to sing before—. It is after myself and the fork he is coming! (*Goes back. Enter* JACK SMITH) Let one of you give him the fork and I will be clear of him now and for eternity!

MRS. TARPEY. The Lord have mercy on us! Red Jack Smith! The man that was going to be waked!

JAMES RYAN. Is it back from the grave you are come?

SHAWN EARLY. Is it alive you are, or is it dead you are?

TIM CASEY. Is it yourself at all that's in it?

MRS. TULLY. Is it letting on you were to be dead?

MRS. FALLON. Dead or alive, let you stop Kitty Keary, your wife, from bringing my man away with her to America!

JACK SMITH. It is what I think, the wits are gone astray on the whole of you. What would my wife want bringing Bartley Fallon to America?

MRS. FALLON. To leave yourself, and to get quit of you she wants, Jack Smith, and to bring him away from myself. That's what the two of them had settled together.

JACK SMITH. I'll break the head of any man that says that! Who is it says it? (*To* TIM CASEY) Was it you said it? (*To* SHAWN EARLY) Was it you?

ALL TOGETHER (*backing and shaking their heads*). It wasn't I said it!

JACK SMITH. Tell me the name of any man that said it!

ALL TOGETHER (*pointing to Bartley*). It was *him* that said it!

JACK SMITH. Let me at him till I break his head!

(*Bartley backs in terror. Neighbours hold* JACK SMITH *back.*)

JACK SMITH (*trying to free himself*). Let me at him! Isn't he the pleasant sort of a scarecrow for any woman to be crossing the ocean with! It's back from the docks of New York he'd be turned (*trying to rush at him again*), with a lie in his mouth and treachery in his heart, and another man's wife by his side, and he passing her off as his own! Let me at him can't you. (*Makes another rush, but is held back.*)

MAGISTRATE (*pointing to* JACK SMITH). Policeman, put the handcuffs on this man. I see it all now. A case of false impersonation, a conspiracy to defeat the ends of justice. There was a case in the Andaman Islands, a murderer of the Mopsa tribe, a religious enthusiast—

POLICEMAN. So he might be, too.

MAGISTRATE. We must take both these men to the scene of the murder. We must confront them with the body of the real Jack Smith.

JACK SMITH. I'll break the head of any man that will find my dead body!

MAGISTRATE. I'll call more help from the barracks. (*Blows Policeman's whistle.*)

BARTLEY. It is what I am thinking, if myself and Jack Smith are put together in the one cell for the night, the handcuffs will be taken off him, and his hands will be free, and murder will be done that time surely!

MAGISTRATE. Come on! (*They turn to the right.*)

Shadow and Substance

A PLAY IN FOUR ACTS

BY PAUL VINCENT CARROLL

"Oh, what a power has white Simplicity!"

KEATS

CHARACTERS

Brigid (*Canon Skerritt's servant*)

Dermot Francis O'Flingsley (*the local schoolmaster*)

Thomasina Concannon (*Canon Skerritt's niece*)

Local Curates:

  Father Corr

  Father Kirwan

Very Rev. Thomas Canon Skerritt

Miss Jemima Cooney (*a local spinster*)

Francis Ignatius O'Connor (*her nephew*)

Martin Mullahone (*the local publican*)

Rosey Violet (*his wife*)

SCENES

The time is the present.

The action passes in the living room of Canon Skerritt's parochial house in "Ardmahone," one of the small towns lying round the feet of the Mourne hills in County Louth, Ireland.

Shadow and Substance was first produced at the Abbey Theatre, Dublin, on January 25th, 1937.

A legend connected with St. Brigid relates how, in order to escape the attentions of persistent suitors, she disfigured the loveliness of her face at Fanghart, her birthplace, near Dundalk, Ireland.

Shadow and Substance

ACT ONE

SCENE: *The living room in the Parochial House of the Very Rev. Thomas Canon Skerritt in Ardmahone, one of the small towns lying round the feet of Mourne, on the borders of Louth.*

The room is excellently furnished, and gives evidence in its accoutrements, its beautiful leaded bookcases, its pictures and other tasteful details, of the refined character of the Canon.

The one incongruous note in the harmony of the whole design is a large gaudy oleograph of the Sacred Heart over the door, left.

A window, back, in French manner, very tastefully curtained to the ground with crimson art brocade, and giving access to the gardens. Through the window, a view of Mourne's rugged peaks. The walls are hung with small Spanish and Roman reproductions of very good quality, including Velasquez, Murillo, El Greco, Da Vinci and Raphael.

As the curtain rises, BRIGID *is ushering in* DERMOT FRANCIS O'FLINGSLEY, *the schoolmaster, a young man, very alert, alive, and intelligent, obviously capable of feeling things acutely, and of passion and pride. He is bright in manner, and has a pleasing sense of humor.* BRIGID *is small, possibly a little stupid-looking, with large eyes; neat, but not to any degree Quakerish. She is obviously not mentally outstanding, but capable of deep affection, and pleasing in her person.*

A table is laid, very carefully and very completely, for lunch, and both it and the chairs, and the table-ware are of excellent quality. There is no sign of tawdriness or of slipshod carelessness about the room.

BRIGID. He said, Master, he might be home for lunch and he mightn't. It's to Dublin he went, I think. It'll be maybe to see one of them Spanish gentlemen that writes to him since the time he was in Spain. Sure just rest a wee while, Master, seein' he's not here yet.

O'FLINGSLEY (*entering carelessly, hands in jacket pocket*). Thanks, Brigid. It's not often I get this far into the great one's privacy. Such privileges are not for schoolmasters.

BRIGID. Ach, sure it's just his way. Are ye goin' to quarrel with him again?

O'FLINGSLEY. No, Brigid, definitely no. But I will, all the same.

BRIGID. Yous hate one another. Sure I know, be now . . .

O'FLINGSLEY. I suppose we do.

BRIGID. Isn't it funny now that I think there's no one like aythur of yous. Would that not mean that the two of yous are maybe the one? Or am I blatherin'?

O'FLINGSLEY. You certainly *are* blatherin', Brigid. If you love him, you hate *me,* and if you love *me,* you hate *him.*

BRIGID (*slowly*). That's maybe the way it would show on paper, but in the mind it's not maybe as true. (*Pause*) St. Brigid wouldn't deceive me like that.

O'FLINGSLEY (*regarding her half-seriously, half-humorously*). Are you still on that nonsense, Brigid?

BRIGID (*hurt*). Don't say it's nonsense, Master.

O'FLINGSLEY. Have you told anyone about this—the Canon or the curates?

BRIGID (*secretively*). No one only you.

O'FLINGSLEY. Why just me?

BRIGID. I don't know. . . . Didn't you tell me yourself, one time, that there's no words at all for some of the things we think and feel?

O'FLINGSLEY (*touched*). I am not worth all this trust, Brigid. Suppose, some night when I'd have a spree, I'd tell it in a snug.

BRIGID (*catching at his arm, tensely*). You—wouldn't do that. . . . (*He smiles at her*) Sure, don't I know. . . . You have the fine thing in you—the same thing that the Canon has.

O'FLINGSLEY (*laughing*). Don't you dare compare me with *him*. (*Pause*) Why don't you tell *him* about—this secret of yours? Or the curates?

BRIGID. Sure, they'd question and cross-question, and then make me promise never to see her again. That would be somethin' too terrible for me to bear—the same as you could bear the burn of a hot poker or of scaldin' water.

O'FLINGSLEY. Then—you *do* see her actually?

BRIGID (*rapt*). Yes . . . often. I'm used to her now. She is always smilin', smilin' and in great humor, as if she was enjoyin' makin' me happy. It's lovely that she's not sour like a nun, at the convent school, or like a priest in the box.

O'FLINGSLEY (*seriously*). I don't want to hurt you, Brigid, but if you're a wise girl, you'll put this thing absolutely away from you. Some day, maybe she or it, whatever it is, will desert you, and you'll go crazy with despair. Are you listenin' to me?

BRIGID (*softly*). Yes . . . but she promised . . .

O'FLINGSLEY. Supposing she's an evil thing? It could well be.

BRIGID. If she was evil, I would feel the fear in me. Doesn't God make us like that?

O'FLINGSLEY. Why don't you ask her for a proof, as I told you?

BRIGID. I did. I asked her one night to make the bed-chair move. Wasn't that what you said?

O'FLINGSLEY. And did she?

BRIGID. No. . . . She just smiled, and her eyes laughed the way she was amused at me.

O'FLINGSLEY. Maybe it was at me she was amused—O'Flingsley, the idiot.

BRIGID. It was never that. She loves you too. I can see it. She told me you had a secret.

O'FLINGSLEY (*startled*). What sort of a secret?

BRIGID. She said—a dark secret, and that you were a blunderer, but that God loved blunderers because they were the children of Peter.

O'FLINGSLEY (*concerned*). Brigid, you dreamed this! You *did!*

BRIGID (*slowly*). No. . . . Sure I know I didn't. . . She told me about the Canon too.

O'FLINGSLEY. *Him?* What did she say about him?

BRIGID. She said that there was great holiness in him, but that his pride would need the tears of a hundred just men and the soul of a child, to soften it.

O'FLINGSLEY (*tensely*). Did she say—what child?

BRIGID. She only smiled and went away.

O'FLINGSLEY. Good God! What creature is this at all? I'm warning you, Brigid. I'm warning you, mind.

BRIGID. I love her too much now to be afraid. . . . (*Pause*) Have you a secret?

O'FLINGSLEY (*secretively*). I have written a book and published it. No one knows it's mine.

BRIGID. Is it a *good* book?

O'FLINGSLEY. It might be. It's a *bitter* book.

BRIGID. She will not be pleased. Why could you not make it full of love?

O'FLINGSLEY (*tensely*). I don't believe in love.

BRIGID. St. Brigid does. She stood near me at the bed last night when the new moon was in it. I said, "There's the new moon, God bless it," and I blessed meself, and she laughed without any noise, and her eyes had the moon in them like a mirror. She stood lookin' out at the big boulders of the hills, and her speakin' low. Then she said when I came close to her that the hills were just like that long long ago, and that they were God's hint to man to build in the heart forever and ever, instead of with stone and mortar and the pride that puts a stone on another stone without meanin'. And a lot more that the words will not come to me for. I fell asleep listenin' to her—her voice was sinkin' me all the time into sleep. (*She looks up at* O'FLINGSLEY. *A shadow of fear crosses her face suddenly. She grips him*) I'm a fool to be tellin' you—a fool, a fool. You'll put it in a bitter book and laugh at it.

o'flingsley (*touched*). No, Brigid . . . not in a book. (*Pause—He catches her arm*) Are you—lying to me, Brigid?

brigid (*pathetically*) No, Master. . . . How could I lie?

o'flingsley. But—how do you remember it all like this?

brigid. Remember it? Sure, how could I *forget* it? (*She looks at him in pain. He soothes her.*)

o'flingsley. There! There! I don't mean to hurt you. I'm just nervous about you. I think you'd better tell the Canon about this.

brigid. Not—not yet. I won't be separated from her. I love her. Some day I shall come to her, she said.

o'flingsley (*worried*). You must keep your mind off that now. You must first live your life here.

brigid. She told me that too.

o'flingsley (*after a pause*). You're a funny little customer, Brigid. There's times when I'd like to pull your hair, and give you a smack on the jaw.

brigid. Sure I would never feel it. . . .

o'flingsley. There's tears for you, and I'm warning you. But you won't heed. Well, I'd better be getting back to the school. I'll come back later and see if he's home.

brigid. Will you lave a message?

o'flingsley. Anything to oblige, Brigid. Ask him when is the school going to get any coal, when I can have the new maps I asked for last year, when the windows are going to be repaired, and if he'll supply me with two pails to catch the raindrops from the ceiling on wet days. And when is he going to relieve *me* of the job of brushing and cleaning out the place?

BRIGID (*breathless*). I'll never remember all of them.

O'FLINGSLEY. Oh, don't let that worry you. *He'll* not remember any of them anyway.

BRIGID (*disconsolately*). I can see another fight comin', and you bein' ordered out again. Yous are never done.

O'FLINGSLEY. Well, what can *I* do? What could anyone do? If only I had enough guts in me, I'd clap on my hat, and walk right out of this place. But I haven't. Actually, Brigid, I'm afraid I'd have no money and be hungry. Amn't I a miserable creature?

BRIGID. If you could have somethin' grand and lovely to rise for, every day, like me with St. Brigid.

O'FLINGSLEY (*tensely*). Maybe I have.

BRIGID. Tell me about it, Master.

O'FLINGSLEY. No. . . . It's all—fire and smoke . . . and things falling.

BRIGID (*reprovingly*). Sure isn't that just like you! (*She laughs*) I'll bet St. Brigid would know.

O'FLINGSLEY. Will you ask her?

BRIGID. I will, if you promise to obey her.

O'FLINGSLEY. I'll—try.

(*He is crossing, and looking back whimsically at* BRIGID *when* THOMASINA CONCANNON *enters briskly. She is a very "bunty" girl of about 22, with full animal spirits, round fat face, all dimples, given to giggling laughter, and eternally sucking sweetmeats.*)

THOMASINA (*as she rushes in*). Is me uncle back yet, Bridgie?

BRIGID. No, miss. But I'm expectin' him any minute. The Master's waitin' on him too.

THOMASINA (*to* O'FLINGSLEY). Oh, you're Mr. O'Flingsley. I'm a school teacher too—just finished a few months, and was doing substitute at Dunaree. I'm pleased to meet you. (*She giggles.*)

O'FLINGSLEY. So am I. How do you do, Miss —

BRIGID. Miss Concannon her name is, Master.

THOMASINA. I'm the Canon's niece, you know. Me mother says I'm a bit like him round the nose. (*She giggles*) Do *you* think so?

O'FLINGSLEY. On the contrary, I think you have a very nice nose.

BRIGID. Oh, Master! (THOMASINA *and* O'FLINGSLEY *laugh together.* BRIGID *goes, quickly.*)

THOMASINA. Well, I have another hold on him anyway. I'm called after him. You see, they thought I'd be a boy, and the name was ready and all.

O'FLINGSLEY (*entering the fun*). And you weren't?

THOMASINA. Why of course I wasn't, stupid! (*She giggles heartily*) So me mother, who lets nothin' bate her, said: "She'll be Thomasina." Wasn't it awful cute of her?

O'FLINGSLEY. It certainly was a great idea, Miss Concannon.

THOMASINA (*holding up poke of sweets*). Do have a liquorice-all-sort, Mr. O'Flingsley, and you may call me Thomasina.

O'FLINGSLEY (*taking sweet*). Th-thanks. *You* can call me anything you like, and quote your uncle as a precedent.

BRIGID (*entering hastily*). The Canon's back on the train. He's in the Post Office below, writin' a postcard. The milkman's after tellin' me.

O'FLINGSLEY (*to go*). I'll come back later when he settles, Brigid.

THOMASINA. Wait till he hears I slept in his room last night!

O'FLINGSLEY. Slept in his room!

THOMASINA. The bed in the spare room has bronchitis. (*With a gasp*) Oh, dear God! I believe I left *Love's Purple Passions* under his pilla. Ex-excuse *me*, Mr. O'Flingsley. (*She rushes off, breathlessly.* O'FLINGSLEY *looks at* BRIGID *in a bewildered way.*)

O'FLINGSLEY. Is that the one that's trying to get in here as my Assistant?

BRIGID. Yis, Master.

O'FLINGSLEY. Good God! The mists thicken, O, Israel. . . .

(*He goes, worried.* BRIGID *looks after him softly, then runs to table, and in a scared way begins rearranging things on the dining table.* FATHER CORR *enters, left. He is a young man, small and round-shouldered with a face easily affected by fervor or sentiment. His mood is melancholic and introspective.*)

FATHER CORR (*kindly*). Well, Bridgie, me heartie, and how's the bones today? (*Flings hat on chair.*)

BRIGID. Oh, Father Corr, do *you* see anythin' missin' on that table? The Canon's back. He's in the Post Office.

FATHER CORR (*careless glance*). Ach sure, isn't it fine?

BRIGID. Oh, but the Canon! If there's a single spot . . .

(FATHER KIRWAN *enters, left, wearing motor goggles and gloves. Athletic, good-humored and well-meaning. Neatly lands his hat on a bookcase, takes off goggles, etc., and then turns very severely to* FATHER CORR—*obviously mimicking the Canon.*)

FATHER KIRWAN. Father Corr, may I ask who owns this—er— motor machine I observe at the front entrance?

FATHER CORR (*with a wave*). Cut out that coddin' and get a shave. The Canon's back.

FATHER KIRWAN (*incredibly*). He's *not*?

FATHER CORR. He is.

FATHER KIRWAN. Heavens! (*Feeling hairy cheek*). Am I bad? Brigid, tell me like a decent woman, do I need a shave, or do I not?

BRIGID. Indeed you do, Father. And I sent you up shavin' water this mornin'.

FATHER KIRWAN. So you did, but seein' the Canon was—not in residence, I used it for softenin' a corn. God made feet, but an enemy came and oversowed corns. . . .

BRIGID. Do *you* see anythin' missin' there, Father Kirwan?

FATHER KIRWAN (*wistfully*). Sure and I do, Bridgie. A whippin' good plate o' cabbage and bacon.

BRIGID. Ah, Father! And the Canon always sayin' we know nothin' about food in Ireland.

FATHER KIRWAN (*mimicking again*). When I was in Spain, my excellent friend, Don Miguel Del Fuego . . . (*All start laughing.*)

BRIGID (*looking from window, suddenly*). Oh, here's the Canon comin' up the lawn. (*All flurried*) Oh, dear me. I hope everythin's right. And I wish I had him told about Thomasina. (*She runs off, scared. The two curates laugh rather nervously.*)

FATHER KIRWAN. Wait till you see his face when he sees that niece of his! She always sends him off the deep end!

FATHER CORR. The girl's a bit of an ass right enough, but there's no harm in her. Now remember we're to tackle him about that filthy book that's on the rounds. I expect you to back me up and not let the confraternity down.

FATHER KIRWAN. I'll do my best. But you know the dry way he can bottle you up. And be Heavens I left the wee car at the gate. He'll have a fit when he sees it!

FATHER CORR. Well, aren't all the curates everywhere gettin' cars? And it's a free country. Come on into the garden and give him time to settle. (*They go out by the window.*)

FATHER KIRWAN (*as they go, dubiously*). I wish that niece had stayed at home, and—I wish I had shaved. . . . (BRIGID *comes in quickly, and nervously sets glasses on table. She stands over the table counting and calculating.* CANON THOMAS SKERRITT *enters, left. Finely built, but a little too full in the stomach, fine face, but a little too red. His eyes are vividly living always, and at times his whole being concentrates in them. He has a perfect bow, his voice is cultured, he can be very charming and courteous, can quickly adapt himself to suit people, and has a kingly walk and dignity. He is excellently dressed. He is wearing a tall silk hat, and carries an umbrella.*)

CANON (*benignly*). Ah, Brigid, you're there!

BRIGID (*soothingly*). Yis, Canon. Your hat and umbrella, Canon. (*She takes them with great care, and looks up at him with childish simplicity combined with womanly prudence*) I hope, Canon, you're grand and well after the week-end.

CANON. You will be pleased to know, Brigid, that the Canon feels excellently.

BRIGID. And did you meet your great friend from Spain, Canon?

CANON. I met him, Brigid. My friend Don Miguel Barzan y Per-dito. It was good, Brigid. It was very good. I mentioned you, Brigid. (*Clapping her patronizingly*) I said to Don Miguel, "My truest friend in this fallen land is Brigid." And he smiled in his excellent way, and said, "Donde esta la verdad esta Dios."

BRIGID. Wasn't that lovely of you, Canon! And what did Don Miguel mean be that?

CANON (*deprecating*). He meant, Brigid, in the crude language of the—Saxon: "Where we have truth we have God."

BRIGID. *It's love*ly. It's like what a saint—I mean a gentleman, would say.

CANON. A saint *and* a gentleman, you mean, Brigid. That is the classic equivalent to the—the odious Northern Officer and gentleman. But go, Brigid, see to lunch immediately.

BRIGID. Yis, Canon. (*She crosses.*)

CANON. Stay, Brigid. There is no news—I hope?

BRIGID. No, Canon, except that—that your niece is here.

CANON (*immediately on edge*). My step-niece, Brigid. I insist on the distinction. What evil brings her here?

BRIGID. It's to see you, special, she said—about the school, I think. She insisted on stayin' last night. She said her mother said it.

CANON (*with suppressed venom*). Her mother! That barbarian who links me by law to a—cattle-jobber. It burns me, Brigid—it *burns* me.

BRIGID. Please now, Canon, don't make yourself ill again.

CANON. You are wise, child. I forget myself. I always forget myself in the face of this recurring decimal of relationship. (*Holding* BRIGID'S *arm*) Consider, Brigid! My name—grave and classical—purloined—that's the word for it—to gain a—nomenclature for a human dumpling who reeks eternally of peppermints.

BRIGID. Sure, you're angerin' yourself, Canon. Sure, maybe if she got married, it would settle her down, and you wouldn't be pestered with her no more.

CANON. There is wisdom there, Brigid. I will consider that. I shall turn that over carefully.

BRIGID. Sure, I try to help ye, Canon.

CANON. As you say, Brigid, you try to help me, and as I say, there is wisdom in you. Let it be written of you, Brigid. You are a good child—an excellent child. Go, Brigid!

BRIGID (*going*). Yis, Canon.

CANON. Wait, Brigid. Where did she stay last night?

BRIGID (*in fear*). She—she said the spare room was draughty and there was a mouse in the wardrobe, and she—she—

CANON. She what?

BRIGID. She took *your* room, Canon.

CANON (*fuming*). Eh? She—she what? Brigid! I am incensed beyond words. You are arraigned! You are in the dock!

BRIGID. But I could do nothin', Canon. Says she to me, "I'm the Canon's niece, and the place for his servant is at me footstool."

CANON. The Canon's niece! That Irish matrimonial luggage label! That ecclesiastical buckle on a female shoe! Go, Brigid! Restore my room to its—austerity.

BRIGID. Yis, Canon. Sure it'll be lovely and grand for you now, if you'll not be vexin' yourself.

CANON (*softening*). There, child, I do not blame you. We are thwarted. We shall die outwitted by boobs and idiots. Mark it, Brigid, mark it! Go, Brigid!

THOMASINA (*calling offstage*). Gooee, Brigid! Did my uncle come?

CANON. God! Must I suffer this?

BRIGID (*fearfully*). Yis, Miss. He's here. (THOMASINA *bounds in, and runs as if to embrace the* CANON. *He skillfully counters this by blowing his nose with one hand and holding out a defensive other hand.* BRIGID *slips out, scared.*)

THOMASINA (*gurglingly*). Oh, Uncle Thomas! I thought you'd never come. Oh, isn't it lovely you're back?

CANON (*vaguely, staring at her*). Ah, it's you. Of course it's you. I was expecting you. You wrote, of course. I remember. You are a good child—an excellent child. . . .

THOMASINA. But I never wrote, Uncle.

CANON. Ah, you never wrote. Of course you didn't. I remember distinctly. It was the last time you wrote.

THOMASINA. I came down, Uncle Thomas, to tell you I finished in Dunaree School on Friday. The teacher is better now.

CANON. Very creditable, very creditable.

THOMASINA. And Father Crone, the parish priest, said to say to you, do you remember Crone, your old crony in Maynooth before you went to Spain. (*She giggles loudly.*)

CANON (*gravely*). Never heard of him.

THOMASINA. But he swears him and you used to keep a pot o' jam in the dormitory against the rules. (*She giggles explosively.*)

CANON (*outraged*). Come, come! I dislike levity in young people.

THOMASINA (*pouting ponderously*). I'm sorry, Uncle Thomas. Sure it was only to show you the great man Father Crone is for jokes. Do you think they'll make a Canon of him, Uncle? I think he'd make a lovely Canon—and it would go so grand with his name too—Kevin Canon Crone.

CANON (*ironic*). No doubt the accumulated wisdom of the Church will endorse your conclusions. (*He sniffs and blows his nose meaningly*) In future, my dear, when seeking a—a—an audience with me, I wish you would compose yourself with some degree of mental sobriety, and in addition fast from peppermints for at least one hour.

THOMASINA (*pouting*). You're not glad to see me, Uncle Thomas. Well, it was me mother kept *at* me, Uncle. "There y'are," she kept girnin', "walkin' about idle for three whole days and nights, and you Canon Thomas Skerritt's niece be law and be blood. A fine state this country's comin' to." That's *her* all the time.

CANON (*with calm brutality*). Your mother, my dear, I regret to say, is, and has ever been, a woman bereft—that's the word, bereft—of one iota of sound sense or dignity. The fact burns me. But it is—irrefutable. (THOMASINA *giggles involuntarily, and then dabs her face with a mint-reeking handkerchief.*)

THOMASINA. Sure, maybe you're right, Uncle. The talk and blatherin' of her—you'd think I had no name o' me own—I'm the Canon's niece to everyone we meet.

CANON (*grimly*). I am well aware of it. But it is a national disease, and I am no surgeon. You must leave me now, and I shall let you know in a few days about the school. (*Consulting watch.*) There is a train back in twelve minutes.

THOMASINA. But sure it's the bus I go by always, Canon.

CANON (*countering*). There is a bus back in *six* minutes.

THOMASINA (*as she is moved off*). Will you appoint me to the school, Uncle, when Miss Driscoll goes to her training next week?

CANON. Possibly.

THOMASINA. I'll just say "yes," instead of "possibly" to me mother. Let me play a wee tune for you on the piano before I go.

CANON. Certainly not!

THOMASINA. But it's a lovely wee thing, Canon. Father Crone sang it at a wee tea-party before I left Dunaree School. It begins, "When first I saw your face of virgin kew."

CANON (*evenly*). You will go now, my dear.

THOMASINA. All right then, Uncle, but I'll come again.

CANON. So you will. (*Almost sotto voce*) *Est Natura rerum.* . . . (*As he moves her on.*)

THOMASINA. What does that mean, Canon?

CANON. You would not appreciate it. (*They go out together. BRIGID comes in and lays serving dishes on table. The two curates, FATHER CORR and FATHER KIRWAN, come in from garden by window.*)

BRIGID. Lunch is ready, Fathers, and the Canon's ready. Will you please sit down?

FATHER CORR. Grand news, Bridgie. What are you going to give us?

FATHER KIRWAN (*as they both sit*). Nothin' Spanish, I hope.

BRIGID (*half secretively*). It's another of them dishes the Canon used to love in Spain. (*She smiles secretively at them and goes.*)

FATHER KIRWAN. *In Nomine De,* when is this goin' to stop?

FATHER CORR (*tired*). Ach, just take it for your sins, and hope for the best.

FATHER KIRWAN. I wish to God I could get a transfer to some old P.P. that loves cabbage and eats peas with his knife, and snores after his dinner.

FATHER CORR. Sssh! (*The CANON re-enters. The curates rise respectfully. The CANON comes slowly to the table, with dignity. He stands at the head of the table.*)

CANON (*courteously, with a slight bow*). Good morning, Fathers.

CURATES (*together*). Good mornin', Canon.

CANON (*acidly*). I didn't quite catch the final "g" in "morning," Fathers. (*Pause. They silently say grace. Further pause*) May I ask, Fathers, who owns that motor-car at the gate?

FATHER CORR. It's ours, Canon.

FATHER KIRWAN. It killed a man, Canon, and the owner wanted rid of it. We got it dirt cheap.

CANON. I am glad to hear it has such excellent capabilities. But— is it necessary?

FATHER CORR. It will come in useful I'm sure. Father Kirwan and I do a lot of running about. And besides we feel entitled to contribute in any way we can to our happiness here.

CANON. You mean it will make your job more comfortable.

FATHER KIRWAN. Job, Canon?

CANON. Yes . . . a word that Columkille and Columbanus knew in another sense. However, there is no Canon law against— owner-driver clerics. You may be seated. (*All sit.* BRIGID *enters and starts serving*) Well, Brigid, did the experiment work again?

BRIGID (*as she serves*). Sure, it's lovely, Canon, and it was easy follyin' your directions.

CANON. Very creditable, Brigid. You have today, Fathers, an extremely delicious Spanish dish, given me some years ago by the chatelaine of my friend Don Juan Almeria y Fernandez. (CURATES *taste dish gingerly and nod to the* CANON.)

FATHER CORR. Very good indeed, Canon.

FATHER KIRWAN. Grand, Canon. (BRIGID *moves about and on and off.* CANON *notices a newspaper sticking out of* FATHER KIRWAN'S *pocket.*)

CANON. The development of a sensitive palate, Fathers, is not the most unimportant of legitimate activities. Father Kirwan, may I ask what—litter is that protruding from the outer pocket of your attire?

FATHER KIRWAN (*touching paper*). Sure it's just the—the *Ballyedminstown Courier,* Canon.

CANON (*suavely*). Would you please adjust the—the—*Ballyelphinstown* Courier, Father, so that it will not detract from the dignity of your person?

FATHER KIRWAN (*pushing paper right into pocket*). Sorry, Canon. (*Pause*) There's a very strong leader in it this week, Canon, on that outrageous book that's just after comin' out. It's called *I Am Sir Oracle.*

FATHER CORR. I was just goin' to mention that, Canon. It's a very grave matter altogether, and I think it calls for action. The people's demandin' it.

FATHER KIRWAN. They say, Canon, the author is a schoolmaster with a spite agin the local P.P. He calls himself Eugene Gibney.

FATHER CORR. Are *you* prepared to take anny action, Canon?

CANON (*acidly*). There is no such word as "anny," except of course the female appellation, and the verb agrees with its subject, always—even in Ireland. (*As* BRIGID *enters*) You may serve the coffee black, Brigid. (*The two curates look very abject.*)

BRIGID. Yis, Canon. It's ready.

FATHER CORR (*apologetically*). If you don't mind, Canon, I'll have tea instead.

CANON (*with withering suavity*). You may serve Father Corr with—tea.

FATHER KIRWAN. And me too, Canon, if you please.

CANON. You are at liberty to poison Father Kirwan also.

BRIGID. Yis, Canon. (*She crosses.*)

CANON. And, Brigid. (*Takes key from pocket and gives it to her*) You know the one, Brigid. It is marked "Vino de Amontillado."

BRIGID. Is that the one, Canon, with the gold silver-paper on it that Don Miguel sent you from Spain?

CANON. Exactly, Brigid. My friend, Don Miguel Barzan y Perdito. (*As* BRIGID *unlocks cupboard under the bookshelves*) Are you having a little wine, Fathers?

FATHER CORR. I'll take a thimbleful, Canon.

FATHER KIRWAN. And I too, thanks. (BRIGID *brings small flagon of rich golden wine, expensively wrapped, which the* CANON *handles with great delicacy.*)

CANON. I'm afraid there are no—thimbles reasonably convenient, Father. Better take a wineglassful. (*As he receives bottle*) Excellent, Brigid. You may bring Fathers Corr and Kirwan the bottle of Empire wine that's on the left-hand side. (*With a sardonic curve of lip.*)

BRIGID. Is it the one, Canon, that Martin Reilly sent up last Christmas for a present?

CANON. Precisely, Brigid. (*Ironically*) It should be considerably matured by this. (*As* BRIGID *gets it*) You were speaking, gentlemen, of the proposed suppression of a book, entitled *I Am Sir Oracle*.

FATHER KIRWAN. The editor of this paper, from my home town, Canon, calls for it to be burned on every market square in Ireland.

FATHER CORR. It demands action too from the Board of Censors.

CANON. (*Lifting glass and examining golden wine carefully*) And on what grounds are we to have this extensive series of rural bonfires?

FATHER CORR (*with fire*). Why, the whole book is a dastardly attack on the Catholicism of Ireland, Canon! (BRIGID *pours out the red port for curates, and then goes softly.*)

CANON (*looking closely at bubbling wine*). Grave news surely out of Bally—Ballyeffelstown. A seamew blunders against a lighthouse and the keeper sends up distress rockets. (*With suave irony*) Your health, Fathers. (*He drinks delicately and with great relish. The curates fling back their port and cough into napkins. As he lies back, enjoying the wine on his tongue*) May I ask if the writer attacks any specific doctrine of the Church?

FATHER CORR. He evades that, Canon. In a Catholic country, like this, a fellow like that should be hung.

CANON (*imperturbably*). Hanged, Father Corr. (*Pause.* BRIGID *serves coffee and tea, etc.*) Were *you* about to make some observation, Father Kirwan?

FATHER KIRWAN. I was goin' to say, Canon, that the men of the

football team I run, are up in arms agin it. And Father Corr
can tell you about the Sacred Heart Confraternity.

FATHER CORR. Martin Reilly's wife, Canon, had the book home
from Dublin, and it's got round the people. The whole men and
women of the Sacred Heart are anxious to burn it in public. And
Father Kirwan and myself agree with them. We'd like your
advice.

CANON. You mean my—direction.

BRIGID (*as she goes*). If you please, Canon, when you want me to
clear away, will you shout?

CANON (*eyelids raised*). Shout, Brigid? Certainly not. I shall
ring.

BRIGID. Yis, Canon. And if you please, Canon, the schoolmaster
is back again wantin' to see you, and he says he's in a hurry.

CANON. Dear me! Even the school teachers are becoming presumptuous. We live, Brigid, in an incongruous age. Tell him,
I shall possibly see him when his hurry is more in keeping with
his status.

BRIGID. Yis, Canon. And if you please, Canon, are ye rememberin'
that Miss Jemima Cooney and her nephew Francis Ignatius is
waitin' since before lunch to show you Francis' new teachin'
certificate?

CANON. Brigid, I fear you fret yourself unduly. Tell them both
to go round into the Church, and say the Rosary, and by that
time I may possibly be in a position to receive them.

BRIGID. But you see, Canon—

CANON. Go, Brigid!

BRIGID. Yis, Canon. (*She goes. The* CURATES *now make to rise. The* CANON *detains them with a finger.*)

CANON. One moment, Fathers. An observation or two is—imperative. (*They settle stiffly.*) Father Corr, I am given to understand that since your arrival here you have attained quite an inordinate amount of popularity mixed with a particularly abhorrent form of sentimentality, and that this copious bathing —shall we say—springs from your antics with bouncing babies, and such like, the prescribing of cures for old ladies' rheumatics and for various diseases in horses and cows. I suggest to you, that since Catholicism rests on a classical, almost abstract love of God, rather than on the frothy swirl of stirred emotionalism that these popular heroics of yours are not, canonically speaking, the duties of a Catholic curate.

FATHER CORR (*blushing and abashed*). I—I was only tryin' to be kind, Canon.

CANON. *I* call it hunting after popular glory—an Irish clerical disease.

FATHER CORR (*rising with fire*). I'm a farmer's son, Canon, and I'm not ashamed of it.

CANON. I am not interested in your antecedents. I am interested instead in the behavior of my curates. You may be seated. (FATHER CORR *sits down, crushed.* FATHER KIRWAN *shifts uneasily in his seat, with one eye on the* CANON *who presently regards him with calm brutality.*)

CANON (*with a slight cough*). Father Kirwan, may I ask if it is the custom in *your* part of the country for the curate to don football-regalia, and—er—kick ball?

FATHER KIRWAN. Sure it's quite common down in Ballyedmins-town, Canon. The curate in me father's place is a very noted center-half.

CANON (*cruelly, leading him on, hand to ear*). I—I didn't quite catch that word, Father Kirwan. Center—what?

FATHER KIRWAN. Center-half, Canon. The fellow, Canon, that the team most depends on when the enemy makes an onslaught.

CANON (*suavely*). Incongruous as it may seem, Father Kirwan, it is *not* the custom here for the curate to be the fellow that—er—does what you say he does.

FATHER KIRWAN. But you misunderstand me, Canon. I strip and play with the men to entice them all into the Sacred Heart Con-fraternity. Sure, Canon, that's a grand motive for a grand end!

CANON. I see . . . And since when has the Sacred Heart of our Redeemer, that kings and emperors and queens like Violante and Don John of Austria and the great Charles V, and the soldier Ignatius, walked barefooted for the love of—since when has it become a sort of snap door chamber where dolts and boobs come to—to kick ball and find themselves tripped up on an altar step instead of a goal post?

FATHER KIRWAN (*aghast*). I—I never looked at it that way, Canon. Doesn't it justify itself if it brings people to the Sacred Heart?

CANON. Am I justified then, in staging amateur theatricals on the high altar to coax boobs along the Latin way of salvation? (*There are awesome ejaculations from the two* CURATES.)

FATHER KIRWAN AND FATHER CORR. God forbid, Canon! There is no comparison, surely!

CANON. To my thinking, there is a parallel. As a consequence, Brigid will be instructed that—er—football regalia is barred from the parochial clothes line.

FATHER KIRWAN. As you wish, Canon.

CANON. There is just one other matter. Is it the custom also in Bally—Bally—eskerstown, to sit down to lunch unshaven?

FATHER KIRWAN. I'm afraid it's not, Canon.

CANON. Interesting to compare the topographical similarities. It is *not* the custom in *this* part of the country either. (*With a sardonic smile and a slight bow, he waves a finger and rises. The* CURATES *rise also.* CANON *now rings bell with dignity.* BRIGID *enters to clear away.* FATHERS CORR *and* KIRWAN *are crossing to go out. The* CANON's *eye lights on the gaudy German oleograph. He almost explodes*) Wait, all! Stay! What—what incongruity is this? (*Points to picture. All look at it.*)

FATHER CORR. The Women's Confraternity presented it to Father Kirwan and meself yesterday. (BRIGID *is very perturbed.*)

CANON. And does it follow that I am to suffer it?

FATHER KIRWAN. But sure it's the—Sacred Heart, Canon.

CANON (*ironically*). I should never have believed it, Father Kirwan. I could have sworn it was the nightmarish conception of some uncouth vulgarian. (CURATES *regard each other nonplussed.* BRIGID *is all "at sea." She fears the* CANON *is ill.*)

BRIGID (*emotionally, her face in pain*). Please, Canon, are ye not well again?

CANON. I am very well, child.

BRIGID. But—it's the Sacred Heart, Canon.

CANON. No. (*Pause.*)

FATHER CORR. We thought, Canon, it would give a deeper religious tone to this room. The pictures are nearly all secular.

CANON. Secular? What word is that? (*Pointing*) There is a beautiful reproduction of Velasquez's "Philip IV Entering Lerida," and *there* another of Murillo's "Immaculate Conception," and *there* is Raphael's bitter "Dispute of the Sacrament." Could any picture in this room be called secular if we know anything of the might of the thing that has given us birth?

FATHER CORR. I was just followin' the pious custom, Canon, of havin' colored pictures of religious subjects near us to give a feeling of sanctity.

CANON. A feeling of sanctity from that! (*He points to the oleograph. A pause. When he speaks again, it is with great quietness*) I am a man, Fathers, who by study, travel and observation, has seen the decline and decay of the great classic ideals and the steady vulgarization of our life by that tributaried stream of barbarians who have taken all that was royal in conception, and given nothing but their vulgar deluge in return. Their achievement is the Nordic civilization, in which the passport to fame is financial scoundrelism, and the scholar of taste is ever the avowed "enemy of the people." They have vulgarized our reading, our music, our art, our very privacy. They have thrust books into the hands of herds who are forever misreading them; they have reduced us all to the lowest social class by teaching us how to get from excess the same emotionalism the classicist used to get from music and art; they have taken away our aesthetic sense and given us in exchange a rather spurious ethical sense, and as you can see here—(*He points to picture*) they deal with a whitewash brush in terms of the divine. Yet you stand aghast when I point it out to you—when I refuse to allow barbarians to impose on me their vulgar conception of Christ and His Saints. If, for a moment, I felt our Redeemer's heart was akin to that monstrosity on the wall, I should go back to Socrates, and be a pagan. (*The two* CURATES *look at him dumbfounded and mystified.* BRIGID *is very worried.*)

BRIGID. Please, Canon, you are not well again.

CANON (*gently*). I am very well, child. Go, Brigid, and have Dave Dooley remove this—this caricature from my room.

BRIGID. I'll get him from the garden, Canon. (*She goes, left.*)

FATHER CORR (*lamely*). It's this funny sort of way you have of looking at things, Canon. It's maybe you being abroad so much.

CANON (*dryly*). Maybe. . . .

FATHER CORR. I'm sorry you don't like it.

FATHER KIRWAN. Sure we'll just hang it up in the church hall, Canon, if you have no objection.

CANON (*tiredly, with veiled contempt*). Where you wish—but not here. Hang it at the crossroads where a people who at least had a classic past, can see their Nordic God, and forget about the Royal Christ of the Renaissance. (*He turns tiredly away. The* CURATES, *nonplussed, look at each other, and go out quietly.* BRIGID *re-enters. She looks at him, very worried.*)

BRIGID (*appeasingly*). Dave Dooley will take it away, Canon, when he comes back from his dinner.

CANON. Dinner! Must there be this delay, Brigid?

BRIGID. Just a little delay, Canon. He'll be here any minute now.

CANON. It is the way of things, Brigid. An important issue confused and involved by the dinner of a boob! You may go, Brigid!

BRIGID. Yis, Canon.

CANON (*softly*). But no, Brigid. Stay! It is good, child, you are here with me. You are not nauseous to me, Brigid, you are clean and simple. Oh, my child, this wilderness. . . . Knaves, fools, spirit-grocers, and their women . . . clerical football-kickers . . . palavering C.C.'s . . . and only one scoundrel. . . . Come here to me, Brigid.

BRIGID (*coming, almost in tears*). Yis, Canon.

CANON. Do you smell it?

BRIGID. What, Canon? (*She sniffs.*)

CANON. The vulgarity of it all.

BRIGID (*not understanding*). Will I open the window, Canon?

CANON. Yes . . . (*She goes and opens it*) . . . and the walls . . . But it will not matter . . .

BRIGID (*returning from window*). I'm terrible sorry, Canon, you're not well again. You're lonely.

CANON (*wearily*). As you say, Brigid, I'm lonely.

BRIGID. It'll be after your friend, Don Miguel, you'll be lonely.

CANON. Yes . . . my friend . . . Don Miguel Barzan y Perdito . . . (*As in a reverie*) I can see the stone tables in the sun where we used to sit . . . and the grave courtesy and grace of the

people and their walk—that heartbreak of these Northern crip-
ples . . . oh, these Northerners, morally afraid, mentally bereft,
physically fatigued and hoof-footed. They have touched us,
Brigid—we who should be great—and given us humps like a
dromedary. Go, Brigid.

BRIGID. Yis, Canon. (*She goes.*)

CANON. Come back, Brigid.

BRIGID. Yis, Canon.

CANON. Do you know what I'm saying to you?

BRIGID (*afraid*). N-n-no, Canon. (*She shrinks.*)

CANON. Then I can safely make you my friend. You are the
Canon's friend, Brigid.

BRIGID. Yis, Canon. Thank you, Canon. (*A pause. She looks at
him timidly*) Can—can I speak to you, Canon?

CANON. You can always speak to me, Brigid. It is your privilege.

BRIGID. Thank you, Canon. I—I— (*She looks at him and then
stops*) It's nothin', Canon.

CANON. Are you sure, Brigid?

BRIGID. Yis . . . no . . . I'll not tell you now, Canon. I'll—go,
Canon. (*She tries to go, but he holds her with his look.*)

CANON. You are hiding something from me, Brigid.

BRIGID. Yis, Canon.

CANON. Is it something I should know?

BRIGID (*pathetically*). Yis . . . No . . . I—I don't know . . .

CANON. If it's a matter of your soul, Brigid, I must know it.

BRIGID. Please, Canon, not—not now, I'll tell you when I'm—able. I—I don't want it taken away from—from me yet.

CANON (*rising*). This is a serious matter, Brigid. I insist. The Canon insists.

BRIGID (*hands to face*). N-no, Canon. I want it. I want it.

CANON. Did I say that I insist, Brigid?

BRIGID (*backing against wall*). Not for a while yet, Canon. Not —not now.

CANON (*coming to her*). I will dismiss you, Brigid, for this disobedience.

BRIGID (*hands to face, back to wall*). Yis, Canon.

CANON. I will cast you down—down!

BRIGID (*pathetically*). Yis, Canon.

CANON. You will be the Canon's friend no longer.

BRIGID. Yis, Canon.

CANON. You will tell me then?

BRIGID. N-no, Canon.

CANON. You will suffer all these things?

BRIGID. Yis, Canon.

CANON (*terribly*). The Canon commands it.

BRIGID. N-no, no, Canon. N-no. I—I couldn't! Not—now . . .

CANON. Put down those hands and look at me. (*She puts down her hands. Head is held up, but tears in her eyes. She is firmly against the wall like one at bay. An incongruous pride sits upon her. The* CANON *observes her strangely, as if deeply moved at a discovery.*)

CANON. You defy me!

BRIGID. N-no, Canon.

CANON. But you—refuse to tell me!

BRIGID (*pathetically but proudly*). Y-yis, Canon. (*Long pause. He stands watching her as if fascinated.*)

CANON (*as if to himself*). My God, my God, that—that is what we have come from . . . Pride . . . loyalty . . . a classic race . . . a royal conception . . . A thousand years ago, someone with that brow and face held up His head and died like a prince. . . . It was that . . . (*He stares at her, his face working visibly*) Come here to me, Brigid.

BRIGID (*as she comes slowly and looks humbly up at him*). Yis, Canon.

CANON. I shall ask you—nothing.

BRIGID. Th-thank you, Canon. (*She looks gratefully at him.*)

CANON (*slowly*). You are the Canon's friend, Brigid. Let it be written of you. Let it be written of both of us. (*They are looking at each other, the* CANON *with deep emotions stirred, and* BRIGID *with the tears glistening in her eyes, as the* CURTAIN FALLS.)

CURTAIN

ACT TWO

SCENE: *Following day.*

The CANON *is discovered reading the castigated novel,* I am Sir Oracle. *Now and again he smiles sardonically, and sips from a glass of wine.*

The picture of the Sacred Heart is removed. BRIGID *knocks and enters. Lays evening paper on table.*

BRIGID. That's the *Evenin' Herald,* Canon.

CANON. Very good, Brigid. (*He reads on.*)

BRIGID. And if you please, Canon, are ye not forgettin' about them two in the waitin' room?

CANON (*tolerantly*). Which two, Brigid? You are always a little vague lately.

BRIGID. The two I told you about, after dinner. Miss Cooney and her nephew with his new teacher's certificate. I told them you'd see them after you were done readin' the Bishop's Pastoral.

CANON (*remembering*). Of course, of course, Brigid. I remember now. I distinctly remember saying to you, "Brigid, I'll see them presently."

BRIGID. That's just what you said, Canon.

CANON. To be sure it was. Tell them, Brigid—tell them to come back tomorrow.

BRIGID. But they've spent the whole day between waitin' on you here, Canon, and follyin' ye about the streets.

CANON. But my dear child, they like doing that. It is a corporate part of our national life. Tell them, Brigid, that the Canon— no, no—say, "His Reverence presents his compliments to Miss Cooney and his heartiest congratulations to Francis Xavier—"

BRIGID. Francis Ignatius, Canon.

CANON. Thank you, Brigid. Let us have accuracy at all costs in these important matters. But be careful of the exact wording. Wording, Brigid, is an art. (*Repeating*) "His Reverence presents his compliments." (*He reads on.*)

BRIGID. Yis, Canon, but sure they're in and out o' the kitchen every minute pesterin' me. Is the Canon here? Is the Canon there? Where is the Canon? What hat has he on? Sure you could get rid of them in a minute, Canon, with a grand word and a clap on the back.

CANON (*rising*). Excellent, Brigid. An answer and a suggestion at once plausible and philosophic. The Canon, Brigid—the Canon shall do exactly as you say.

BRIGID. Will I show them in then, Canon?

CANON. By all means, Brigid. And Brigid, if by any ill chance, they weary me beyond their time— (*He raises a finger meaningly.*)

BRIGID. Sure, you needn't tell me, Canon. (*She goes.* CANON *lays down the book resignedly, and mutters in Latin.* BRIGID *re-enters followed by* MISS JEMIMA COONEY *and her nephew* FRANCIS O'CONNOR. FRANCIS *is a sheepish, obsequious youth, his whole being in*

*the grip of an inferiority complex. He is awkward and without
confidence.* JEMIMA *is a thin, gaunt spinster, secretly vicious but
very virtuous before the* CANON. *The storm of "Yis, Canons" and
"No, Canons" should be played very rapidly*) This is them,
Canon. (*She goes.* JEMIMA *and* FRANCIS *advance awkwardly ges-
ticulating and very obsequious. The* CANON *rises with calm dignity, embraces his nose with a silk handkerchief, and gives them
a curt bow, tempered with a quite unreadable smile.*)

JEMIMA. Sure, Lord, Canon, are we disturbin' ye?

FRANCIS. Sure, now, Canon, anny time would do!

JEMIMA. Sure, now, Canon, are ye after leavin' off sayin' your
office for us?

FRANCIS. Sure, Lord, Canon, we could have come back anny
time at all.

JEMIMA. Sure, Heavens, Canon, Francis is that up in the air
about his new certificate!

FRANCIS. Sure, Canon, you'll be thinkin' me a nuisance!

CANON (*in a lull, dignified*). You may be seated. (*Silence while
they sit.* CANON *heroically contains himself, again embraces his
nose, and seats himself opposite them. With scoundrel grace*)
And now, Miss Cooney, I hope I see you well. And you too,
Francis, none the less, mark! In short, I hope I see you *both*
well. (*He smiles sardonically.*)

JEMIMA. Sure, Lord, Canon, I'm lovely now. Sure I never felt
so well since I came home from the hospital.

FRANCIS. And I'm like a two-year-old, Canon, ready to attack
me work.

CANON (*with bow*). Excellent. I assure you this news is a *great* satisfaction to me.

JEMIMA (*exploding*). Sure, you're too good, Canon. Run, Francis now, and show His Reverence your teacher's certificate.

FRANCIS (*opening scroll, and going awkwardly to* CANON). I just got it from the college yisterday mornin', Canon.

CANON (*viewing the certificate without touching it*). Creditable, Francis. Very creditable. I see in this the seal of—of scholarship, and the beginning of attainment. I congratulate you, Francis. (JEMIMA *beams*.)

FRANCIS (*explosively*). Canon, will you please do all you can for me about the school?

JEMIMA (*irascibly*). Francis, will you mind your manners now? Sure don't you know you don't need to ask the Canon that? (*To the* CANON, *apologetically*) Sure he—he's over-exuberant, Canon.

CANON (*with bow to* JEMIMA). As your Aunt Jemima so wisely observes, Francis, your request is superfluous, since I *must* do my best for you. Is it not written, Francis, in your Penny Catechism that we must all of us come to the aid of each other?

JEMIMA. There now, Francis.

FRANCIS (*backing awkwardly to seat*). Sure, I'm a—a—an ass, Canon.

CANON. Not a bit, Francis. *Quandoque bonus dormitat Homerus.*

JEMIMA (*impulsively running to the* CANON *with photograph of* FRANCIS). Look, Canon. A wee surprise. I got it taken in Dublin before we left, in a grand place in Talbot Street. (*Pointing*)

That's Francis's certificate in his hand, and the wee book in his waistcoat pocket is the prayer book you gave him yourself for servin' Mass for eight years.

CANON (*benignly regarding photograph as if it were a new uncategoried animal*). Very good! Uncommonly good! And very farseeing of you, Miss Cooney, to—to have Francis's scholarly achievement—er—permanently recorded.

JEMIMA (*driveling*). Wouldn't his ma, God rest her, be proud of him there, Canon.

FRANCIS (*blushing and smirking*). Sure, I'm nothin' at all, Canon.

CANON (*with preliminary grave bow to* JEMIMA). Your mother, Francis, was a good woman. (*With great gravity*) In fact, a very good woman.

FRANCIS. Thank ye, Canon.

CANON (*gravely*). In fact, Francis, in the light of my home and foreign experience, I might even say—an excellent woman.

JEMIMA. There now is news for you, Francis!

FRANCIS. It's awful kind of you to say the like of that, Canon.

CANON (*handing back photograph to* JEMIMA). Very creditable, Miss Cooney. And now, Francis, you must be a little patient. We must *all* be a little patient. Your Aunt Jemima with her invaluable experience of life, as we live it, and of the—the idiosyncrasies of our checkered existence, will have impressed *that* upon you, I feel sure.

JEMIMA. Sure, Lord, Canon, isn't it all now in the will o' God!

CANON (*bowing delightfully*). Excellent, Miss Cooney. Your Aunt Jemima, Francis, has just made a very wise observation. It is—if I may repeat, Miss Cooney?—in the will of God. Did I say, Francis, that your mother was a good woman?

FRANCIS. You did, indeed, Canon. A very good woman, you said.

CANON. So I did, Francis. I distinctly remember the remark now. I want to add to it, Francis. (*With great gravity*) I want to observe that your Aunt Jemima is a woman, to my knowledge, of incomparable wisdom, piety and virtue.

JEMIMA (*head down, blushing*). Sure, I'm not worth that, Canon.

FRANCIS. Indeed, she's the best in the world, Canon. Sure, I'd be nothin' only for *her*.

CANON. As you say, Francis, you might be nothing but for *her*. And look what you are! *Hoc opus! hic labor est!* (CANON *smiles delightfully*.)

FRANCIS (*blushing and confused*). Yis, Canon, indeed yis. I owe her everythin'.

JEMIMA. You didn't happen to see, Canon, the piece in the *Dundalk Sentinel* about him? Sure, the editor was a great college friend of Francis's before he failed for the teachin' and fell back on bein' an editor.

CANON. I regret, Miss Cooney, I missed it. I must inquire from Father Corr. I believe *he* buys the—the *Dundalk Semaphore*.

FRANCIS. *Sentinel*, Canon.

CANON. *Sentinel,* Francis. *Sentinel,* to be sure. Accuracy, Francis, accuracy always.

BRIGID (*entering*). If you please, Canon, there's a gentleman waitin' with a soft hat and an umbrella.

CANON. Ah, yes, Brigid. Presently, my child, presently. Francis and his aunt are just going. (*They take the tip and rise to go.* CANON *claps* FRANCIS *on back*) And now, Francis, I hope to have excellent news for you shortly. I can say nothing further now. The tongues of none of us are free. But keep within easy call, and employ your waiting time properly.

JEMIMA. Indeed, Canon, he'll spend his time of waitin' your command in makin' a novena.

FRANCIS (*outrageously*). Sure, Canon, *orare est vigilare.*

JEMIMA. Well, will you listen to that, Canon. And him only a child.

CANON (*beaming*). Excellent, Francis. I can see you are deeply versed in the profundities of the classics.

JEMIMA. Come on now, Francis, we're keepin' the Canon. And he'll pray for you, Canon. We'll both pray for you.

CANON (*bowing repeatedly as they go out*). Excellent. . . . (*They go. He sinks wearily into chair.* BRIGID *comes in quickly and opens up window.*)

BRIGID. I knew you'd want the window open, Canon.

CANON. You are a very understanding child, Brigid. The law of Nature's compensation is not after all a myth. (*He looks up at her as she stands solicitously watching him*) Brigid, promise me you'll never leave me.

BRIGID (*shrinking*). I—I couldn't do that, Canon.

CANON (*startled*). What? . . . What is this, Brigid? Are you not happy here?

BRIGID. Oh, yis, Canon. It's not that. I'm always happy.

CANON. Well? . . .

BRIGID. I might want to go away in a little while, Canon.

CANON. For what purpose, Brigid?

BRIGID. I—I don't know how to say it, Canon . . . It's the way I feel.

CANON. You are not well, child. You must take a good rest.

BRIGID. It's not that, Canon.

CANON. Nonsense! It *must* be that. Listen, Brigid. When I die, you will get every penny I have. There now! There's a secret out. Don't breathe it!

BRIGID. But Canon, it's not money I'll be wantin' where I—I think I'm goin'.

CANON. What talk is this? Where are you going?

BRIGID (*falteringly*). Please, Canon, I want to be a nun.

CANON (*flabbergasted*). Eh? You—you want to be a nun, eh? My God, am I not sufficiently stocked with boobs that *you*, Brigid, *you* must add the final straw.

BRIGID. You're vexed with me, Canon.

CANON. Displeased, Brigid. . . . Displeased that you would go and leave me here alone. And you my friend! You the—the Canon's friend.

BRIGID. It's not just *you*, Canon, but everythin' I'd be leavin'.

CANON (*clapping her affectionately*). Brigid, you have been doing too much lately, and you are overwrought. Excess in anything is bad, Brigid—in work, in play, in religion—it is not—classical. I am going to send you away for a holiday. And you must have a new hat too—a new hat with—with a feather in it. There now!

BRIGID (*amused*). But sure, Canon, feathers is not worn anywhere now.

CANON. Do you tell me that, Brigid? That—that—that's astonishing—astonishing, Brigid.

BRIGID. It's a wee white dog at the side they have now and a nose veil.

CANON (*gravely*). A—a white dog and a nose veil, Brigid? I—I must make a careful note of that, and you must certainly have them both. And it must be size six or seven or whatever you want.

BRIGID. Sure, Canon, with them shallow crowns that's out now, you can't depend on sizes. I'd need a fit-on.

CANON (*gravely*). You'd need a fit-on, Brigid. So you would. These shallow—shallow crowns are certainly a bit of a problem. We'll arrange that too.

BRIGID. Thank you, Canon.

CANON. There now, you've forgotten already. When you get your holiday you will be again classically simple and quiescent. (*Pause*) Brigid, do you know where we keep the Baptismal Registers in the Cloak Room?

BRIGID. Yis, Cannon. In the cupboard behind the door.

CANON. Go, Brigid, and bring me the Register for the year nineteen—nineteen and eight.

BRIGID. Yis, Canon. Nineteen and eight. (*She goes.* CANON
*lifts the book again, and looks at the page he left open. He smiles
sardonically. He then begins to read aloud. It is near the end
of the book.*)

CANON (*reading*). "The Canon lay dying. The mists came white
and wraithlike from the bogs to tell him so . . ." (*Puts down
book*) Not a bit. On the contrary, the Canon feels well—feels
in fact very well. (*As* BRIGID *comes in and hands him Register*)
It may interest you to know, Brigid, that the Canon feels—
excellently. (*He smiles sardonically.*)

BRIGID. Sure, thanks be to God, Canon.

CANON (*as he opens Register*). Amen, Brigid, amen. . . . Let
me see now. (*Turns pages rapidly*) Mallin, Melling, Nagle,
Nolan, O'Brien, O'Connell, O'Kelly . . . ah, here we are—
O'Flingsley. (*He moves his finger along a line of data*) June
8th, 1908, Dermot Francis O'Flingsley.

BRIGID (*looking*). Is that the Master's birthday, Canon?

CANON. That's it, Brigid. (*Gleefully as he reads on*) His father's
name was Francis Eugene O'Flingsley. Mark the princely name,
Eugene. Ah, and his mother bore the—storied name of Gibney.
Could you credit that now? . . . Incomprehensible in fact. . . .
Let me introduce you, Brigid, to Mr. Eugene Gibney—er—
author, amateur theologian, Catholic reformer, public moralist,
student of Northern apologetics, erstwhile schoolmaster, ex-
peasant and—gentleman.

BRIGID (*sensing fear*). What does that mean, Canon?

CANON. To you, Brigid, it shall mean—*nothing*. Put that Register back, Brigid, and not a word to any one. (*As she goes*) Did I say a *word*, Brigid?

BRIGID. Yis, Canon.

CANON (*gravely*). I meant a syllable, Brigid.

BRIGID. Sure, I won't even breathe, Canon.

CANON. Excellent, Brigid.

BRIGID (*turning as she crosses with Register*). Please, Canon, is there anythin' wrong with the Master?

CANON. You're *breathing*, Brigid.

BRIGID. Yis, Canon. . . . No, Canon. . . . (*She crosses disconsolately.*)

CANON. And Brigid. Send Dave Dooley down to the school to tell Mr. O'Flingsley that I wish to see him in the morning.

BRIGID (*almost in tears*). Y-yis, Canon. (*She looks at him for a moment, as if wishing to speak, then goes off sadly with Register.* FATHER CORR *and* FATHER KIRWAN *enter from the window, carrying their hats.*)

FATHER CORR. Father Kirwan and meself, Canon, would like a word with you, if you're not busy.

CANON. I *am* busy.

FATHER CORR. It's about a meeting we've just had of the Confraternity over that scurrilous book. A—a resolution was passed, Canon.

FATHER KIRWAN. Unanimously, Canon.

CANON. Well, what of it? It's a national pastime, isn't it?

FATHER KIRWAN. The members of the Football Club, Canon, are very excited. (*Worriedly*) *They're* the worst. They're gettin' out of hand.

CANON. No doubt, it's the warm weather, Father Kirwan. (*He crosses*) And I note you haven't as yet found time, even between resolutions, to shave. (CANON *goes out slowly.* CURATES *look after him perplexed.*)

FATHER CORR. For Heaven's sake, can you not go and shave and not be makin' things harder for us?

FATHER KIRWAN. Ach, can a man not get wearin' his own hair if he wants to! Sure he's so contrary if I shaved every day, he'd grumble because I hadn't a beard like Don-the-Divil's-Father! Is he an Irishman at all?

FATHER CORR. His father was Irish. It's his mother was the Spaniard. They met in Brussels.

FATHER KIRWAN. It's a pity she didn't stay at home instead of gallivantin' about the continent. Sure you'd think he hadn't a drop of Irish Ireland blood in his veins. I'll bet me boots he'll side with that book agin the Confraternity and the Football Club.

FATHER CORR. With a book like that! My God, at least he's a priest.

FATHER KIRWAN. Did you see the schoolmaster?

FATHER CORR. I did, and he was worth seein'. He's all for us burnin' the book in public, and he thinks that the Canon is the proper one to do the actual casting into the flames.

FATHER KIRWAN (*noticing open book*). Great Scott! Will you look at what's here!

FATHER CORR (*with a start*). The book!

FATHER KIRWAN. It's open at the last chapter where the P.P. dies miserably. He must have been readin' it.

FATHER CORR (*with passionate aversion*). I loathe the thing. It's accursed and vile. (*He flings it venomously on the floor.*)

FATHER KIRWAN ("*dribbling*" *with the book with both feet*). He was certainly no lover of clean sport and the team spirit. (*Still dribbling*) Suppose now yon door was the net. Wait till you see a grand penalty from the touch line. (*He kicks with judgment, and it is hurled against the doorway just as the* CANON *re-enters. He suddenly sees the* CANON *and sinks visibly into himself.* FATHER CORR *is very confused. The* CANON *regards them with extreme frigidity. A definite pause.*)

CANON (*tensely*). You may both be seated. (*They obey silently. With cold hauteur*) My property, Father Corr.

FATHER CORR (*defiantly*). I—I refuse to touch it. It's—vile.

CANON. My property, Father Corr. (FATHER CORR *is defiant for a definite moment, then emotionally lifts the book and hands it to* CANON. *He then reseats himself. The* CANON *lays the mutilated book on table*) I suppose I am to regard this outbreak of hooliganism in my study, as a typical spasm of—Catholic action.

FATHER CORR (*flashing out*). Canon, that book is a disgrace and a shame. The Irish Press in Dublin says it's an insult to the Catholic nation.

CANON (*courteously*). Didn't catch that word, Father Corr. (*Hand to ear*) The Irish what?

FATHER CORR. The Irish Press, Canon.

CANON. Never heard of it. (*He pours out a small glass of golden-colored wine at sideboard, and examines it.*)

FATHER KIRWAN. Sure, the *Ballyedminstown Courier* quotes whole columns from it every Saturday, Canon.

CANON (*sipping wine*). In that case, Father Kirwan, I must concede it has a definite claim to our attention.

BRIGID (*entering*). If you please, Canon, there's four o' the parishioners here wearin' badges, and they'd like a talk with you.

FATHER CORR. I'd like very much, Canon, if you'd receive them. They're a deputation.

FATHER KIRWAN. Sure the whole country's takin' action, Canon.

CANON. Mm . . . I am presumably to agree to a—a descent into Lutheranism and a sort of Kirk Session. Say, Brigid, the Canon says No.

BRIGID (*repeating*). The Canon says No. (*She makes to go.*)

FATHER CORR. Sure, after all if it was only for appearances' sake.

BRIGID. Canon, would you not just give another clap on the back and a grand word?

CANON. What *are* we come to? (*Pause*) Very well then, very well, let the—the neo-theologians come in, but let it be at their peril. I shall ring, Brigid.

BRIGID. Yis, Canon. I'll keep them in the waitin' room. (*She goes.*)

CANON. Who are these people, Father Corr?

FATHER CORR. They're all strong Confraternity and football members, Canon. There's Miss Cooney and her nephew Francis—

CANON. Is *he* here? Who are the other two?

FATHER KIRWAN. Martin Mullahone, Canon, the referee of our football team, that has the public house and farm on the Dublin Road, and his wife, Rosey Violet.

CANON. His wife who?

FATHER KIRWAN. He calls her Rosey Violet, Canon.

CANON. I think I recall her, but if my recollection is correct, she was neither rosey nor a violet. (*He rings the bell*) Be seated, Fathers, and offer no comments until these people are gone. (FATHER CORR *and* FATHER KIRWAN *sit at either end of the empty chairs for the deputation. The* CANON *sits magisterially at the large writing desk.* BRIGID *enters with the deputation behind her.* MISS COONEY *and* FRANCIS O'CONNOR *are as obsequious as usual.* MARTIN MULLAHONE, *a large awkward man, with a large stomach and a red nose, is followed by his wife who is typical in dress and voice of the "social status" aspirants in rural Ireland.*)

BRIGID. This is them, Canon.

CANON (*curtly*). Good afternoon, all. You may be seated. (BRIGID *goes. All sit in chairs opposite the* CANON. *They smirk and bow to the* CANON *and look as virtuous as possible. The* CANON's *sardonic eye surveys them pitilessly. They wilt and shift uneasily. His eyes on* MARTIN) Are you the man, Martin Mullahone?

MARTIN. I—I am then, Canon.

ROSEY VIOLET (*chipping in sweetly*). And I'm his wife, Canon.

CANON. Martin Mullahone, where are your hands? (MARTIN *whips them violently out of his pockets.*)

MARTIN. Sure, I—I never thought, Canon. Sure, God's—

ROSEY VIOLET. Sure, I'm always tellin' him, Canon.

CANON. Sit erect and don't loll or sag. Decorum and personal dignity are not by any means the least of the Christian virtues. (*All sit fearfully erect*) And now to the point. You have come— or should I say you have taken it upon yourselves to come— about a certain book.

MARTIN (*explosively*). Sure, it's a—a terror, Canon. A—a terror and a fright to the world, Canon.

CANON (*with suave irony*). Having learned from your husband, Mrs. Mullahone, that this book is a—a terror and a fright—two quite incomprehensible epithets to me—do you wish to—er— supplement his observation?

ROSEY VIOLET. If you please, Canon, I agree with what Father Kirwan said when he thumped the table at the meetin', that no clean sportin' man with the team spirit in him could write such a book. (FATHER KIRWAN *is confused.*)

CANON (*ironic, with side glance at* FATHER KIRWAN). An *excellent* observation, Mrs. Mullahone.

ROSEY VIOLET. Sure, if you please, Canon, me eldest son, Dan, is the fullback in Father Kirwan's team.

CANON (*cruelly*). Didn't catch that word, Mrs. Mullahone. (*Hand to ear*) The—the what? (FATHER KIRWAN *is very confused.*)

ROSEY VIOLET. The fullback, Canon.

CANON. Ah! of course. The—the fullback. I must ask Father Kirwan for a glossary of these terms. (*Side glance at* FATHER KIRWAN) And you, Miss Cooney, have *you* any observation?

JEMIMA. Sure, Canon, I only came because Father Corr told me it was me duty to God and Ireland. (*Grasping* FRANCIS's *arm*) Say it in Irish for the Canon, Francis. Go on now! (FATHER CORR *is confused.*)

FRANCIS (*rising awkwardly*). *Do cum gloire De, agus onora na h-Eireann.*

CANON (*hand to ear*). Didn't catch that, Francis. Cum—cum what?

FRANCIS (*unconscious of cruelty*). *Do cum gloire De, agus onora na h-Eireann.*

CANON (*scoundrelishly*). Excellent, Francis. Excellent! You may be seated. Any other observation, Miss Cooney?

JEMIMA. Sure, I'll just listen now to you, and learn, Canon. Isn't that me duty?

CANON. Very creditable, Miss Cooney. An attitude at once wise, womanly and prudent. And you, Francis?

JEMIMA (*hurriedly*). He'll just do the same as meself, Canon. Not a word now, Francis, before His Reverence.

FRANCIS. Sure, it's for *you* to say, Canon.

CANON. Commendable, Francis. You have a good—a very good counselor.

ROSEY VIOLET (*not to be outdone*). Sure, if you please, Canon, me brother, Father Jamsie, says it was no one but the divil guided the hand that wrote that book.

CANON (*startled*). Your who—the what? Speak up, Mrs. Mulla-hone.

ROSEY VIOLET (*exuberantly*). Why, me brother, Father Jamsie, Canon, that's up in Dunaree with Father Crone. Sure, Canon, it was Father Jamsie that anointed your sister, Thomasina's mother, when she near died and didn't, last Christmas.

CANON (*shaking head*). Never heard of him.

ROSEY VIOLET (*sentimentally*). Ah, sure poor wee Father Jamsie, Canon. Sure, God help him.

CANON. What's the matter with him?

ROSEY VIOLET (*surprised*). Sure, nothin' at all, Canon. Sure, Lord, what would be the matter with him?

CANON (*with an effort*). Very well then.

ROSEY VIOLET. Sure, he's happy and lovely in Dunaree, Canon.

CANON (*heroically*). Very well then.

MARTIN (*blunderingly interposing*). Sure, will you not be sick-enin' the Canon, bargin' in every minute about Father Jamsie because he's your brother.

ROSEY VIOLET (*bursting into tears*). If you please, Canon, Mar-tin's always insultin' and belittlin' me in public.

CANON (*with great gravity, eyeing* MARTIN *who quails and shifts about*). Martin Mullahone, what *grave* charge is this I hear as to your conduct and public morals?

MARTIN. Sure—sure, Canon, you'd think by the talk of her mornin' and night that he was a Canon like yourself, and him with the—the cloth on him only a month.

ROSEY VIOLET (*crying*). Me heart's broke with him, Canon.

CANON. You are a good woman, Mrs. Mullahone, and you have pleased me considerably.

ROSEY VIOLET. Sure, everyone loves me, Canon.

CANON. As for you, Martin Mullahone, I am gravely incensed (MARTIN *squirms*) and not a little pained.

ROSEY VIOLET. Oh, thank you, Canon. Martin badly needed that talkin' to.

CANON. Very well then. We digress. How many of you have read this book? (*Negative murmurs and shaking of heads.*)

ROSEY VIOLET. Sure, what Catholic could read a book like that, Canon?

CANON. I take it then that none of you has read this book?

ALL (*shaking heads, murmurs*). Not a one, Canon.

CANON. And you come here to condemn a book you have not read! What nonsense is this? (*Taps desk*) Preposterous and ridiculous! The deputation is dismissed. (*The* CANON *is just rising when* FATHER CORR *jumps up.*)

FATHER CORR. If I may say a word, Canon—

CANON. Be seated, Father Corr. (FATHER CORR *sits.*)

FRANCIS (*rising*). If you please, Canon—

JEMIMA (*seizing him and flinging him down*). That's enough, you pup! Sit down!

CANON (*sitting back, eyeing* FRANCIS, *benignly*) We shall allow him the privilege on this occasion, Miss Cooney. Proceed, Francis.

FRANCIS (*awkwardly*). I was just goin' to say, Canon, that is, as a—a certified teacher, I—I read the book—judiciously.

CANON (*hand to ear, cruelly luring him on*). What—what word was that, Francis?

FRANCIS. Judiciously, Canon.

CANON. Ah! Enlarge upon that, Francis. It is a little vague.

FRANCIS. Well, Canon, if I—I felt a part was gettin' bad, I skipped.

CANON. You—you skipped, Francis. (*He smiles.*)

ROSEY VIOLET (*interposing*). I done that too, Canon.

JEMIMA. If you please, Canon, when I saw that Francis was determined to—to study it, I felt it me duty to read it before him and turn down some of the pages.

CANON (*face masklike*). I understand—exactly. And you, Martin Mullahone?

MARTIN (*hoarsely*). I can't read, Canon. It's me wife is the scholar in our family.

ROSEY VIOLET (*interposing, gushingly*). I was three years in the convent, Canon, before Martin won me.

MARTIN (*hoarsely*). It was the little fella that has the bike shop, Canon—wee Joey Hardy, that was readin' out bits of it at the counter on Friday, and I—I couldn't help hearin' them, Canon. Out—outrageous and terrible, Canon! A fright to the world!

CANON (*rounding on them*). I am to take it then that four of my parishioners, deliberately—I might even say, wantonly—and without right or lawful authority from me either in person or by proxy, committed themselves to the reading of a book gravely alleged to be pernicious, immoral and—subversive. (*He sizes up the four, severely*) Of these, one is the sister of a priest (ROSEY VIOLET *sobs*) Another presumptuously aspires to the position of teacher of the young (JEMIMA *gives* FRANCIS *a vicious elbow dig in the ribs*), a third is or should be a father and a husband (MARTIN *sags visibly*), and a fourth—(JEMIMA *bows her head and sniffs*)—I can find no words to castigate the curiosity that tempted the fourth to this grave indiscretion. (*He rings the bell*) I shall deliver my directions to the two Fathers here who will communicate them to you for your unswerving acceptance. You will leave immediately. I shall contemplate whether it is humanly possible to pardon any or all of you. (CANON *rises, as* BRIGID *appears. The deputation also rises. The* CANON *waves. They go out in confusion following* BRIGID. *The two* CURATES *turn nervously to the* CANON. *Curtly*) Be seated. (*They sit.* CANON *resumes his seat*) I may take it, I suppose, that you two have also presumed to read this book.

FATHER CORR. I frankly considered it my duty, Canon.

FATHER KIRWAN. So did I, Canon.

CANON. Bad theology, Fathers, bad theology. And equally bad theology of course to have any—er—unofficial conflagrations on the public street without my express approval. (*Pause*) The author of this book which I have read, Fathers, is obviously a very young man. I fear his education cannot be more—adequate than that of the average young man of the present, either lay or—er—clerical. (*He coughs*) The theme I take to mean that Ireland has dangerously materialized the outlook of the Church, and that its profound spiritual essence has been stolen by a

small band of learned men whom it does not even recognize. A
dangerous theme, Fathers, I grant you.

FATHER CORR (*blazing out*). A blasphemous lie on Catholic Ireland!

CANON (*calmly*). A theme, Fathers, that in the hands of an abler
controversialist with a claim to scholarship or a classic status,
might possibly cause alarm amongst us, especially when we have
presently no known Irish Catholic scholar with that delicacy
of touch, subtlety of culture and profundity of classical knowledge to defend and even rescue the Church intellectually. Coming in contact with such an immaturity as this the insufficiently
scholared mind, fed mostly on sentimentalisms in the form of
learning, is often shocked, and—vulgarly agitated. Violent emotionalism results, followed by a quite ridiculous hubbub, tawdry
heroics, even bigoted physical violence under holy names, and
generally a quite ludicrous procedure that the classic dignity
of the mind of the Church recoils from. As I have no desire,
Fathers, to make a presumptuous young man bogusly important
in an age that is itself bogusly important, or to condone a procedure too undignified to be Catholic, I therefore decree that no
action of any sort be taken in the case of this book, except such
action as I, in my official capacity, shall think fit to perform.
(*Pause*) That, I think, Fathers, will be all.

FATHER CORR (*livid*). Are we then actually to take it that our
efforts to deal with this disgraceful libel are banned?

CANON. You are!

FATHER KIRWAN (*touching* FATHER CORR, *as he is about to burst
out*). That's enough now. You'll only be sayin' things you'll be
sorry for.

FATHER CORR (*in a temper*). I'll say what I like.

FATHER KIRWAN. Now, can't you see that's wild talk?

FATHER CORR (*cooling*). I suppose it is. But he's never done belittlin' and humblin' me. But I'll try not to mind. It's in my nature to be humble.

CANON. Inoculated would be a better word. Inoculated with the prevalent deluge of sentimentalism.

FATHER CORR. I'm afraid, Canon, there's nothin' for me to do but ask the Bishop for a shift and to give my reasons.

CANON. And in spite of your impertinences, Father, I shall be prepared to give his Grace an—adequate report on your work. (FATHER CORR *abruptly leaves the room, left. The* CANON *looks after him quietly and then turns to* FATHER KIRWAN) And you, Father Kirwan? Are you also going to the Bishop?

FATHER KIRWAN (*confused, and crossing*). I'm goin' for a—for a shave, Canon.

CANON. Dear me! We—progress! (FATHER KIRWAN *goes awkwardly, left. The* CANON *turns away tiredly, goes to the leaded bookcase, unlocks it and extracts a volume. He settles with it in an armchair. But the dusk is falling fast, and in a moment he looks up towards the lamp. He reaches for the bell, and is about to shake it when, with a cry,* BRIGID *runs in.*)

BRIGID. Canon! Canon! (*He rises rapidly and goes to her. She tries to recover and looks up at him pathetically.*)

CANON. What on earth is the matter, child?

BRIGID (*breathing hard, but trying to recover*). It s nothin', Canon, nothin' at all. I—I'm all right now.

CANON. Did something frighten you?

BRIGID. Y-yis, Canon. But it's nothin'.

CANON. You should have the lamp lighted in there at this time. There, you are tired and overwrought.

BRIGID. Canon, may I—ask you somethin'?

CANON. Certainly, Brigid.

BRIGID. Do you—do you love St. Brigid?

CANON (*looking at her uncertainly*). Why, of course I do, child. Sure we *all* love St. Brigid.

BRIGID (*happy*). Yes . . . I'm glad you do. She'll be pleased.

CANON (*solicitously*). Brigid, you are ill. You are not well.

BRIGID. Yis, Canon, I'm well.

CANON. I'm afraid not, child.

BRIGID. It's just, Canon, that I—I still want to be a nun.

CANON. There now! I *knew* you weren't well.

BRIGID (*pleadingly*). But if I could just be a nun, Canon.

CANON. Don't you know, Brigid, that nuns must be very, very strong and brave? They must be cruel to themselves and they must give all.

BRIGID (*tensely*). I will give all, Canon. I will! I promised her.

CANON. What nonsense is this? Promised whom, child?

BRIGID (*her eyes aglow*). St. Brigid, Canon. I—I was dryin' the cups in the kitchen when she touched me on the shoulder and says she, "You're holdin' the dish-towel wrong, Brigid." And when I held it right, she whispered to me, "Ask him if he loves me more than the rest." (*The* CANON *stares at her, walks irascibly away, and then returns to her, collected.*)

CANON (*gravely*). Brigid, you are, I fear, stubborn, disobedient, and even defiant, and—I am seriously annoyed and displeased with you.

BRIGID (*simply*). I—I knew you would, Canon.

CANON. If you were a boob, Brigid, or a footling trifler, I should expel you from my presence. But you are my friend, and I try to bear with you.

BRIGID (*sadly*). Yis, Canon.

CANON. I have borne all day with fools, Brigid, knowing that at the end you would come to me, and ask my wants and find no fault in me. There now. You see how it is with me.

BRIGID. Yis, Canon. (*Sadly*) I'm a wretch and a villain.

CANON. On the contrary, child, you are a good girl, and you have wisdom and grace. God, Brigid, is not *always* pleased with girls who want to be nuns. Sometimes He expects them to remain at their posts as His soldiers.

BRIGID (*pathetically persistent*). If only I could just be a nun instead of a soldier! Soldiers make so much noise.

CANON. Brigid, I am afraid your nerves are all shaken. You must go to bed now and on Friday I shall send you to Bray to a friend of mine for a holiday. Miss Cooney will take your place for a few weeks. You must get plenty of sleep and rest. Rest to the body, Brigid, is like prayer to the soul. And you will then forget these imaginings of yours.

BRIGID. But in bed, how can I forget, if her face is there in the curtains and the mark on her cheek where she struck the loveliness out of her face.

CANON (*irascibly*). Now, now, now! I am trying not to be angry. There is no historical authority for that at all. The Church in its wisdom does not confirm it. It is probably just a myth. A myth, Brigid. Doesn't that show you!

BRIGID (*pathetically*). What is a myth, Canon?

CANON. A legend, child. (*Pause.*)

BRIGID (*venturing*). And what is a—a legend, Canon?

CANON. Brigid, this is very trying! An old tale, that may or may not be true.

BRIGID. Then—it *could* be true, Canon?

CANON. Now which of us knows best about these things, Brigid?

BRIGID. You, Canon.

CANON. Well now, I say this thing you foolishly think you see is not—not of God. Dismiss it!

BRIGID (*in pain, her head in her hands*). Canon! . . . oh, Canon! . . . how—how could you be sayin' that?

CANON (*sympathetically*). There, there! God tempts most those whom He loves best. You should be proud. The soul's great battles are not fought by common boobs. The great Ignatius was tempted like this, and so were Theresa and Augustine and Dominic, but they were not deceived. They rose up and conquered the tempter. So must you conquer this, Brigid.

BRIGID (*tearfully*). But I—I love her so much. She is so lovely and beautiful.

CANON. Not more beautiful, Brigid, than the demon that twisted himself round the crucifix St. Ignatius prayed before. He had to lie on his face to save himself. You too, Brigid, must turn away from this thing you think you see. You must be wise. Wise, Brigid, and brave. Promise me, Brigid.

BRIGID (*sobbing*). I want to die, Canon. . . . I want to—to die. . . .

CANON (*softly*). Come now, Brigid. That is not being brave! That is being merely heroic, like these modern vulgarians. Say, Brigid, "I want to live and conquer." (*She is silent*) Say it, Brigid. Be proud like a soldier and say it.

BRIGID (*sadly*). I want to live and—conquer. . . .

CANON (*clapping her on back*). Ah, Brigid, excellent! Go now, Brigid, to bed and sleep. And none of these dreams, remember, or foolishness. To sleep is safe, to dream is dangerous. I shall go out and send Dave Dooley for Miss Cooney to take your place.

BRIGID (*emotionally*). Yis, Canon. (*He crosses to window, opens it and passes out, into the garden.*)

CANON'S VOICE (*without*). Dooley! Are you there! Come here, Dooley! (BRIGID'S *emotional stress now visibly shakes her, as she stands undecided and forlorn in the deepening shadows. She sobs pathetically, her head down, like a child. She gives the impression of having lost someone very beloved. She lifts her head suddenly, and stares stealthily over her own shoulders at the slightly swaying curtains, that reach to the ground. Her body shudders, and she covers her face with her hands.*)

BRIGID (*sobbing*). I'm not to look at you. . . . I—I promised
him. . . . I'm not to see your face. . . . No, no. I—I mustn't
. . . I daren't . . . I must keep my eyes covered from you . . .
I must be—be wise and brave . . . I must sleep but not dream
. . . but I—I . . . (*She draws her hands from her eyes, shakingly, stretches out her two arms to the curtains, and with a sob,
rushes to them as to a loved one*) But I—I love you . . . I love
you . . . I love you. . . . (*Her face is buried sobbingly in the
great curtains, and her arms are about them pathetically, as the
curtain falls slowly.*)

CURTAIN

ACT THREE

SCENE: *The same. A few days later.*

The CANON *is seated at table finishing breakfast.* FATHER CORR *is standing at the writing-desk, quietly examining a Register of Births.* JEMIMA, *with an apron on, is flitting fearfully about the table, obsequious and uncomfortable in the* CANON'S *presence.*

JEMIMA (*sweetly*). Is there anythin' else, Canon, if you please?

CANON (*beamingly*). You leave nothing to be desired, Miss Cooney. Thank you.

JEMIMA. Thank you, Canon. (*She crosses.*)

CANON. One moment, Miss Cooney. Has Brigid had a good night?

JEMIMA. She had, Canon. A wee bit feverish maybe and her eyes are shineyish, but the doctor says it's nothin' to worry about.

CANON. As a good woman, Miss Cooney, what do *you* think yourself?

JEMIMA (*squirming a little under his gaze*). Sure I'd say, Canon, I'd say nothin' much. I'd put it down, if you'd allow me, Canon, to what—what she came from. Her mother, Canon, was none too strong— (*Hoarsely*) in the mind I mean, Canon. They had to—remove her in the end.

CANON. Remove her? Enlarge on that, Miss Cooney.

282

JEMIMA. Sure—take her away, Canon: to—to Dublin, I mean. It was before your time, sure.

CANON (*understanding*). Ah! . . . And her father?

JEMIMA (*hoarsely*). Sure they say, Canon, he didn't die a Christian death in Scotland. But sure God's good, Canon.

CANON. As you say, Miss Cooney, God is good. (*Pause*) I want you to give Brigid very careful attention night and day.

JEMIMA. Sure if it's your wish, Canon.

CANON. Expressly so! That will be all. (*She goes after bowing. The* CANON *watches* FATHER CORR *at the Births' Register, as he finishes his coffee*) I understand you heard Brigid's confession this morning, Father Corr?

FATHER CORR (*raising head from book*). That's correct, Canon. At eight o'clock. She asked for me.

CANON. Did you—instruct her on these matters we discussed, on the lines I recommended?

FATHER CORR. I carried out your instructions to the letter, Canon, even if I did think myself you were unnecessarily extreme and severe.

CANON. The latter half of your observation, Father Corr, is superfluous.

FATHER CORR. Not so much as you might think, Canon, if you examine this Register of Births.

CANON. I knew from the manner in which you were poring over that book that there was a sort of necromancer's air about you. Well? And what are the—the "signs and wonders"?

FATHER CORR (*impressively*). Would it surprise you to know, Canon, that Brigid was born on February the first, almost twenty-one years ago? That's St. Brigid's day!

CANON. And you are going to infer vulgarly that there is anything more than mere coincidence in that? (*He sips his coffee slowly.*)

FATHER CORR (*coming forward slowly*). Since I heard of this—contention of Brigid's, Canon, I've been worried and disturbed.

CANON (*sipping*). I thought you would. The danger with you, Father Corr, is that some trivial happening is always liable to hurl you headlong into violent emotionalism.

FATHER CORR. Sure, I'm doin' nothin' violent, Canon—I'm as calm as any priest could be. I'm only just quietly turnin' over a few things in my mind, such as, for instance, the fact that Brigid was born on St. Brigid's day, and that St. Brigid lived and worked in this very locality here in Fanghart.

CANON. I dislike your attitude. If a leaf turns unaccountably in these credulous days ten thousand ferrety nonentities cock their ears and gibber.

FATHER CORR. Suppose, Canon, that Brigid—*did* see this—well, this vision?

CANON. If Brigid saw ten thousand visions, our attitude to the accumulated wisdom of the Church should be unaltered. I wish you, in particular, and this country in general, could digest just *that* much, and cease chasing emotional red-herrings. (*Pause.* FATHER CORR *shifts uneasily.*)

FATHER CORR. With all respect to you, Canon, I don't think you understand this country.

CANON (*acidly*). I understand the mind of the universal Church, and that alone concerns me. (*Pause*) Besides, didn't you hear Miss Cooney just now on the matter of Brigid's antecedents?

FATHER CORR. That might mean nothing.

CANON. It generally means everything. But you *will* strain after miracles, in spite of my previous observations. One can conceivably understand her father dying an unchristian death in a barbarous nation like Scotland, but there is no escaping the significance of the fact that her mother was—removed, as Miss Cooney so Celtically phrased it.

FATHER CORR. That may be, Canon. What worries me, is her insistence that she saw the face and eyes of the Saint. Poor Brigid is not a liar.

CANON. Brigid, as you observe, is not a liar. But the reflections, Father, in an unstable mind are not—shall we say theologically significant? (*As* JEMIMA *enters*) Let us dismiss the subject.

JEMIMA. Please, Canon, you said you wanted to see me nephew, Francis. He's here now.

CANON. Let him come in, Miss Cooney.

JEMIMA. Sure, let him wait till Father Corr is finished with you, Canon.

FATHER CORR (*to* JEMIMA). You can send him in. I'm going now. (*She bows and goes*) Canon, I've written to the Bishop for a transfer. I don't, and probably never will, understand you. I don't want you to think I'm doin' it behind your back.

CANON (*slowly*). It is not important. (FRANCIS *comes in awkwardly with his cap in his hand. Neither priest takes the slightest notice of him.*)

FATHER CORR. Very well, Canon. (*He bows and goes. Very preoccupied, the* CANON *looks at* FRANCIS *for quite a time, unseeingly.* FRANCIS *sweats.*)

FRANCIS. Am I too—too soon, Canon? Sure, I could go back and wait! . . .

CANON (*coming slowly to consciousness*). Ah, Francis, you've come. Of course. You wanted to see me, Francis?

FRANCIS (*open-mouthed*). But sure it—was *you* wanted to see *me,* Canon!

CANON. Oh, it was *I* wanted to see *you,* Francis! Why, of course it was. I remember now. I distinctly remember. Be seated, Francis. (FRANCIS *sits awkwardly, squeezing cap.*)

FRANCIS (*in a typical Irish whisper*). Is there—anny news?

CANON. There is, Francis, and there isn't. Contradictory, Francis? But no! I mean by it, there *is* news—relevant news, but there is the necessity for absolute secrecy.

FRANCIS. Sure you can swear me on the book, Canon. (*Magnanimously*) Or if ye lek, Canon, don't tell me a word, if you think fit.

CANON. Excellent, Francis. But—you will be told everything. I trust you. To be exact, moral issues—issues, Francis, of a moral nature, are involved.

FRANCIS (*all at sea*). I—I see, Canon. . . .

CANON. Your aunt will understand more fully than you, Francis. Moral issues *are* involved, and where such are met with, we must tread warily. We must tread, Francis, with the subtlety of angels. But to proceed. You have met my niece—my step-niece, Thomasina Concannon?

FRANCIS. I—I had the honor, Canon, a good few times, in the hall and at concerts she came down to see.

CANON. As you say, Francis, you've had the honor. A—a gentle-manly expression, Francis. For some time past, I have promised her the first vacancy in the school here. And as Miss Driscoll goes to training next week, I must fulfill that promise, Francis. We must *all* fulfill our promises.

FRANCIS (*very crestfallen*). Well, sure, thank you annyway, Canon. I know you did your best for me, and sure you can't please everyone.

CANON. Wait, Francis, wait! There is something further. What remains is confidential. But I have your word, Francis.

FRANCIS. Sure me lips is sealed, Canon, and as for me Aunt, sure she's a—a gravestone.

CANON. As you say, Francis, your aunt's a—a gravestone. I may therefore, proceed. I intend, Francis, dismissing the man, O'Flingsley. (FRANCIS *gives a gasp and half rises*) A grave step, Francis—a very grave step, but necessary. We must never hesi-tate in our duty. That is the sum and the essence of conduct. Note it down, Francis.

FRANCIS. I'll write it in me "Things to Remember" book this very night, Canon.

CANON. Excellent, Francis. That will be another vacancy. Now that position of Principal, Francis, I would give to no one sooner than you.

FRANCIS (*gasping*). P-principal, Canon!

CANON. But mark what it results in! Mark my problem, Francis, my dilemma, my moral embarrassment. An attractive young man and a comely young girl in the one building all day. Mark it gravely, Francis!

FRANCIS (*wide-eyed, dismayed*). There—there would be scandal, Canon, and . . . and talk. I see it all.

CANON. Let us say instead, Francis, with the dignity demanded by the phenomenon, that moral issues of grave import are involved.

FRANCIS (*aghast*). I see it all, Canon. . . .

CANON. You see it all, Francis! You have insight! You inherit it, I have not the *slightest* doubt, from your Aunt Jemima. Now, if my step-niece were a benevolent old lady, the problem would not only solve itself—it would have no existence in fact.

FRANCIS. That's the trouble, Canon, with Thomasina young and—if I may make so bold, Canon—attractive.

CANON. Attractive is the word, Francis, or if you wish—sussusceptible. An excellent word, Francis. You see my difficulty?

FRANCIS. Sure it's plain, Canon.

CANON. It's plain, Francis. It's more than plain. It's unsurmountable. Unless of course, Francis, you could hit on a way out. Your brain is young and nimble, Francis, not like mine.

FRANCIS. If only I could, Canon! Sure it's grand of you strivin' to help me, and perplexin' yourself.

CANON. Not a bit, Francis. "The labor we delight in physics

pain." You remember that great inspirational line, Francis, in your studies.

FRANCIS. Indeed I do, Canon. Sure, I know Lord Macaulay inside out.

CANON. So you do, Francis! I can see that.

FRANCIS. If the two of them was married, Canon?

CANON (*apparently perplexed*). Which two, Francis?

FRANCIS. The two in the school, Canon.

CANON. Oh, the two in the school, Francis. If they were married. But they're not, Francis. If they *were,* the conditions would be an approximation to the ideal. But we must deal in facts, Francis.

FRANCIS (*uneasily*). If I could maybe, Canon, ask me aunt to ask Thomasina to—to discuss things. . . .

CANON (*obtusely*). For—for what purpose, pray, Francis?

FRANCIS. I mean, Canon, that is if *you* have no objection, to see if Thomasina would consider a—a match between us.

CANON (*admirably playacting*). A—a match! A—a match! . . . Francis, what on earth is this? What is that brain of yours propounding?

FRANCIS (*laughing*). But you asked me to hit on a way out, Canon!

CANON. I asked you to hit on a way out, and you—you bring the house down about my ears without warning! By my soul, Francis, you're a—a scoundrel; a—a desperado! I insist on your Aunt Jemima taking you in hand this instant! (*Goes to door and calls*) Miss Cooney! Come here instantly! (JEMIMA *runs in nervously*.)

JEMIMA. You want me, Canon?

CANON (*with mock severity*). Miss Cooney, take Francis out of my sight, and never let him into my presence again. He's a scoundrel!

JEMIMA (*aghast*). Did—did he insult ye, Canon? Did he have the—the cheek—! (*Tempestuously, finger up*) Stand before me, Francis, this minute! (CANON *and* FRANCIS *laugh heartily*) Sure is—is it mockin' me yous are, Canon?

CANON (*touching her shoulder*). No, Miss Cooney. But Francis has mentally, and I might even say morally, winded me. He wants me to make a match with my step-niece and take over the school!

JEMIMA (*excitedly*). Make a match! . . . Take over the school! . . . Canon, if it's takin' liberties he is in your presence, it's your own fault. You're far too kind and free with him, and you don't keep him in his place.

FRANCIS. But you see, Aunt Jemima, O'Flingsley's bein' put out.

JEMIMA. O'Flingsley? Put out! Is that for you to *say,* or the Canon? The cheek of you, Francis. I'll slap your jaw.

CANON. It's true, Miss Cooney. But in strict confidence as yet, remember!

JEMIMA (*involuntarily*). Praises to God! . . .

CANON. But I can't appoint Francis alongside my step-niece, because of moral issues.

JEMIMA (*awarely*). You can *not,* Canon. I can see *that.*

FRANCIS. But if we were married, Aunt? The Canon says he has no objection.

JEMIMA (*gravely*). Did—did you say that, Canon?

CANON. I certainly did, Miss Cooney. But the suggestion is not mine, Miss Cooney. I—wash my hands. (*Laughter.*)

JEMIMA. It's God, Canon, that's Who it is! And Thomasina was in the kitchen to see you not three minutes ago.

CANON (*aghast*). What? She—she's back?

JEMIMA. She came in, Canon. But she left a book she was readin' behind her on the bus, and she's away flyin' down to the Depot to get it.

FRANCIS (*exuberantly*). I'll go down after her, and help her to get it!

JEMIMA. You'll stay where y'are, till you learn the Canon's wishes. Direct him, Canon.

CANON. I refuse to commit myself by *one* word. Did I not say I had washed my hands?

FRANCIS. I'll go. I—I insist on me independence, in this, Aunt Jemima. (*As he goes, excitedly*) And sure, Canon. *Fortis cadere, cedere non potest!* (CANON and JEMIMA *laugh affectedly, as* FRANCIS *goes.*)

JEMIMA (*proudly*). Imagine the nerve of him, Canon, hurlin' the Latin back at you!

CANON. There is no presumption where there is no malice, Miss Cooney. Francis is a good boy. That will be all, Miss Cooney.

(*He lifts book and crosses*) I shall be seated at the lower end of the garden if Mr. O'Flingsley calls. I'm expecting him.

JEMIMA. I'll come for you at once, Canon. Sure, it's God's blessin', Canon. You're gettin' rid of him, and him that cheeky and impertinent to you. (*The* CANON *crosses and takes no notice of her remark. She notices this and goes quickly.* CANON *pauses a moment to look out pensively at the hills, then opens the window and with his book passes out. A moment later, the door bell rings and almost immediately* JEMIMA *ushers in* DERMOT O'FLINGSLEY. *Sourly*) Sit there, and I'll run into the garden and see if the Canon will be willin' to see you.

O'FLINGSLEY. I'll stand. And don't *run*. You might break your neck.

JEMIMA (*very sourly*). Yours is bruck if you only knew it.

O'FLINGSLEY (*squeaking*). Coo-ee, Jemima! Your petticoat's hangin'! (*She stamps out in a fury.* O'FLINGSLEY *laughs heartily, throws his hat on a chair, and makes a tour of the bookcases and the pictures.* BRIGID, *wrapped in a dressing-gown and bare-footed, comes in left, noiselessly. She crosses until she is right beside him. She looks feverish and frail*) How anyone can have all that beauty about him, and still be a bear! (*He sees* BRIGID *beside him and jumps*) Brigid! Where on earth did you drop from? Are you not well?

BRIGID·(*softly*). Yis, Master, I'm well. It's just that the Canon says I'm not.

O'FLINGSLEY (*looking at her*). I think now, Brigid, that *for once* he's right. Let me feel your hand. (*He takes her hand gently.*)

BRIGID. I knew you'd be here.

O'FLINGSLEY (*staring at her*). Eh? You what?

BRIGID. I knew it. I could—see you. I was dreaming about you. I thought you were going down a long road and waving back to me. So I came down. I—I— (*She suddenly sobs and buries her head in his breast. He is very shaken and tries to control himself by being humorous.*)

O'FLINGSLEY. There, silly! I'm not going away. I'm going to stay here and grow a mustache, and play bowls with the Canon.

BRIGID (*looking at him*). No . . . you're going away . . . You're to—"to take up your bed—"

O'FLINGSLEY (*startled*). Brigid! Is that the message?

BRIGID (*simply*). Yis, Master . . . and you're to try to love people when they're dirty because any ass can love them when they're clean.

O'FLINGSLEY (*after a pause, vigorously*). You dreamt that!

BRIGID. No . . . she said it. She'd have said more only Miss Cooney was annoyin' her dustin' and cleanin'. She went away then . . .

O'FLINGSLEY (*pensively*). Take up my bed and walk . . . I wonder what exactly that means?

BRIGID. I don't know . . . she said *you'd* know. . . .

O'FLINGSLEY. Yes . . . maybe I do. Brigid, I *am* going away.

BRIGID. I knew . . .

O'FLINGSLEY. If I could just shake this fear off me—this fear of hunger . . . of money . . . of the cold. . . .

BRIGID. It will be terrible, Master, when I see you comin' up the school road, and you not comin' at all. But I'll still have the Canon.

O'FLINGSLEY. The Canon! That man!

BRIGID. Yis, Master . . . Oh, I know you have the dagger for him because he can hurt and say killin' words . . . *You* see him when he's proud, but I see him when he's prayin' in his little place and the tears on his cheeks; *you* see him when he dines but *I* see him when he fasts; *you* see him when his head is up and fiery like a lion, but *I* see his head when it's down low and his words won't come . . . It's because of that, that *you* hate him and *I* love him . . . St. Brigid says that if we could all see each other all the time in big hangin' mirrors, the whole hate of the world would turn into dust.

O'FLINGSLEY (*touched*). I'll remember that always, Brigid. And I'll remember you too.

BRIGID. It wouldn't matter not rememberin' *me,* if you'd remember *it.* (*They are staring at each other as the* CANON *appears at the window. His brow clouds. He comes forward into the room and for a moment regards them both.*)

CANON (*sharply*). Brigid, what is this? How dare you leave your bed in your sick state and in this attire? (BRIGID *looks from the* CANON *to* O'FLINGSLEY *and back again. She continues to look at both of them. They are a little uncomfortable, and eye each other surreptitiously.*)

BRIGID. I wanted to come down . . . to see—the two of yous.

CANON. For what purpose?

BRIGID. I—I don't know, Canon . . . I just wanted to—to be

sure that I loved the two of yous and could serve yous always. (*Pause.* JEMIMA *comes rushing in.*)

JEMIMA. Canon! (*She stops short on seeing* BRIGID.)

CANON. Preposterous! Miss Cooney, I cannot congratulate you on your care of Brigid.

JEMIMA. It was when I was out findin' you, Canon, that she left her bed.

CANON. Brigid, I am displeased.

BRIGID. Yis, Canon . . . and so is the Master.

CANON (*with glance at* O'FLINGSLEY). Brigid, go back to bed with Miss Cooney.

JEMIMA (*taking her arm*). Come on now. Annoyin' the Canon like this.

O'FLINGSLEY. Good-bye, Brigid.

BRIGID (*turning*). Master! . . . (*She turns to get back, but* JEMIMA *won't let her.*)

JEMIMA. Never mind *him*. Come on when you're told.

CANON. Let her come, Miss Cooney. (JEMIMA *releases her. She comes back to* O'FLINGSLEY, *and gives him her hand. She looks up at him.*)

BRIGID. Good-bye, Master. And—I love you. (*She looks up at him emotionally. He bends and kisses her hair softly. The* CANON *stands like a statue, his feelings masked completely.* BRIGID *turns and goes with* JEMIMA.)

CANON (*as* JEMIMA *takes* BRIGID's *arm*). That could have been gentler, Miss Cooney. I will have it so.

JEMIMA. Sure I'm not sayin' a word at all to her, Canon. (*They go.* O'FLINGSLEY *and the* CANON *both regard each other in silence for a moment. One can see them as if shedding their finer feelings and donning their fighting equipment.*)

O'FLINGSLEY. Well, Canon? You sent for me.

CANON (*quietly*). You may be seated, O'Flingsley. (O'FLINGSLEY *sits frankly and without nervousness, in a chair. The* CANON *goes to desk and sits in his large chair. A pause*) O'Flingsley, for some time past, I have had ample grounds for complaint both against your person and your work.

O'FLINGSLEY. *I* have a goodly few complaints also. Perhaps they will cancel each other out.

CANON (*eyebrows raised*). *You* have complaints, O'Flingsley? I did not think it was considered a—a suitable attitude in a teacher to have complaints.

O'FLINGSLEY (*stung*). You forget, Canon, that I am "that man O'Flingsley" first, and your schoolmaster second.

CANON (*ironically*). Very novel, and shall we use that hateful word, modern?

O'FLINGSLEY. If it's something ancient, very ancient you want, here you are:—(*Very rapidly on his fingers*) No coal, no handle on sweeping-brush, no caretaker for the school, no windows that aren't stuck fast; eighteen crumbling desks, six broken panes of glass, no lighting on dark days, and the public highway of the Saorstat Eireann for a playground. And these complaints render my attitude—unsuitable.

CANON (*unperturbed*). Your enunciation is very imperfect for a teacher, O'Flingsley. I missed quite half of them. Besides, these alleged deficiencies are not complaints. They are officially termed "Recommendations in Writing to the Very Reverend Manager."

O'FLINGSLEY. Or alternately, "Words Scrawled on the Sands by an Innocent."

CANON (*coldly*). I will not—descend to you, O'Flingsley.

O'FLINGSLEY. You sent for me, Canon, to say something and you haven't said it yet.

CANON. I'll say it now, O'Flingsley. I'll say it now..(*Bending over*) Your mother's name was Gibney.

O'FLINGSLEY (*with a slight start*). So it was, Canon.

CANON (*grimly*). Your father's second name was Eugene.

O'FLINGSLEY (*now reckless*). It was. And if you're as interested as all that in my genealogy, I had a grandmother that was called Poppet, an uncle that could spit over his own shoulder, and a paralyzed aunt that was christened Delia Diana. But I never had a niece that was called after me, thank God.

CANON (*controlling his anger*). I'll be—calm, O'Flingsley. I'll be—logical. I—I won't descend to you. (*Holding up press cuttings from desk*) I note from these cuttings of *your* book *I Am Sir Oracle,* that the Church in Ireland is controlled by a—a red army of turkey-cocks.

O'FLINGSLEY. If you have, Canon, that's always a big step forward.

CANON (*grimly, his eye gleaming*). And I see that our educational system is the—the sewage of European culture. I'd never have thought it, O'Flingsley. Could you tell me, on what page of your teacher's Penny Catechism I could find it?

O'FLINGSLEY (*with venom*). On the page, Canon, the Bishops won't add until they're made.

CANON (*striking desk*). Damnation! I'll not have—*that!* (*He jumps up fiercely.*)

O'FLINGSLEY (*also jumping up*). And hell and blazes, but you'll have to! (*They face each other on the floor, the masks now off completely. A pause as they regard each other venomously. The* CANON *composes himself with a great effort.*)

CANON (*with composure*). O'Flingsley, do you know Francis Ignatius O'Connor?

O'FLINGSLEY. Who doesn't? (*Imitating* FRANCIS) "Sure, Lord now, Canon!"

CANON (*grimly*). I—I'm expecting him.

O'FLINGSLEY. I rather thought you were. And his—virgin consort, Aunt Jemima too, of course.

CANON (*fuming*). In my—my forty years as a priest—

O'FLINGSLEY. You played the turkey-cock with your teachers, and made them your slavish handymen.

CANON (*with some composure*). No . . . I—I will not stoop! I will not argue. To argue is to assume equality.

O'FLINGSLEY. And equality of course would mean the end of your precious managerial system of education that's the laughing-stock of Europe. That would never do, Canon. By all means, spit on me.

(FRANCIS O'CONNOR *comes to the door, left, awkwardly. He is rather excited.*)

FRANCIS. Can I come in, Canon? I'm back with good news!

CANON. Good news will keep, Francis. Be seated.

FRANCIS (*exuberantly*). Sure—I—I can't keep it, Canon. Your niece has done me the honor of promisin' to be me wife. Everythin's lovely and grand, Canon! (O'FLINGSLEY *chuckles merrily*.)

O'FLINGSLEY. Hurrah for the Catholic ideal! A rebel knocked out; a niece married off; and a school made safe for a stagnant tradition all in the one move! Canon, you deserve a seat in Maynooth. (FRANCIS *stares at him goggle-eyed*.)

CANON. Take no heed of that man, Francis. He's an occasion of sin. Allow me instead to congratulate you. (*To* O'FLINGSLEY, *grimly turning*) Need I say any more, O'Flingsley? Need I say that Francis will—take over your duties at the end of the month?

O'FLINGSLEY. And I'm—fired?

CANON (*dignifiedly*). "Dismissed" is the word, O'Flingsley. (*They regard each other grimly*.)

O'FLINGSLEY. I somehow feel we'll meet again, we two.

CANON. I trust not.

O'FLINGSLEY (*to Francis*). And now, O'Connor, you're an Irish schoolmaster! In other words, a clerical handyman, a piece of furniture in a chapel house, a brusher-out of barn schools, a Canon's yesman.

CANON (*as* FRANCIS *goggles*). You heard that—that man, Francis!

FRANCIS. He'll never have anny luck, Canon. Sure, leave him to God.

CANON. An excellent suggestion, Francis, and it will save me from descending to him. (*To* O'FLINGSLEY) At the end of the month, then, O'Flingsley . . . And that will be all, thank you. (O'FLINGSLEY *crosses.*)

O'FLINGSLEY (*turning*). I'll leave tomorrow, Canon, without pay, and give over the school to your handyman, if you'll answer me one question before I go.

CANON. Your question, O'Flingsley, may have an answer from us if it is—suitable.

O'FLINGSLEY. As a scholar who knows what he won't publicly admit, you loathe and detest the whole miserable fabric of things here. You detest that disgraceful apology for a school down there, even more than *I* do. I know that because I'm not a fool whatever else I am. Why then do you deliberately prepare to perpetuate it through that poor spineless imbecile there beside you?

FRANCIS (*outraged*). Canon! He's insultin' me. I'd make him take that back. (*The* CANON's *eyes meet* O'FLINGSLEY's *eyes challengingly, in a silent tense duel. Pause.*)

CANON (*tensely*). That will be all, O'Flingsley.

O'FLINGSLEY (*venomously*). Afraid, Canon? But the heartbreak is there all the same. *You* know it, and I know it. However, I'll always owe you something for taking me by the scruff of the neck out of a mouse's hiding place and putting me back on the high road. Good-bye, Canon, you will be remembered, if at all, not as a classicist, nor as a priest, but for your love for a poor little miserable child.

CANON (*his voice trembling with passion*). That will—be all,

O'Flingsley. (O'FLINGSLEY *turns and snapping up his hat, walks quickly off. The* CANON, *oblivious of* FRANCIS, *stares after him unseeingly.* FRANCIS *is standing flabbergasted and open-mouthed.*)

FRANCIS. Is he mad or what, Canon?

CANON (*after a pause*). Conceivably, Francis . . . conceivably. . . .

CURTAIN

ACT FOUR

SCENE: *The Same. The following morning.*

On the window, back, there are beautiful long white curtains reaching to the ground, and on the table a great vase of white lilies. The CANON *rises from the dining table and wipes his mouth with a napkin.* MISS COONEY *enters with a wrapped box.*

JEMIMA. This, Canon, came in from Driscall's of Dundalk. It's the hat and veil you sent in for.

CANON. Just leave it. (*She puts down box*) And undo the string. Are the Fathers finished Mass yet?

JEMIMA. Father Kirwan's takin' off his vestments, Canon. He'll be in for breakfast in a minute. Father Corr had his, this hour since.

CANON. Very well then. And Brigid?

JEMIMA. She was asleep when I riz at seven, Canon. And she didn't call since.

CANON. You should have brought her a cup of tea.

JEMIMA. She was twistin' and fidgetin' durin' the night, Canon, and I thought it best to let her sleep on. It's what the doctor said. (*She suddenly sees the white curtains and starts visibly*) Canon! Who—who changed the curtains? It was the rose-red ones that was on, and I goin' through to your own Mass at

302

seven, and I never noticed nothin' till now. Oh! and them lilies on the table too!

CANON (*staring at flowers and curtains*). Was it not yourself?

JEMIMA. It was not, then, Canon. I'm sure o' that. They didn't need changin'. (*Pause*) It—it was *her*, I'll bet. (FATHER KIRWAN *comes in bareheaded through the window. He stands and looks on.*)

CANON. Who is *her*? Explain yourself.

JEMIMA. Brigid, I mean, Canon. She done it maybe, and I out at Mass.

CANON. What grounds have you for such a statement?

JEMIMA. It was the meanderin' talk of her durin' the night, Canon. She kept sayin' that someone went always in white a long time ago.

CANON. Am I to take it then, that this sick child whom I have placed in your care, has been wandering about in this cold room, bare-footed and undressed?

JEMIMA. But sure, Canon, I had to go to Mass.

CANON. You should have missed Mass in the circumstances.

JEMIMA. But I was makin' a novena for poor Francis.

CANON. I don't care if you were making fifty novenas.

JEMIMA (*sniffing*). You're wrongin' me, Canon. But sure no matter. I'll not defend myself.

CANON. I want none of this palaver. I want practical wisdom and sound sense. Go to Brigid now and see to her comfort.

JEMIMA. It's what you say, Canon. (*To* FATHER KIRWAN) Will you serve yourself, Father?

FATHER KIRWAN. Sure, and I can. Go ahead and see after Brigie. (MISS COONEY *goes, left.* FATHER KIRWAN *sits and starts his breakfast.*)

FATHER KIRWAN. What is it all about, Canon?

CANON. Brigid seems to have risen during my Mass and put up white curtains and decorated the table with flowers. (FATHER KIRWAN *looks at the curtains and flowers.*)

FATHER KIRWAN (*smiling*). She gets the funniest notions. . . . They say her mother, before she was sent away, used to wear her boots on the wrong feet for pure contrariness. (MISS COONEY *re-enters hurriedly.*)

JEMIMA (*fearfully*). Canon! She—she's not there!

CANON (*sharply*). Not where?

JEMIMA. In the bed, Canon.

CANON (*irascibly*). What new sort of stupidity is this?

FATHER KIRWAN. Did you try the kitchen?

JEMIMA. I did, Father. She's nowhere about the house.

FATHER KIRWAN. I'll bet she crossed the fields over to St. Brigid's Shrine. This is her feast day—the first of February.

JEMIMA. Sure, it's an Irish mile if it's a yard, Father. Maybe it's down to the schoolmaster she went.

FATHER KIRWAN. That low scum! I hope not, for her own sake.

JEMIMA. Troth, Father, she had a likin' that didn't become her at all for that fella. I was goin' to warn His Reverence. . . .

CANON (*irascibly*). This conjecturing is both ludicrous and undignified. It is obvious that the child's mind is in a very weak state, and that she has wandered aimlessly on to the roads. Miss Cooney, I haven't the slightest hesitation in reprimanding you for neglect of duty.

JEMIMA. It's not for me to answer you back, Canon, but I advised you a few times that she was wake in the mind, as her mother was, and that she needed . . .

CANON (*cutting in*). I am not concerned with your advice, Miss Cooney. Go out and search for her instead. And you, Father Kirwan, if you are free will also join . . .

FATHER KIRWAN (*rising enthusiasm*). I'll take the wee car, Canon, and I'll cover the whole parish in a flash. The new gear box, Canon, that . . .

CANON. You will walk! I am averse to cinematic exhibitions on the parochial roads, because our servant has—mislaid herself. And if I may add, Father . . . (*The* CANON *stops abruptly to stare at* BRIGID *who suddenly comes in by the window. She is dressed all in white, is neat and comely, matter-of-fact and practical in manner, and is smiling slightly. She leans against the curtains—a white picture in a white frame. All turn and stare at her.*)

CANON. Brigid! What does this mean?

BRIGID. Please, Canon, I had—things to do. So I riz.

CANON. I am incensed and angry.

BRIGID. Not *this* day, Canon, please. Tomorrow maybe . . . (*Pause*) Do you like my white curtains?

FATHER KIRWAN. So it *was* you changed them!

BRIGID. Yes . . . just at dawn and the sky whitenin'. It had to be then.

JEMIMA. The curtains didn't need changin' at all, until Friday, Canon.

CANON. Have you any answer to that?

BRIGID. I just—felt they did. I thought them red ones would be a show before—before anyone comin'. (*She hangs her head.*)

CANON. Brigid, I want no nonsense, but sound sense. In leaving your bed you were disobedient.

BRIGID. Yis, Canon. I thought, Canon, that the flowers and me white curtains and me white dress would please you. And—anyone comin' too.

CANON. Instead, you have gravely *dis*pleased me. Where have you been?

BRIGID. In the chapel, Canon. Sure you gave me Communion yourself. (FATHER CORR *appears back, and comes in through window bareheaded.*)

CANON. Eh? I—I what?

BRIGID. Sure, you didn't know me in me white dress. I was near laughin'. . . . Father Corr wouldn't have seen me either only he plopped down beside me behind the pillar. (*A pause.* BRIGID *hangs her head.*)

BRIGID (*hesitant*). You—you're angry, Canon.

CANON. I am more than angry. I am disgusted.

JEMIMA. Will I put her back to bed, Canon?

BRIGID. Please no, Canon. I hate bed.

CANON. Very well then, for the present. Take her, Miss Cooney, and give her breakfast. And then, Brigid, I wish to speak to you.

JEMIMA. Come on now, and no nonsense.

BRIGID (*going to* CANON). *I* want to speak to *you* too, Canon, if you'll let me.

CANON. All of the speaking will be done by me. You will go now.

BRIGID. But—I don't want any breakfast.

CANON. What's that?

FATHER CORR. She specially wants to fast till midday, Canon. I spoke to her against it, but it was no use.

CANON. The Church requires no such penance from a sick child. You will go, Brigid. I forbid this.

BRIGID. But I—I can't, Canon. I promised.

CANON. Miss Cooney, prepare Brigid's breakfast and inform me when it is ready.

JEMIMA. I will, Canon. And that's the right way. Such contrariness and stubbornness! Her mother too—

CANON. You will go, Miss Cooney. (JEMIMA, *with a gulp, goes, left.* FATHER KIRWAN *rises from breakfast and crosses.*)

FATHER KIRWAN (*apologetically*). If you'll excuse *me*, I have a meetin' of the Football team to attend. (*To* FATHER CORR) Aren't *you* comin', too, Father? It's near ten. We'll take the car.

FATHER CORR. Get the engine started up, and I'll be out after you.

FATHER KIRWAN. Hurry then. We'll have to stop at Ryan's for petrol. (*As he crosses*) Brigie, if you go in and wallop a plate of bacon and eggs, I'll give you a whizz this evenin' in the car. There now!

BRIGID. Not this day, Father, but another day.

FATHER KIRWAN. Go on now. You're annoyin' the Canon. And I'll learn you to drive as well.

BRIGID. But, Father, I've promised and given me word. . . . Do you think I could bear to break it, and me with a white dress on me too. It would be terrible.

FATHER KIRWAN. Ach, you're a blather! I'll buy you a football jersey. (*He goes out with a wave.* FATHER CORR *walks uneasily about. He is ill at ease under* BRIGID's *gaze.*)

BRIGID. Please stay—with us here, Father Corr, and—don't go.

FATHER CORR. Brigid, won't you just be a good girl and leave *us* to look after our own business?

CANON. What is going on here that I am not aware of?

FATHER CORR (*evasively*). Just a meetin' of the football team, Canon. (*A tense pause.*)

BRIGID (*bursting out*). If—if Mr. O'Flingsley done one thing wrong, he'll surely do twinty things right. (*Both turn and stare at her. The* CANON *is mystified.* FATHER CORR *is confused.*)

CANON. O'Flingsley? . . . What—what on earth is this?

BRIGID (*in pain*). The men's havin' a meetin', Canon. There's goin' to be talk and then stones and sticks.

FATHER CORR (*sharply*). What talk is this *you* have?

CANON. What? . . . What do you know of this, Brigid?

BRIGID. If I told you, Canon, you would say I—I wasn't well.

CANON. Pht! Of course you are not well! You are ill! You are very ill! (*To* FATHER CORR) What truth is there in this, Father Corr?

FATHER CORR (*stiffly*). Instead of answering that, Canon, might I ask instead why *we* weren't told that that scoundrel, O'Flingsley, was the author of that blasphemous book we read?

CANON. Because it was sufficient for the purposes of the Church that *I* knew of it.

FATHER CORR. These are new times, Canon. Neither we nor the people down there consider that satisfactory.

CANON. There is only one time in God's Church, Father Corr. (*Grimly*) And I expect my rulings to be obeyed.

FATHER. In canonical matters, yes.

CANON. In all matters affecting the dignity of the Church.

FATHER CORR. We made it our business to warn this scoundrel to be clear out of this parish by this morning. If he is still here it is *his* look-out. I will try to moderate the feelings of the people, but I warn you I cannot cork them up in a bottle.

CANON. This is defiance!

FATHER CORR. No, Canon. It is legitimate action, since *you* won't move.

CANON. *Move?* I've dismissed the man summarily.

FATHER CORR. In our opinion, it is not enough.

CANON. It is a most severe sentence in any civilized community. The man's bread and butter.

FATHER CORR. Any bla'guard like *him* can get bread and butter, aye and honey too, in Ireland by slingin' mud at the Church.

CANON. Mud, Father Corr, sticks only to mud. But I would hardly expect that much philosophy from *you*.

FATHER CORR. I'm not here to talk sophistry, Canon. It glosses over unbearable insults. I'm a plain, blunt man.

CANON. Like Luther and Cromwell.

BRIGID. If the Master, Canon, was a bla'guard with terrible things in him, and not just a blunderer the same as Father Corr . . .

FATHER CORR. How dare you, Brigid!

CANON. That will do, Brigid. As usual, Father Corr, you are intemperate in your language, and chaotic in your feelings. I place both you and Father Kirwan under a strict rule of obedience. Any attempt at Dublin's holy hooliganism in *my* parish, will be rigorously met by *me*. Go down and acquaint this meeting of *that*. And in my name, dismiss it.

FATHER CORR. But what do you imagine they will think of me when . . .

CANON (*imperiously*). I insist, Father Corr!

FATHER CORR. Very well, Canon. I'll—deliver your message.

(*Very sulkily he goes, left.* BRIGID *goes close to the* CANON, *and looks at him solicitously.*)

BRIGID. It's a mortal sin for us all, Canon, worryin' and annoyin' ye.

CANON (*softly*). It is a worrying age, child. But what of it? As Don Miguel used to be fond of saying, "*Dios quie da la llaga, da la medicina.*"

BRIGID. And what does that mean, Canon?

CANON. It means, Brigid, that when God sends us evil, He sends with it the weapon to conquer it.

BRIGID. It's lovely. (*Pause*) Is a weapon, Canon, a sword?

CANON. God could make a weapon of anything, child.

BRIGID (*as in a dream*). Yis. . . . *She* said that too . . . and she was sad. . . . (MISS COONEY *enters, left.*)

JEMIMA. Brigid's breakfast is ready, Canon. And this letter's just come in for you. (*She hands* CANON *the letter which he proceeds to open and read.* BRIGID *looks very appealingly at him.*)

CANON (*his eyes on the letter*). Go, Brigid, and have a full meal. (BRIGID *goes dejectedly towards door, and then looks back pathetically at* CANON, *who is immersed in his letter.*)

JEMIMA (*at door, waiting*). Are ye goin' to be all day comin'?

BRIGID (*low*). I'll be after ye in a minute. Sssh!

JEMIMA. I'll not ssh! at all. It'll be cold. Canon, how much more of her nonsense are we to put up with?

CANON (*finishing letter and looking up*). You may go, Miss

Cooney. Brigid will follow in a moment. (MISS COONEY *goes.*
BRIGID *regards the* CANON *wistfully. He looks at her, half-ruffled,
half lovingly*) Brigid, are *you* going to be a good girl?

BRIGID. Yis, Canon.

CANON. Excellent, Brigid. Come here! (*She comes to him softly*)
This letter will give you a good appetite. It is from a great
friend of mine in Bray. You will go up there, Brigid, for an
excellent holiday, and I will put a whole five pound note in
your bag. There now! And your hat! Why, I was forgetting all
about your hat! (*Pointing*) There it is! It has a veil over your
ear, Brigid—

BRIGID. My nose, Canon.

CANON. Your nose, Brigid. Your nose to be sure. And an orna-
ment stuck at the side.

BRIGID. Is it a little white dog, Canon?

CANON. A dog? I believe it *is* a dog. I distinctly remember the
manageress saying that dogs were the fashion.

BRIGID. So they are, Canon.

CANON. Excellent, Brigid. I consider dogs are in excellent taste
myself. But you are not to see the hat now—not till you get
your breakfast. Come now, are you pleased?

BRIGID (*softly*). I—I could cry, Canon. I'll—anger you again and
vex you. I—I know it.

CANON. No, Brigid. God will help you not to. You will be my
friend instead. It is good to have a friend on a dark day. If anything is ever said of me, child, I want it to be that I found your
face always full of grace and comely.

BRIGID. Don't say anythin' nice about me face, Canon, or I would want it to be like St. Brigid's face with the niceness torn out of it with pain.

CANON (*chidingly*). There! There! Your mind must not dwell on these myths and fancies. What is God's, nothing can destroy. Go now, child, and have a good breakfast, and then we shall fit on your hat and arrange about your train. (BRIGID *moves towards door, and then comes back pathetically.*)

BRIGID (*shrewdly*). Canon, if—if you made a great promise to—to Don Miguel or Don Pedro, would you keep it in face of everythin'?

CANON. Keep it? Why, most certainly, Brigid. A gentleman *always* keeps his promises, under penalty of dishonor. (*She looks at him pleadingly.*)

BRIGID (*after a pause*). That's why I don't want to—to eat till midday, Canon. I—I promised St. Brigid. (*The* CANON *starts visibly, realizing he is caught. He controls his feelings.*)

CANON. Brigid, you are very trying. Will you eat if I, as the Canon, give you a special—a very special dispensation?

BRIGID. But it's for—the love of her, Canon, not as a penance. She asked me to prove I loved her.

CANON. To say she asked you is—inaccurate, Brigid. What you mean is that in praying to St. Brigid, you *told* her you would fast yourself. In that you were harder on yourself than the Church allows. Anything excessive, Brigid, is not classically Catholic.

BRIGID. She *did* ask me, Canon. But you won't believe me.

CANON (*ruffled*). I thought, Brigid, we finished with this matter long ago!

BRIGID. I tried, Canon. But—she kept pleadin'—as if everythin' else was standin' waitin'. . . . She said I was to offer my Communion this mornin' for *you,* and my fast till midday for *you* too.

CANON (*after a pause*). Brigid, for offering your Communion for me, I am indeed grateful. It is the act of my friend. But you must not think any *figure told* you to do this. The Church *frowns* at such imaginings, and she is very, very wise.

BRIGID. But there's—somethin' else, Canon. It's—killin' and killin' me. . . .

CANON (*holding himself in*). I feel you're going to make me angry, Brigid.

BRIGID (*trembling*). I—I know . . . I'm tremblin'. . . .

CANON (*touching her*). There! My poor child, there! You are ill, and I will say no word. You may tell me. I will contain myself, Brigid. I will bear with you. Let it be written of me.

BRIGID. She told me to ask you, Canon, to—come with me, wearin' your surplice and soutane, and I in this white dress, into the chapel yard today at twelve when the Angelus is ringin' and the people are comin' and goin'. (*The* CANON *is staring at her, holding himself desperately in leash.* BRIGID, *with tearful eyes, is looking up pleadingly at him*) We are to kneel down on the seventh flag from the door and I am to keep sayin' the prayer to St. Brigid. And you are to invoke her three times, and then kiss the stone and say, "Mary of the Gael, show us the way through the dark." And she promises that a stream of water, waitin' there for years, will gush out over the flagstone, and that the fingers of everyone will dip into it forever. (*Pause*) That—that's all, Canon. (*She stands visibly trembling, looking up at the* CANON *whose face is strained and masklike*) Please don't—shout and be angry with me, C-Canon. Just—just say, "G-go, B-Brigid!" (*The* CANON, *his hands clenched to his sides, turns and walks irascibly to the window and stares out. He is fighting desperately to control himself.* BRIGID *keeps watching him—her hand to her trembling mouth. In a few moments, he walks back to her with evident composure.*)

CANON (*slowly*). No, Brigid. I shall not shout or be hard on you. That would be unjust. Even if I am angry. Even if I am *very* angry. But I forgive you, Brigid. You are very ill. You are even more ill than I suspected.

BRIGID (*passionately*). Canon, believe me! Believe me! I am weak tellin' you. I am not—able.

CANON. Brigid, by the grace of God, I am holding away my anger from you, for you are not deserving of it. If you were not ill, I should be disgusted. I make you my friend, and in return you ask me to be a—boobish sort of conjurer who draws rabbits out of a hat or water out of a stone for the gratification of oafs and idiots.

BRIGID. But sure, Canon, St. Brigid wouldn't belittle *you* and deceive *me*. She—she *couldn't*.

CANON. As you rightly say she couldn't, Brigid. As I explained, child, she wasn't—there.

BRIGID. But I saw her, Canon. And the mark on her face and all.

CANON. I know, Brigid. Our poor sick minds play with terrible pictures. But *you* know nothing of such things. When you return from your holiday, you will say to me, "Canon, I was a little fool in the wind, and you were a big tree that gave me shelter." (*Enter* MISS COONEY.)

JEMIMA. What will I do with Brigid's breakfast, Canon! It's goin' to loss.

CANON. Bring it here to this table, Miss Cooney, on a tray.

JEMIMA (*staring*). Is it the—the priests' table you mean, Canon?

CANON. Obviously, Miss Cooney. (*With a perplexed bow, she goes.*)

CANON. Come and sit down with me, Brigid, till I tell you something. (*He seats her on a couch and seats himself near her.*)

BRIGID (*wretchedly*). I am weak and useless. . . . I am not able. . . . St. Brigid will brush me name off her lips as if it was a piece of soot in the wind.

CANON (*chidingly*). Brigid! Brigid! These morbid fancies! How now, can I speak to you if you go on giving rein to them like a willful child?

BRIGID. She said she wanted a miracle, Canon, since the world had become so hard. Somethin', she said, that would give us all new life and strength.

CANON (*gently*). Listen to me, Brigid. When a woman in marriage gives birth to men, she proves herself a mother. Her men are all about her—justifying her. Suppose, Brigid, a fool came along and said, "Prove yourself a mother again," what would happen?

BRIGID. Sure they'd laugh, Canon.

CANON (*touching her shoulder*). They'd laugh! Excellent, Brigid. You are following me with intelligence. Now, it is just like that with the Church. Her children have justified her eternally. She is venerable with holiness and heavy with the wisdom of ages. And yet, Brigid, you want her to give birth to a new child—to prove herself by a new miracle. St. Brigid would laugh heartily at such a thing. She, Brigid, that redeemed the world, you want her to produce rabbits out of a boob's hat!

BRIGID (*in tears*). It wasn't like that, that I meant it, Canon.

CANON. You are just very young, Brigid, and your poor mind is ill. If you were as wise and old as me, Brigid, you would know that out there where you cannot see, there is a whole world of spiritual rowdies willing to sell themselves to anything that can produce signs and wonders to please their vanity. And there you are, Brigid, in the center of them, backing them up —you, the Canon's friend who should know better.

BRIGID (*woefully*). Please, Canon, don't say that to me. . . . It's terrible. . . . I don't know where I am or what to think. It's like people that you love pullin' agin each other. . . . It's hard, Canon, the things that you love goin' crashin' down, as if they were timber fallin'.

CANON. You must learn to laugh, child, at the big shaky things that our poor sick minds build up, and our healthy minds pull down. There is great safety in the right kind of laughter. (MISS COONEY *enters and puts a tray of breakfast things on the dining table.*)

JEMIMA. Please, Canon, make her take that now. I had to make fresh tea.

CANON. This very moment, Miss Cooney. (MISS COONEY *goes, left*) Come, Brigid. The Church very wisely tells us that our food is also important. (*He takes her to the table by the arm*) And you will sit at the top in the Canon's chair. (*As she seats herself shyly*) There now!

BRIGID. Please, Canon, *must* I eat?

CANON. Yes, Brigid.

BRIGID. Would you be angry if I didn't?

CANON. *Very* angry. And so would the Church. And St. Brigid too. St. Brigid, if you know anything of her, was a *very* sensible saint indeed.

BRIGID (*resigned*). I'll—eat, then, Canon.

CANON. Excellent! A good meal now, and then we'll discuss your holiday and—your hat, Brigid. We mustn't forget your hat. That *too* is important. (*As he moves away*) I am going upstairs to attend to—a little matter.

BRIGID. Is it up to the little place off your bedroom that—

CANON (*hand up*). That will do, Brigid. It is—my affair.

BRIGID. Yis, Canon. Please, Canon, will you—pray for me—too?

CANON (*after a pause*). I will, child. For both of us. (*He goes out pensively.* BRIGID *lifts the teapot uncertainly, her hand trembles and she puts it down again. She looks toward the door fearfully. She sits a few moments in torment. There is a noise off. She shakingly pours out some tea. She adds sugar and cream in a dazed way. She lifts the cup halfway to her lips, puts it guiltily down, and buries her face in her hands.*)

BRIGID. It's not fair . . . after me promisin' . . . and me white dress on me too. . . . (*She rises, her eyes on the curtains, and walks center*) I'm miserable and not able. . . . What name have you for me in your lovely mouth? Soot maybe, or clabber of the ground or maybe dung that smells. . . . (*Pathetically*) Oh, please no, not that! . . . Make it somethin' that has been burned in the fire . . . somethin' burned black with flame. . . . (*She turns sorrowfully back to table.* MISS COONEY *comes to the door.*)

JEMIMA. Are ye done there yet? It's near half-eleven already. Why, you didn't begin yet! If it's goin' on bein' contrary you are, I'll tell the Canon. (*Looking around*) Where *is* the Canon?

BRIGID. He's not to be disturbed.

JEMIMA. Did he say that?

BRIGID. No, Miss Cooney, but I know he meant it.

JEMIMA. Indeed! And them's *your* orders, are they?

BRIGID (*softly*). How could I be givin' orders?

JEMIMA. You're daft enough for anythin'. And you're goin' to Dublin, are ye?

BRIGID. It's whatever the Canon says.

JEMIMA. Aye, well you'll not be the first in your family that's seen Nelson's Pillar.

BRIGID (*staring at her, very hurt*). There's some terrible meanin' in that. You must be wicked and cruel. I can feel it in you.

JEMIMA. You hurry up there, or you'll feel me a good bit more.

BRIGID (*coweringly*). Yis . . . I'll—eat now—in a minute. If only the Angelus would ring! . . . (THOMASINA CONCANNON *and* FRANCIS O'CONNOR *come in, arm-in-arm, in high spirits.*)

THOMASINA. Is me uncle about, Jemima? Francis and meself want a word with him.

FRANCIS. It's about the weddin' arrangements, auntie.

JEMIMA. Sure he was here no time ago. Where did you say he went, Brigid?

BRIGID. He—didn't say.

JEMIMA (*sharply*). Which way did he go?

BRIGID. He went out into the hall.

JEMIMA. He'll maybe be in his room. Wait now and I'll see.

THOMASINA. We just want to be sure, Jemima, he'll marry us himself, and not push us over to one of the curates. It's never just the same.

JEMIMA. Sure, surely to God. he wouldn't have a curate marryin' his own niece!

FRANCIS (*with a sheet of paper*). And we want his leave, auntie, to put in the paper, "beloved niece of the Very Rev. Thomas Canon Skerritt. P.P."

JEMIMA. Sure just put it in, and say nothin' till after. Look at the fix you'll be in, if he says no. Have you *my* name in it too?

FRANCIS. Imagine askin' that, auntie!

JEMIMA. And have your own middle name, Francis. The scuts o' the country have as many names as ourselves nowadays.

FRANCIS. It's all fireproof, auntie, Lord Macaulay couldn't do better.

JEMIMA. I hope so, after all the schoolin' and collegin' you got. I'll run up and get him for you. (*She goes off, left.* THOMASINA *and* FRANCIS *cross to* BRIGID, *who is moodily sitting with her head in her hands at the table.*)

THOMASINA. Well, Brigid, are ye better?

BRIGID. Sure, I wasn't ill, Miss Concannon.

THOMASINA. Not ill? Sure the last time I was in, you were . . .

FRANCIS (*digging* THOMASINA). You're dreamin', Thomasina. Brigid wasn't ill.

THOMASINA (*with a giggle*). Ach, sure of course she wasn't. It's me bein' in love, that's what it is!

BRIGID. Please take some tea, Miss Concannon. It's just fresh wet.

THOMASINA (*eagerly*). I will in troth. (*Taking cup*) I could eat a cow! It's this love! Are ye finished with the cake there?

BRIGID (*eagerly*). Yis. Please ate them all. Help her, Francis, if you like. The Canon gets mad when he sees food left over.

FRANCIS. Sure and I will. (*Taking a cake*) I had always a sweet tooth. Make a note o' that, sweetest one! Yum! This is a co-coanut one! (*Both start eating vigorously.* BRIGID *watches them evidently relieved.*)

THOMASINA (*munching*). I wonder if that's true about O'Flingsley—I mean what Dave Dooley was tellin' us below at the bridge, Francis?

FRANCIS. About the people goin' to give him a battherin'? Maybe it is. Anyway, he'll be a good riddance.

BRIGID (*trembling*). Did—did you hear that? Are the people—sayin' it?

THOMASINA. Ach, behave yourself, Brigid! If they are itself, he deserves it.

BRIGID. But it's cruel and terrible. The Canon wouldn't see that done on him.

FRANCIS (*munching*). The Canon? Sure, you could ate all the Canon likes of him.

BRIGID (*in pain*). It's not true. . . . The Canon doesn't hate like that . . . and the Master doesn't hate like that either . . . I know what I'll do. I'll— (*Before the others can restrain her, she passes rapidly like a white vision through the white-curtained window. They stare after her, with pieces of cake in their hands and mouths. Then they look at each other and laugh spontaneously.*)

FRANCIS. That one will get hurt if the stones start flyin'.

THOMASINA. The poor thing. It must be terrible to be∙mad in the head. Is it true, Francis, that they smother mad people in Dublin between blankets? (*Before* FRANCIS *can settle the point, the* CANON *enters, left. He is irascible and ruffled.*)

CANON. Who wants me here? And for what purpose?

THOMASINA. Sure, it's just me and Francis, Uncle.

CANON. That much, I observe.

FRANCIS. Did we disturb ye now, Canon? Sure just say the word, Canon, and we'll come back any time.

CANON. I gave orders that I was not to be disturbed.

FRANCIS (*seizing* THOMASINA). Come on now, Thomasina, and let us not be maddenin' His Reverence. We can come back later by the Canon's leave.

THOMASINA. But me mother's comin' on the two o'clock train, and she'll be mad to know everythin'.

CANON (*acidly*). You will ask your questions concisely and without superfluity, and I shall answer them in—like manner. Proceed! (MISS COONEY *comes in to collect tea-tray.* THOMASINA *and* FRANCIS *regard each other uncertainly.*)

FRANCIS. Sure, Canon, if you'd rather—

CANON. I said, proceed!

THOMASINA (*breathlessly*). We want to know, uncle, if *you'll* marry us yourself?

CANON (*rapidly*). No! Next question.

THOMASINA. But me mother will have a fit, uncle, if you don't.

CANON (*acidly*). Superfluous! I have already suitably defined your mother.

JEMIMA (*at table, obsequiously*). If I might humbly put in a word, Canon . . .

CANON. You might not, Miss Cooney. (MISS COONEY *goes, humbly*.)

FRANCIS. Then I suppose, Canon, you won't allow us to put your name in the marriage notice in the papers?

CANON. Exactly, Francis. And that holds for birth notices too. Where is Brigid?

THOMASINA. She went out through the window, Canon, after we came in.

CANON (*irascibly*). For what purpose?

FRANCIS. She heard Thomasina and meself, Canon, talkin' about that man O'Flingsley, and the things the people were sayin' down the town.

THOMASINA. And away she went like a madhead.

CANON (*irascibly*). Why wasn't I told of this immediately instead of wasting time on trivialities? Run both of you instantly, and find her. The child is most unwell. .Tell her the Canon wants her this very minute. (*He rushes them out by the window. As he returns,* FATHER KIRWAN *enters hurriedly by the door, wearing gauntlets.*)

FATHER KIRWAN. Canon, I flew up in the wee car for you. Father Corr and I want your help.

CANON. Am I to be continually reminding you, Father Kirwan, that I don't give help? I give direction. (*Pause*) What new stupidity is afoot now?

FATHER KIRWAN. It's not our fault really, Canon. It's the men insisted on marching to that O'Flingsley fellow's house.

CANON. For what purpose?

FATHER KIRWAN. To warn him, as was resolved at the meetin', to be gone out of this district.

CANON. On what authority?

FATHER KIRWAN. Sure, Canon, the authority of angry men. (*Loud booing and cheering from the distance*) Listen! There they're boohin' and shouting. Father Corr is trying to hold them down from anny violence.

CANON. And where might I ask is the Sergeant of Police, when a brawl of this nature takes place?

FATHER KIRWAN. His wife's havin' a baby, Canon, and he can't come.

CANON. The sergeant a midwife, and my curates turned American lynchmen! Excellent! (FATHER CORR *enters rapidly by the door. He is excited.*)

FATHER CORR. Canon, that fellow O'Flingsley is jeerin' at the people instead of goin' when he's told. He has them as angry as bulls. If you'd just come out and show yourself for a minute . . . (*More booing and shouting from the distance.*)

CANON (*severely*). Did you and Father Kirwan march this— mob to O'Flingsley's house?

FATHER CORR. We did, Canon. It was—was up to us. But they're no mob, and they were in excellent order, till *he* started jeering.

FATHER KIRWAN. That's the down truth, Canon.

CANON. You are a sentimental youth, Father Corr, or you would know that all men in the mass are barbarians. Every year scores of decent Christians in America sprinkle Negroes with petrol and burn them because they love God and his justice. Yet, you *will* indulge in this—free Presbyterianism, this Lutheran zeal that the Church has never had any nonsense with in history. And in *my* parish, too. (*Further bursts of booing and shout-*

ing, and the noise of sticks and stones in the distance. MISS
COONEY *comes in rapidly.*)

MISS COONEY (*very scared*). Canon, did ye ever hear the like!
The milkman's after tellin' me about Brigid. She's below holdin'
on to the man O'Flingsley on the road, and a crowd peltin'
him with sticks and stones.

THE CURATES (*startled*). Canon!

CANON (*seized with fear*). Brigid! This—this is defiance! . . .
My hat and stick instantly. (MISS COONEY *rushes off. The* CANON
draws himself up to his full height and regards the CURATES *imperiously*) I have long enough suffered boobs gladly both without and within. Now, I the Canon, will act, and I will have
obedience and authority!

FATHER KIRWAN (*boyishly*). Sure, it wasn't our fault at all,
Canon. The men only got out of hand when that fellow,
O'Flingsley . . .

CANON (*with a wave*). Enough. (MISS COONEY *runs in with his
stick and two hats, a soft one and a tall silk one. She fumbles
nervously.*)

MISS COONEY. Is it this one, Canon, or the tall one?

CANON (*hurling soft hat across room and taking the tall one*).
The tall one. (*He dons it with an awesome sweep of the arm*)
I will show these neo-theologians and football kickers of yours
that the bulk of the people are not to do but to be done by.

FATHER KIRWAN (*stupidly*). I'll whip ye down in the wee car in
a jiffy, Canon.

CANON (*irascibly*). Get behind me, fool. I'll walk. (MISS COONEY *and the two* CURATES *cower back as he marches intently towards the window, back. Before he reaches it, there is a commotion.* O'FLINGSLEY *appears in the opening with* BRIGID *lying in his arms. His hair is disheveled and his face streaked with blood and mud.* BRIGID'S *head is almost covered by a large white cloth— in fact, an apron—and there are bloodstains upon her white dress. She is limp and inert.)*

MISS COONEY (*hysterical*). Canon! It's Brigid! They've kilt her!

FATHER CORR (*in anguish*). It's not—not true! . . .

FATHER KIRWAN (*hand to face, shakingly*). No! . . . No, no!

CANON (*hoarsely, doffing hat*). In the name of God, O'Flingsley . . .

O'FLINGSLEY. I'm not asking protection for myself, Canon. But get a doctor for Brigid at once.

CANON (*controlling himself*). Rush, Miss Cooney, for Dr. Connell. Say I said instantly. Fly, woman, dash!

MISS COONEY (*rushing out*). I'll race, Canon. Mother o' God . . .

CANON (*arranging couch*). Set her here, O'Flingsley.

FATHER KIRWAN (*in pain, bursting out*). Canon, we didn't mean annythin'. God knows we didn't . . .

CANON (*almost inaudibly*). Quiet, quiet. (O'FLINGSLEY *gently stretches* BRIGID *on the couch. He stands on one side and the* CANON *on the other. Each is striving desperately to control himself. The* CURATES *stand bowed with fear and remorse.)*

CANON (*shakingly*). God of mercy, do not take this, my one

consolation away from me. . . . (*His voice breaks*) Is—is it
serious, O'Flingsley?

O'FLINGSLEY. I'm afraid it is. (*They avoid each other's gaze.*)

CANON (*as in a dream, huskily*). What happened? T-tell
me. . . .

O'FLINGSLEY (*passionlessly*). She got half a brick that one of
your hirelings intended for *me.*

CANON (*pathetic*). They were not *my* hirelings, O'Flingsley.
We are surely better enemies than that. (*Pause*) Where is the
wound?

O'FLINGSLEY. Side of the head and upper part of the face. I'm
afraid of concussion. It was a cruel blow. . . . As I ran with
her, a woman poured a bottle of oil over it and tied her apron
about her to stop the bleeding.

CANON (*bending, in pain*). And this in the name of the Communion of Saints . . .

FATHER CORR (*emotionally breaking down*). Canon, I can't bear
it! I can't bear it! . . . God knows I meant no blood or violence . . . that I wouldn't hurt anythin' livin'. . . . I—I never
thought . . . I never thought . . .

FATHER KIRWAN (*soothing him*). There now, there! Let ye hold
on to yourself now. Sure the Canon knows. And Brigie will be
all right in a minute.

FATHER CORR (*hysterical*). I did it! I did it! . . . I wasn't wise
like—like the Canon . . . I—I only meant, Canon—

CANON (*not unkindly*). Father Corr, you will control your
emotion.

FATHER CORR. Y-yes, Canon.

CANON. And cease allowing it to run you into fresh idiocies.

FATHER KIRWAN. I'll take him out to the fresh air, Canon.

CANON. You will both go out to these people, and order them in my name to return instantly to their homes and their work.

FATHER CORR. Very well, Canon. (*They go out, back,* FATHER KIRWAN *assisting* FATHER CORR. *The* CANON *bends in fear over to the couch.*)

CANON. Will that doctor ever come! . . . Could we do anything of ourselves? God would guide us surely.

O'FLINGSLEY (*cautiously*). Better not. If the blood started . . .

CANON (*drawing bandages slightly*). My God, my God, what have they done? Did she speak at all, O'Flingsley?

O'FLINGSLEY. She whispered something about the Angelus Bell and you. Then she sank into this.

CANON (*huskily*). We are all in this—this dark she lies in, only deeper than her. . . . Brigid, I am with you, the Canon, your friend. . . .

O'FLINGSLEY. There may be hope, if only that doctor is not playing golf. . . .

CANON (*wringing his hands*). It is like that—always—stupidities lying in the way. . . . God! Hasten him! Hasten him out! . . . (*At this moment, the Angelus Bell begins ringing clearly from the Church tower outside.* BRIGID *groans, stirs weakly and moves her head. They regard her emotionally.*)

O'FLINGSLEY (*softly*). Brigid . . . it's the Canon and I.

BRIGID (*weakly*). The man O'Flingsley. . . . (*Moving painfully*) The—the Angelus . . . the Angelus . . . and I'm not—able. . . . Canon, make me able. . . .

CANON. I am here, Brigid. But you must not speak. You are very ill, poor child.

BRIGID (*as in a dream*). There's blood on the Master's head. . . . I felt it. . . . Then the stone came . . . with the pain in it . . . and I knew my face was like St. Brigid's then . . . torn and hurt. . . . My mouth is burnin' . . . me. . . . (*The* CANON *pours a little of his Spanish wine into a glass and brings it towards her.*)

O'FLINGSLEY. The Canon is right this time, Brigid. You must lie very still and not talk till the doctor comes.

BRIGID. But how can I rest . . . and that bell ringin'. . . . The Canon knows . . . Canon! . . .

CANON. There, child! I am here with you. . . . You must take a sip of this wine to strengthen you. . . . (*She takes a few sips from the glass.*)

BRIGID. Don Miguel's wine. . . . He said to the Canon, "Where there is truth there is God." . . . I wish I could rise up, and be *true* to her . . . and not false. . . . But I'm not able. . . .

CANON. (*striving to hold in his emotions*). Brigid, if you will live for me, live on as the Canon's friend, I will do what you want. I will bend for you. The Canon will bend. He will stoop. He will—believe. . . .

BRIGID (*weakly, struggling*). C-Canon! . . . I—I want to live for that . . . I must live. . . . I must show you the stone . . . and my white dress on . . . me. . . .

o'flingsley (*tenderly supporting her*). Yes, Brigid, but not till the doctor examines you.

brigid (*weakly moving*). But there is no time, Master . . . no time. . . . The Angelus will soon not be ringin'. . . .

o'flingsley. She's fighting hard as if there was something that mattered a lot.

canon. So there is. . . . (*Emotionally*) So there is. . . .

brigid (*rising a little, painfully*). Make me able, Canon. I want to keep faith with her. I want her to see me face like hers. . . . I want to be a white rose in her mouth . . . not a smut of soot brushed away. . . . (*She rises still more—only her eyes and brow and hair visible and glowing above the bandages*) I want to see your face stooped, Canon, in the way she said . . . and the love of the little things in it. . . . I want to dip me fingers in the new water, and to say what she told me, "Mary of the Gael, show us the way . . . through the dark." . . . (*For a moment her face is poised eloquently. The Angelus bell ceases. She suddenly collapses back, and lies still. The* canon *buries his face in his hands.* o'flingsley *stifles a sob.*)

canon (*shakingly*). Tell me, O'Flingsley. No, no. Don't—don't say it. . . .

o'flingsley (*simply*). It's one of the things must be said, Canon. She's dead. . . .

canon. God . . . God . . . Have I blundered? (o'flingsley *takes up a coverlet to draw it over* brigid's *face, but the* canon *pathetically intervenes, childishly*) No, no. Let—let *me*, O'Flingsley. . . . Let *me*.

O'FLINGSLEY (*slowly*). Let both of us. . . . (*Terribly*) It will be —worthy of us. . . . (*Together they draw the coverlet over* BRIGID's *face. Their eyes meet fully for the first time, and hold each other over* BRIGID's *body. Then each moves slowly back in different directions.*)

CANON (*huskily, as* O'FLINGSLEY *nears the door*). No, no. . . . Do not leave me, O'Flingsley. . . . I am alone. . . .

O'FLINGSLEY (*turning, slowly*). I must. (*Very low*) We must work this out. . . . Innocent blood. . . .

CANON (*hands to face, shakingly*). Am I just an embittered old man . . . living here with shades too glorious to forget? (*For a moment,* O'FLINGSLEY *regards him from the doorway, his face a study—in mingled hate, pity and respect. He turns slowly and goes out. A moment passes. The* CANON *sits down heavily. He lifts heavy weary eyes to the couch and the empty room.*)

CANON (*his head down again, slowly*). I am not well. . . .

SLOW CURTAIN

COMPLETE LIST OF TITLES IN

THE MODERN LIBRARY

For convenience in ordering use number at right of title